FreeHand 9

AUTHORIZED

macromedia®
PRESS

FreeHand 9 Authorized
Macromedia, Inc.

 Published by Macromedia Press, in association with Peachpit Press, a division of Addison Wesley Longman.

Macromedia Press
1249 Eighth Street
Berkeley, CA 94710
510/524-2178
510/524-2221 (fax)
Find us on the World Wide Web at:
http://www.peachpit.com
http://www.macromedia.com

Printed and bound in the United States of America

ISBN 0-201-70034-4

9 8 7 6 5 4 3 2 1

CREDITS

Author and Instructional Designer
Tony Roame, Illustrated Concepts

Artwork
Tony Roame, Illustrated Concepts

Editor
Kelly Ryer and Wendy Sharp

Copyeditor
Judy Ziajka

Production Coordinator
Kate Reber

Compositors
Rick Gordon, Emerald Valley Graphics
Myrna Vladic, Bad Dog Graphics
Debbie Roberti, Espresso Graphics

Indexer
Karin Arrigoni

Cover design
Mimi Heft

This edition is based in part on materials originally created by:
Karen Tucker, Macromedia
Julia Sifers, Glasgow & Associates
Thomas Faist, Datrix Media Group
Craig Faist, Datrix Media Group
Lori Faist, Datrix Media Group
Steve Botts
Stewart McKissick

Thanks to the following people:
Brenda Roame, Illustrated Concepts; Alisse Berger, Brian Schmidt, David Mendels, Suzanne Porta, Karen Silvey and Joanne Watkins at Macromedia; Nancy Ruenzel, Marjorie Baer, Kate Reber, and Kelly Ryer, Peachpit Press; and Ian Kelleigh at The FreeHand Source.

table of contents

Macromedia's FreeHand 9 is a powerful and comprehensive drawing and layout program that provides a complete set of tools for creating dynamic graphics, illustrations, and page designs for print, multimedia, and Internet publishing projects.

This Macromedia Authorized training course introduces you to the major features of FreeHand 9 by guiding you step by step through the development of several sample projects. This 12-hour curriculum includes these lessons:

Lesson 1: FreeHand Basics
Lesson 2: Combining Text and Graphics
Lesson 3: Working with Paths and Points
Lesson 4: Using Layers and Styles
Lesson 5: Creating More Complex Artwork
Lesson 6: Blending Shapes for Shading
Lesson 7: Page Layout in FreeHand
Lesson 8: Multiple-Page Documents
Lesson 9: Setting Up Animation
Lesson 10: Web Site Storyboards

Each lesson begins with an overview of the lesson's content and learning objectives, and each is divided into short tasks that break the skills into bite-size units.

Each lesson also includes these special features:

Tips: Shortcuts for carrying out common tasks and ways to use the skills you're learning to solve common problems.

Power Tips: Extra background and advanced techniques for those who are ready to absorb additional information.

Boldface terms: New vocabulary that will come in handy as you use FreeHand and work with graphics.

Menu commands and keyboard shortcuts: Alternative methods for executing commands in FreeHand 9. Menu commands are shown like this: Menu › Command › Subcommand. Keyboard shortcuts (when available) are shown in parentheses after the first step in which they can be used; a plus sign between the names of keys means you press keys simultaneously: for example, Ctrl+Z means that you should press the Ctrl and Z keys at the same time.

Appendices A and B at the end of the book provide a quick reference to shortcuts you can use on Windows and Macintosh systems, respectively, to give commands in FreeHand. Appendix C provides a quick FreeHand reference for users of other vector illustration applications.

As you complete these lessons, you'll be developing the skills you need to complete your own designs, layouts, and illustrations for print, multimedia, and the Internet. At the end of this course, you should have mastered all the skills listed in the "What You Will Learn" list in this introduction.

All the files you need for the lessons are included in the Lessons folder on the enclosed CD. Files for each lesson appear in their own folders, titled with the lesson name. You can use the lesson files directly from the CD, or you can copy the Lessons folder to your hard drive for quicker access.

Each lesson folder contains three subfolders: Complete, Media, and Start. The Complete folder contains completed files for each project so you can compare your work or see where you are headed. The Media folder contains any media elements you need to complete each lesson, such as graphics or text required to complete a layout. The Start folder contains any prebuilt files you will need to complete the lesson. The completed, media, and starting files you will need are identified at the beginning of each lesson. (Some lessons may not require starting files or media elements, so in some lesson folders, these subfolders will be empty.)

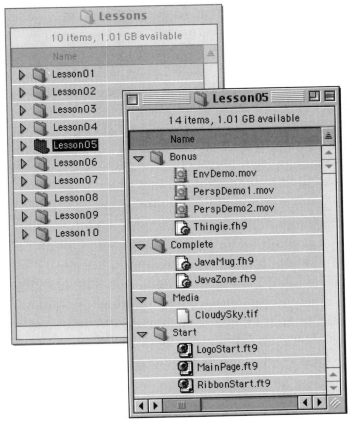

Files for each lesson appear in their own folders, titled with the lesson name. The Complete folder contains completed files for each lesson. The Media folder contains the media elements you need to complete each lesson. If a lesson requires a prebuilt file, you will find the file in the Start folder.

AUTHORIZED TRAINING FOR MACROMEDIA

Each book in the Macromedia Authorized series includes the complete curriculum of a course originally developed for use by Macromedia's authorized trainers. The lesson plans were developed by some of Macromedia's most successful trainers and refined through long experience to meet students' needs. We believe that Macromedia Authorized courses offer the best available training for Macromedia programs.

The instructions in this book are designed for graphic artists, illustrators, designers, and others interested in creating stunning graphics, typography, and layouts for print, multimedia, and the World Wide Web. This course assumes you are a beginner with FreeHand but are familiar with the basic methods of giving commands on a Windows or Macintosh computer, such as choosing items from menus, opening and saving files, and so on. For more information on those basic tasks, see the documentation provided with your computer.

Finally, the instructions in this book assume that you already have FreeHand 9 installed on a Windows or Macintosh computer, and that your computer meets the system requirements listed on the next page. This minimum configuration will allow you to run FreeHand 9 and open the training files included on the enclosed CD. If you do not own FreeHand 9, you can download a demo version from Macromedia's home page. You will be able to complete the lessons with the training version of the software, but the demo version will function only for 30 days, after which the program will no longer launch without a serial number. Follow the instructions in the downloaded Read Me file to install the demo version of the software.

note *Three TrueType font families included on the FreeHand 9 software CD you received when you purchased FreeHand 9 are used throughout the lessons in this course. To accurately reproduce the projects with the original fonts, install the News Gothic T, URW Garamond T Normal, and URW Imperial Normal font families on your system before starting the lessons. Windows users should drag those font files into the Fonts folder in the control panel. Macintosh users should drag those font files into the Fonts folder in the System folder. In addition, Chapter 7 uses two fonts that are not included on the CD, Utopia and Meta Plus Bold Italic. If you do not own these fonts, simply substitute Times and Trebuchet, respectively. (Trebuchet can be freely downloaded from the Microsoft Web site.)*

If you do not install these specific fonts, simply choose other fonts available on your system and adjust type size and formatting as needed to make your projects similar in appearance to the lesson files. Working without the original fonts installed will not interfere with your ability to complete the lessons.

Welcome to Macromedia Authorized. We hope you enjoy the course.

WHAT YOU WILL LEARN

By the end of this course you will be able to:

- Create, combine, and transform graphic elements in FreeHand
- Incorporate graphics and text into your projects
- Create single- and multiple-page layouts
- Take advantage of powerful and easy-to-use special effects features
- Import and export files for easy integration with other applications
- Organize a document into layers
- Import, format, and flow text within a layout
- Prepare files for a commercial printer
- Create blends of multiple shapes
- Apply gradient and lens fills to enhance your illustrations

- Combine elements by joining them together or pasting them inside other paths
- Paint graphics onto the page
- Create blends for shading
- Customize your working environment
- Convert FreeHand artwork to Web page graphics
- Create Shockwave Flash graphics in FreeHand
- Use FreeHand to design and create Web pages

MINIMUM SYSTEM REQUIREMENTS

Windows™

- 120 MHz Intel™ Pentium™ processor or higher
- Windows 95, 98, 2000, or NT 4™ (with Service Pack 3) or later
- 64 MB of application RAM
- 50 MB available disk space (70 MB or more recommended)
- CD-ROM drive
- 800 by 600 color monitor
- PostScript printer (recommended)
- For Lesson 10 only, a Web browser

Macintosh™

- PowerPC™ processor
- Mac OS 8.1 or later operating system
- 32 MB of application RAM (64 MB or more recommended)
- 50 MB available disk space (70 MB or more recommended)
- CD-ROM drive
- 800 by 600 color monitor
- PostScript printer (recommended)
- For Lesson 10 only, a Web browser

a quick tour

FreeHand basics:

FreeHand's drawing and layout tools can be used to develop everything from the simplest illustrations to the most complex designs. Its extensive control over graphics, colors, type, and imported artwork makes FreeHand a powerhouse for any graphic design project.

FreeHand is an object-oriented drawing program. Object oriented means that your document is created from graphic objects, or shapes, rather than from individual

This simple robot figure is constructed from a series of shapes created with FreeHand's basic shape tools. You will see how in this lesson.

LESSON 1

pixels as with a bitmap drawing tool. Object-oriented graphics are also known as vector graphics. Unlike bitmap graphics, vector graphics can be scaled to any size for output resolution with no loss of quality.

In this lesson you will draw a simple robot using graphic objects created by FreeHand's basic shape tools, including Rectangle, Ellipse, and Line. You will also use the Pointer tool to select and move graphic objects.

If you would like to review the final result of this lesson, open Robot.fh9 in the Complete folder within the Lesson01 folder.

WHAT YOU WILL LEARN

In this lesson you will:

- Create a new document
- Identify and organize tools and controls
- Customize application settings
- Create basic shapes such as rectangles, ellipses, and lines
- Change the appearance of objects by adding color and changing line thickness
- Group and align objects
- Create additional copies of existing elements
- Create a mirror image of an element or group
- Rotate elements on the page

APPROXIMATE TIME

It usually takes about 1 hour to complete this lesson.

LESSON FILES

Media Files:
None

Starting Files:
Lesson01\Start\Robot1.fh9 (optional)

Completed Project:
Lesson01\Complete\Robot.fh9
Lesson01\Complete\Robot2.fh9

CREATING A FOLDER ON YOUR HARD DRIVE

Before you begin building anything, you will create a folder to hold all the projects you will create as you work through the lessons in this book.

Create a folder called MyWork on your hard drive.

You will save all of your work in this folder.

Now you are ready to begin.

CREATING A NEW DOCUMENT

To begin working on a new project, you must first launch FreeHand and either create a new document or open an existing document.

1] Open the FreeHand application.

Open the application by double-clicking the FreeHand icon. The FreeHand toolbox, toolbars, and menu bar appear, but without an open document window. A few floating windows may appear on the screen as well; you will learn about these later in this lesson.

On Windows systems, a Welcome Wizard appears, enabling you to create a new document or open an existing file with a quick click of the mouse. If you're a new Windows user, you may find FreeHand's Wizards very useful when working with your own documents; you will learn more about the Wizards later in this lesson. If you prefer that the Wizard not appear the next time you start FreeHand, turn off this option near the bottom of the Welcome Wizard screen.

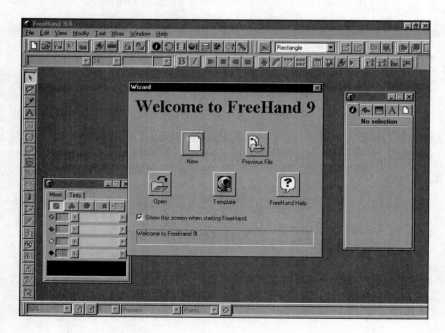

2] Create a new document by clicking the New button on the Welcome Wizard screen (Windows) or choosing File › New (Windows Ctrl+N, Macintosh Command+N).

A document window appears with a new page. The page is sitting on FreeHand's pasteboard, which is a work surface that contains all of the pages in your document. The pasteboard initially contains one page. The 222-inch by 222-inch pasteboard (18.5 feet square) can hold more than 675 letter-sized pages. You will be creating a robot illustration in this window later in this lesson.

You will be learning about the elements on this screen throughout this lesson.

tip *If you cannot see the entire page, choose View > Fit to Page.*

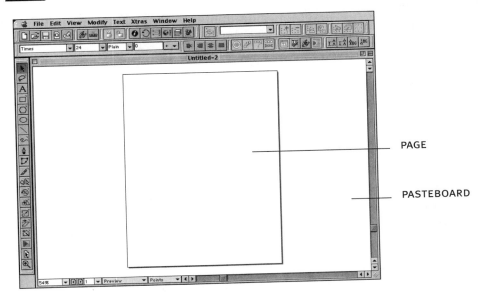

PAGE

PASTEBOARD

tip *If you see other control windows floating on your screen that are not shown here, close them by clicking the close box in each window's header bar. You will explore these panels later in this lesson.*

EXPLORING THE CONTROLS

FreeHand provides a wide variety of tools and controls for you to use to create your own artwork and graphics. In getting started with FreeHand, you first must learn where to find these controls.

1] Move the cursor over the main and text toolbars across the top of the screen. Rest the cursor over a button to see its name.

The main toolbar contains many of FreeHand's basic functions. The text toolbar contains buttons and menus for the most frequently used text commands. If you point to a button and hold the mouse still for a few moments, the button's name will appear.

The toolbar defaults are shown here. Don't worry if your toolbars do not look exactly like these. You will learn in upcoming lessons how to customize FreeHand's toolbars, Toolbox, and shortcuts.

tip *If the main and text toolbars do not appear on your screen, you can display them by selecting Window > Toolbars and then Main or Text.*

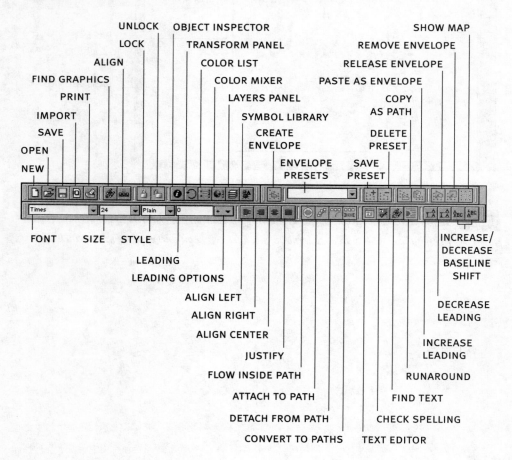

2] Move the cursor over the tools in the Toolbox at the left side of your screen. Rest the cursor over a tool to see its name.

The Toolbox contains FreeHand's drawing and transformation tools. It is docked, or attached, to the left edge of the screen by default.

You select a tool in the Toolbox by clicking on the tool once. Move the cursor into the document window to use the tool.

tip   *If the Toolbox does not appear on your screen, you can display it by selecting Window > Toolbars > Toolbox.*

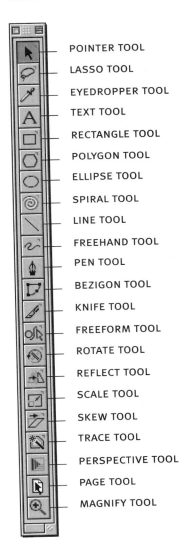

POINTER TOOL

LASSO TOOL

EYEDROPPER TOOL

TEXT TOOL

RECTANGLE TOOL

POLYGON TOOL

ELLIPSE TOOL

SPIRAL TOOL

LINE TOOL

FREEHAND TOOL

PEN TOOL

BEZIGON TOOL

KNIFE TOOL

FREEFORM TOOL

ROTATE TOOL

REFLECT TOOL

SCALE TOOL

SKEW TOOL

TRACE TOOL

PERSPECTIVE TOOL

PAGE TOOL

MAGNIFY TOOL

3] Move the Toolbox away from the left edge of the screen by dragging the horizontal bar located at the top or bottom edge of the Toolbox.

When you undock the Toolbox from the side of the screen, it changes shape and floats in front of your document window.

DRAG FROM HERE...

...TO HERE

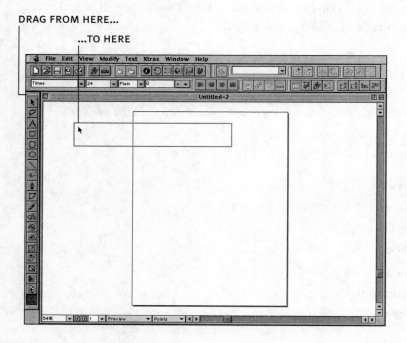

4] Change the size of this floating Toolbox by dragging the size box at the bottom-right corner of the Toolbox.

You can resize this floating Toolbox the same way you can resize any window. This is one of the ways FreeHand enables you to organize your working environment to suit your individual preferences.

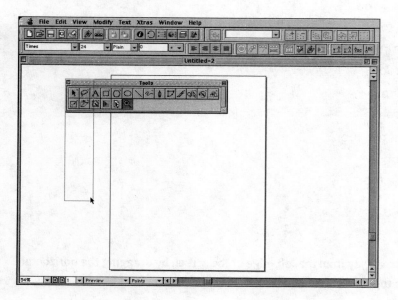

5] Dock the Toolbox against the left edge of the screen again by dragging the header bar at the top of the floating Toolbox window to the left edge of the screen.
FreeHand automatically resizes the Toolbox and attaches it to the left edge of the screen. You can move the tools up and down along the left edge of the screen by dragging.

tip *You may find it convenient to use the Toolbox in the docked position, because then it is not floating over your document window where it may hide part of your artwork as you work.*

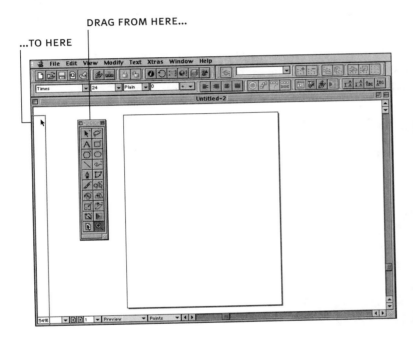

DRAG FROM HERE...

...TO HERE

tip *All toolbars, including the main and text toolbars, can be undocked from the top of the screen in the same manner. Dragging them back to any edge of your screen will dock them again. If you have a dual-monitor system, you can also dock toolbars on your second monitor.*

CUSTOMIZING APPLICATION PREFERENCES

FreeHand lets you set a wide array of preferences for customizing your working environment. You can customize the way elements are displayed, the number of Undo levels, and the way text and graphics can be edited, among many other settings.

Before beginning work with FreeHand, you will change one preference setting that will make it easier to learn the program and see your results clearly.

1] Choose File › Preferences to display the Preferences dialog box. Select General from the preference categories and make sure your General Preferences options are set as shown here.

In the Preferences dialog box that appears, you choose a category of preferences from the tabs at the top (Windows) or the list on the left side (Macintosh). The options in the dialog box change with the category you select.

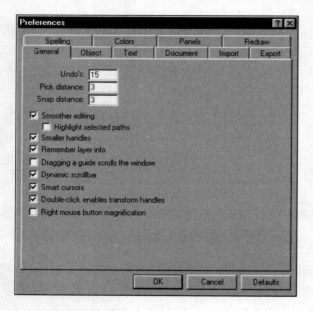

2] Select Redraw from the preference categories. Make sure that the option High-resolution image display is turned on (checked).

This will give you a better screen display of imported images. On some systems, this option can slow down screen redrawing significantly when you are working with very-high-resolution images, but it should not cause any problems for the images you will use in these lessons. The Redraw options apply only to the screen display and do not have any effect on your printed results. The default settings of the other Redraw Preferences options are shown here.

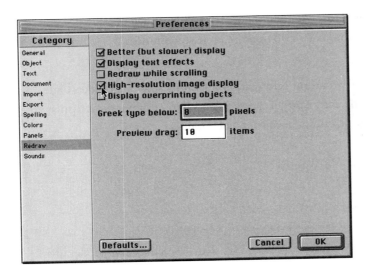

3] Click OK to close the Preferences dialog box.

You will not see the results of the High-resolution image display preference setting until you start working with images on the page.

WORKING WITH PANELS

Many FreeHand drawing settings can be set in panels: floating collections of tools and formatting controls that you can open, close, customize, and move around on your desktop. Unlike dialog boxes, FreeHand's panels can remain on the screen as you work so you can quickly and easily edit document settings.

Earlier in this lesson you learned that undocking the Toolbox turns it into a floating panel. In this section, you'll be introduced to some other useful panels: the Inspectors, Color Mixer, and Color List. You will use these panels often in the lessons that follow.

1] Display the Object Inspector by clicking the Inspector button on the main toolbar or by choosing Window › Inspectors › Object.

OBJECT INSPECTOR

FreeHand's Inspector panels are grouped together by default; when you open the Object Inspector, you see them all. Two or more panels combined in this way are called a panel group.

The Inspector panels display current information regarding selected objects and allow you to change the characteristics of those objects. No information is displayed in the Object Inspector at this time, because no element is selected.

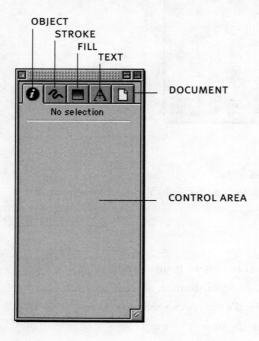

tip   *The five Inspectors (Object, Stroke, Fill, Text, and Document) contain important controls for editing FreeHand graphics. Virtually every FreeHand drawing task involves one or more of these Inspectors. These Inspectors are on movable panels and can be arranged to suit your individual preference.*

2] Click the tab for the Document Inspector to activate that set of controls (bringing that Inspector to the front of the group).
The Document Inspector contains controls for specifying page size and orientation and for adding or removing pages from the document.

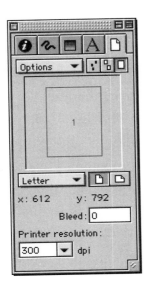

You can switch to any of the other Inspectors by clicking its tab at the top of the panel group.

tip *In addition to the toolbar controls, you can display any of FreeHand's Inspectors by selecting Window > Inspectors and choosing the Inspector you want to use.*

3] Hide the Inspector panel group by clicking the close box in the header bar at the top of the panel.

You can display and hide panels as needed.

Now look at the Color Mixer panel.

4] Display the Color Mixer by clicking its button on the main toolbar or by choosing Window › Panels › Color Mixer.

COLOR MIXER

The Color Mixer enables you to create and modify colors that can be applied to elements throughout the document. You will see how this tool works later in this lesson.

The Color Mixer is initially grouped with the Tints panel. The Tints tab can be seen at the top of this panel group.

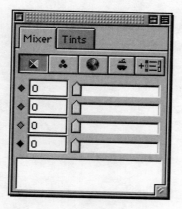

5] Click the Tints tab at the top of this panel group.

The Tints panel comes to the front of the group, hiding the Color Mixer. The Tints panel enables you to create tints, which are lighter shades of a color, expressed as a percentage of the base color. (Tints are also referred to as screens.)

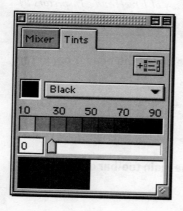

6] Hide the panel group containing the Tints and Color Mixer panels by clicking the close box in the panel group's header bar.

Each panel group can be displayed or hidden as needed when working on a project.

7] Display the Color List by clicking its button on the main toolbar or by choosing Window › Panels › Color List.

The Color List appears, showing the names of the colors that have been defined for this document. Adding colors to the Color List makes it easy to apply those colors to other elements in the document without having to re-create them in the Color Mixer for each use.

The Color List is grouped with the Layers and Styles panels by default. The Layers and Styles tabs can be seen at the top of this panel group.

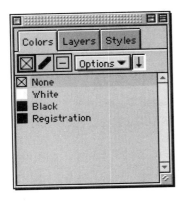

8] Click the Layers tab at the top of this panel group.

The Layers panel comes to the front of the group. In other lessons, you will use Layers to organize artwork in a complex illustration.

19

9] **Drag the Layers panel out of this panel group by pointing to the name Layers on the tab at the top of the panel and dragging the tab out onto the pasteboard. Then release the mouse.**

Layers now appears as a separate panel, so you can access the Color List at the same time as Layers. You have ungrouped these two panels.

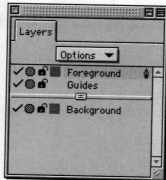

10] **Drag the Layers tab onto the Color List panel and release the mouse.**

This combines the two panels into a panel group again. As you can see, panels can be separated or combined by dragging their tabs.

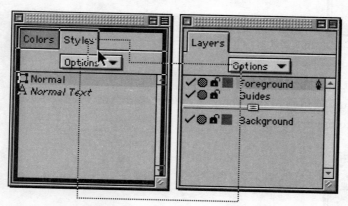

11] **Click the Colors tab to bring the Color List to the front of the panel group. Then hide the Color List by clicking the button on the main toolbar again.**

You can also hide panels as needed using the buttons on the toolbar.

tip *In addition to using the toolbar controls, you can display any of FreeHand's panels by selecting Window > Panels and choosing the panel you want to use.*

ORGANIZING THE WORKSPACE

Next you will see how you can align panels to one another and connect panels together to customize your working environment.

1] Display the Color List and Color Mixer panels again by clicking the two buttons on the main toolbar.

FreeHand has built-in capabilities to help you align panels to keep your working environment organized.

2] Move any edge of the Color List panel toward an edge of the Color Mixer panel by dragging the header bar at the top of the Color List panel.

Notice that as you move the Color List close to the Color Mixer, it snaps into position so that the two panels are aligned. These panels are not connected together, but are neatly aligned at the edges. When you drag a panel or group by its header bar to within 12 pixels of another panel or group, FreeHand automatically aligns them with one another. Panels snap to the top, bottom, or sides of other panels when you move any edge of a panel to within 12 pixels of another panel.

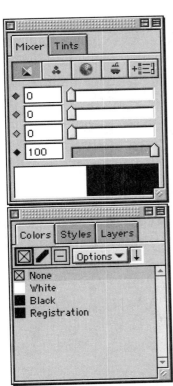

You can also align panels to the edge of your workspace by dragging them to within 12 pixels of the monitor border or to the border of the application.

3] Move the Color List away from the Color Mixer and release the mouse. Then hold down the Shift key and move the Color List back toward the Color Mixer. Release the Shift key.

The panels do not snap together. Pressing Shift while dragging a panel (Shift-drag) temporarily disables snapping. Panels automatically snap to one another when you move panels without holding down the Shift key.

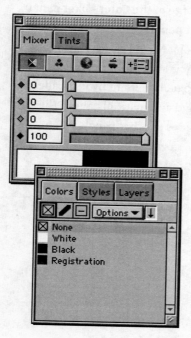

4] Move the top of the Color List toward the bottom of the Color Mixer by dragging the Color List's header bar while holding down the Control key (on both Windows and Macintosh computers).

This docks the panels, connecting them together so they behave as if they are one. Unlike a panel group, docked panels are all displayed at the same time. Notice the panel dock, a small bar connecting the two panels together.

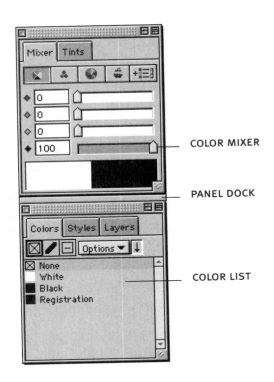

COLOR MIXER

PANEL DOCK

COLOR LIST

5] Try moving one of the docked panels. Then collapse one of the docked panels by clicking the Minimize button (Windows) or Zoom box (Macintosh).

Docked panels move and collapse together, making it easier to work with several panels at once.

Docked panels also are displayed and hidden together, so hiding or displaying either the Color List or Color Mixer while the panels are docked will hide or display both docked panels.

6] Expand the collapsed panels and then undock them by clicking the panel dock between the two panels.

The panels are now independent again. You can also undock the panels by holding down Control while dragging the header bar of a docked panel away from its adjacent panel.

7] Close all open panels.

As you work with FreeHand, you can position, group, dock, and collapse panels as desired. Remember that you can also show and hide panels quickly with the buttons on the main toolbar.

The flexibility that FreeHand offers with panels makes it easy for you to organize FreeHand's controls in a way that is comfortable for you.

CREATING AN ELEMENT ON THE PAGE

In creating any great masterpiece, the most important step is getting started. Here you will begin by creating a rectangle on the page.

1] Select the Rectangle tool near the upper left of the Toolbox by clicking it once.

2] Position your cursor anywhere on the page. Hold down the mouse button and drag diagonally downward and to the right to create a rectangle. Release the mouse when your rectangle is about the size of a playing card.

The rectangle you created appears on the page with a border and no fill. (If your rectangle looks different, don't worry. You will be changing its characteristics shortly.)

Small boxes, called selection boxes, appear at the corners, indicating that this element is selected.

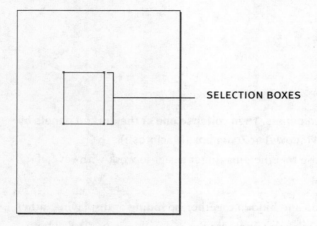

SELECTION BOXES

In the next few steps, you will learn how to move, resize, duplicate, and delete a selected element and how to change its appearance.

tip *If the selection boxes do not appear at the corners of the object, click once on the object's border with the Pointer tool to select the object.*

First you will move the rectangle to a new position on the page.

3] Select the Pointer tool in the Toolbox. Position the cursor on the border of the rectangle (but not on one of the selection boxes) and drag the mouse approximately two inches to the right.

Dragging from the middle of the selected element's border will move the rectangle to a new position on the page. This rectangle is empty, so there is nothing to grab inside the border when you want to move the object. Filled objects can be moved by grabbing anywhere in the middle of the object and dragging the mouse. You will learn how to fill an object later in this lesson.

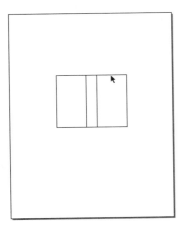

Next you will change the size of the selected element.

4] Position the tip of the Pointer tool on the bottom-right corner selection box of the rectangle. Hold down the mouse button, drag downward about an inch, and release.
The height of the rectangle has been increased about one inch. Dragging any selection box enables you to resize an object.

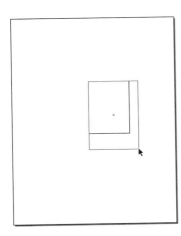

tip *It may help to remember Move = Middle (drag the middle to move an object) and Size = Selection box (change an object's size by dragging a selection box).*

Now you will create duplicates of a selected object.

25

5] With the rectangle still selected, choose Edit › Copy. Then choose Edit › Paste to add a duplicate of the rectangle to the page.

The pasted item appears in the center of the screen. You can duplicate a selected item with the Copy and Paste commands. You can paste duplicates of the most recently copied object into the current document or into other FreeHand documents as needed.

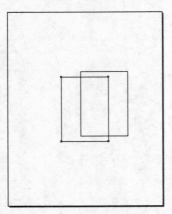

6] Choose Edit › Duplicate to add another copy of this rectangle on the page.

Duplicate is a one-step command you can use when additional copies of the selected element are needed in the same document. The duplicate is positioned down and to the right of the object duplicated.

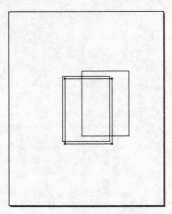

In the next step, you will learn how to delete unwanted elements from the page.

7] With one of the rectangles still selected, press the Delete key.

The selected object is deleted, leaving the other two rectangles on the page.

Now you can create and manipulate elements on the page. You will learn how to change the appearance of elements a bit later in this lesson.

8] Use the Pointer tool to move one of the new rectangles off the page onto the pasteboard. Then move the other rectangle off the page as well.

If these two actions are mistakes, or if you simply change your mind, you can use FreeHand's Undo command, which reverses the most recent changes.

9] Choose Edit › Undo to reverse the most recent change. Then choose Edit › Undo once more to reverse the next most recent change.

Both of the rectangles should be restored to their original positions on the page. FreeHand supports multiple levels of Undo. The default setting is 10 levels of Undo, but you can specify the number of Undo operations by selecting File > Preferences > General and entering a new value (up to 100).

tip *Specifying a higher number of Undo operations may add to FreeHand's RAM requirements.*

CHANGING THE VIEW

As you work on your FreeHand documents, you will find it helpful to zoom in to see the artwork in more detail and zoom out to see the entire illustration. FreeHand offers several features for viewing your artwork on the screen.

1] Select the Magnify tool at the bottom of the Toolbox by clicking it once. Then point to one of the rectangles on your page and click to zoom in on that spot.

Clicking with the Magnify tool enlarges the spot where you click. Another way to zoom in is to hold down the mouse button and drag the Magnify tool cursor to surround the desired area with a marquee, a dotted line that surrounds the area you define by dragging the mouse; when you release the mouse, FreeHand will zoom in on the surrounded area.

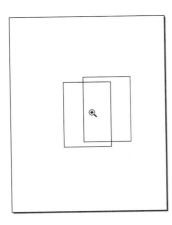

2] Press and hold the Alt (Windows) or Option (Macintosh) key and click with the Magnify tool to reduce the view. Then choose the Pointer tool from the toolbox.

tip   *It is often helpful to change to the Pointer tool when you complete your work with the Zoom tool (and any other tool as well). This prevents an accidental click of the mouse from zooming you in somewhere in the workspace after you had just changed to the perfect view. You cannot use Undo to return to a previous view.*

The Zoom tool displays a plus or minus sign to indicate whether it will magnify (+) or reduce (–) the view. If the magnifying glass cursor appears without either a plus or minus sign, you are zoomed in or out as far as possible. FreeHand supports a zoom range of from 6 to 25,600 percent of the drawing size, so you shouldn't see the empty cursor very often. Notice that the magnification value appears in the lower-left corner of the screen.

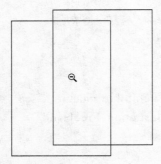

3] Choose View › Fit to Page to see the entire page again (Windows Ctrl+Shift+W, Macintosh Command+Shift+W).

The top three choices on the View menu allow you to change your view of the page immediately with specific results. Fit Selection zooms to fill the document window with any selected elements, Fit to Page resizes the view so you can see the entire page, and Fit All reduces the view so you can see all of the pages in your document at once. (Right now, Fit All and Fit to Page would have the same results, because your current document contains only one page. If you don't have an element selected, Fit Selection will resize the view so you can see the entire page.)

4] Choose Edit › Select › All (Windows Ctrl+A, Macintosh Command+A) to select both of the rectangles on your page. Then choose View › Fit Selection (Windows Ctrl+0 [zero], Macintosh Command+0 [zero]).

This zooms the view so that the selected rectangles fill the document window. The Select All command allows you to select all of the elements on the page at one time.

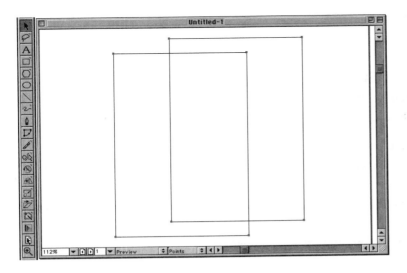

5] With both rectangles still selected, press the Delete key to remove both of the rectangles from the page.

Your page should now be empty again.

6] Point to the arrow in the lower-left corner of the document window and hold down the mouse button to display the magnification menu. Select 100% and release the mouse button.

This menu contains popular preset magnification values. You can select a value from this menu, or you can type a specific number directly in the magnification value field. When changing magnification values by these methods, FreeHand always puts selected elements in the center of the screen. If no elements are selected, FreeHand zooms on the middle of the active page.

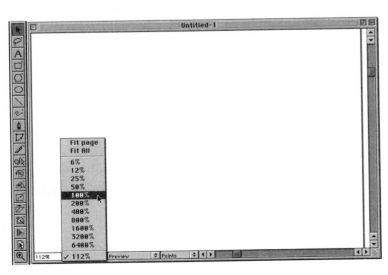

29

As you can see, FreeHand offers several ways for you to achieve the same results, so you can work in the way that is most convenient for you.

CREATING BASIC SHAPES

Now you will begin creating your first project: a simple drawing of a robot. This next task will introduce concepts you will use in every FreeHand project.

If you prefer to re-create the robot more closely, you can work from the template provided. Choose File > Open and open Robot1.fh9 in the Start folder within the Lesson01 folder. This document contains gray outlines of the robot's elements for you to follow. Remember, though, that your main goal in this lesson is to learn to use the drawing tools, not to match the sample exactly. Don't worry if your version of the robot looks a little different from the one shown here.

You will start by creating a rectangle for the torso.

tip *Make sure that your magnification is set to 100% so you can create these elements at actual size.*

1] With the Rectangle tool, create a rectangle of any size on the page.

The rectangle appears on the page with a border and no fill. (If your rectangle looks different, don't worry. You will be changing its characteristics shortly.)

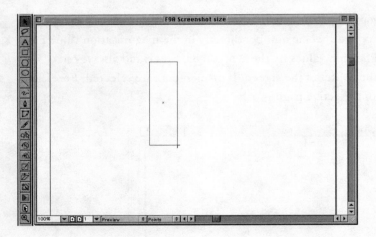

Rather than manually adjusting the size of the rectangle as you did earlier in this lesson, you will use the Object Inspector to specify a precise size for this element.

tip *Zoom in to see the artwork clearly as you work.*

2] Display the Object Inspector by clicking its button on the main toolbar.

The position and size of the selected element are displayed in the Object Inspector.

3] Change the unit of measure for this document to Inches by using the Units menu at the bottom of the document window.

This menu defines the unit of measure used throughout the document (except for the type size, which is always measured in points). Notice that now the values in the Object Inspector representing the position, width, and height of the selected object are displayed in inches.

note *If you're using the Robot1.fh9 file, the unit of measurement is already inches.*

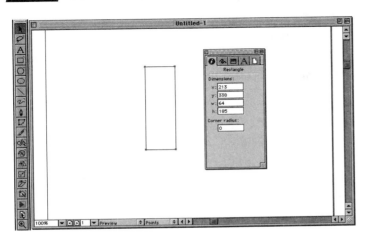

4] In the Object Inspector, select the current w value and type a width of 0.75. Press the Tab key to highlight the h value and type a height of 2. Press the Enter key to apply these changes.

This will change the size of the selected rectangle to the desired size for the robot's torso.

31

When this book says to press Enter, you can press the Enter key on the numeric keypad. PC users can also press Enter on the main keyboard, and Macintosh users can also press Return. For simplicity, this book refers only to the Enter key.

5] Create another rectangle above the torso for the shoulders. Make this rectangle wider than it is tall, as shown here. Then use the Pointer tool to move the shoulder element by pointing to the edge of the rectangle (not on a selection box), holding down the mouse button, and dragging. Visually position the shoulders over the torso.

The precise size of this rectangle is not important, and don't worry if your elements are not centered perfectly above one another; you will fix that shortly.

tip *Remember that to move this element, you must point to the border of the element (without pointing to a selection box) and drag. Because this rectangle is empty, there is nothing to grab inside the border when you want to move the object.*

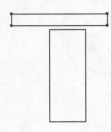

6] Select the Ellipse tool and use this tool to create a perfect circle for the head by holding down the Shift key as you drag diagonally. Then move the circle into position over the shoulders using the Pointer tool.

Holding down Shift enables you to draw perfect circles with the Ellipse tool and perfect squares with the Rectangle tool, and constrains lines created with the Line tool to 180-, 90-, and 45-degree angles. Make sure that you release the mouse button before you release the Shift key, or the constraints will be released.

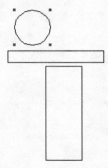

7] Draw another horizontal rectangle below the torso for the hips of the robot. Then use the Line tool to draw a vertical line connecting all of these shapes; this is the spine of the robot. Make sure to hold down the Shift key to keep the line vertical.

You now have five elements on your page.

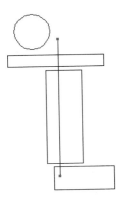

8] Choose the Pointer tool in the Toolbox.

It is always a good idea to return to the Pointer tool when you finish with other tools. Then an accidental click will not add a tiny rectangle, line, or ellipse, change your view, or perform any other operation on your artwork.

◉ POWER TIP *There are faster ways to choose the Pointer tool than clicking in the toolbox. You can press the 0 (Zero) key on the numeric pad or the main keyboard, or you can press the V key.*

note *If you are typing in a text block, you must first deselect the text block, then press the 0 or V key.*

SAVING THE DOCUMENT

Saving your work frequently is a good habit. You should save at least every 15 minutes or each time you finish a significant task. This will prevent you from losing hours of work if a power outage or computer malfunction occurs.

1] Choose File › Save to display the Save As dialog box (Windows Ctrl+S, Macintosh Command+S). Alternatively, you can click the Save button on the toolbar.

Because this is the first time you have saved this document, FreeHand will ask for a location and name for the file.

2] Select the location where you want to save this document. In this case, choose the MyWork folder you created on your hard drive.

3] Type a name for the document, such as MyRobot, and click Save.

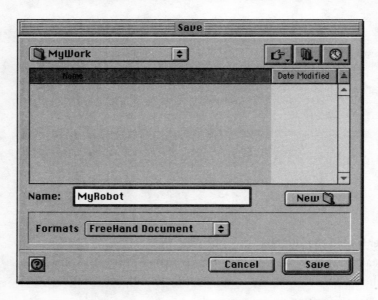

When FreeHand is finished saving the file, the name you entered will appear in the title bar at the top of the document window.

tip *Always choose the location before entering a name for a document. This ensures that you know exactly where your document is saved.*

APPLYING BASIC FILLS AND STROKES

The circle and rectangles you have created are empty shapes with thin black outlines. In this task, you will fill in each of these empty shapes with one or more colors or shades. Applying colors to the inside of an element is called applying a fill. You will also change the border, or stroke, of each element.

1] Open the Color Mixer by choosing Window › Panels › Color Mixer or by clicking the Color Mixer button on the main toolbar.

You will use the Color Mixer to create new colors to apply to elements in your documents. The buttons across the top allow you to select the type of color you want to define.

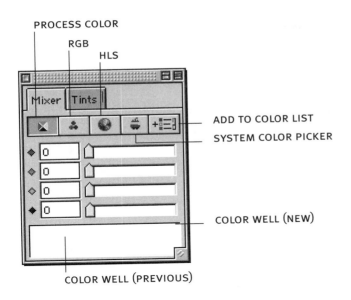

PROCESS COLOR

RGB

HLS

Mixer | Tints

ADD TO COLOR LIST

SYSTEM COLOR PICKER

COLOR WELL (NEW)

COLOR WELL (PREVIOUS)

2] Click the top-left button in the Color Mixer to display the four color controls—Cyan, Magenta, Yellow, and Black—used to define process colors (if they are not already visible in the Color Mixer). Drag the sliders to create a green color, such as 100 Cyan, 0 Magenta, 100 Yellow, and 0 Black.

You can define a color by dragging the sliders or entering values for each color component directly and pressing Enter. If you are typing values directly, you can press Tab to move between fields.

3] Point to the color well at the bottom of the Color Mixer, hold down the mouse button, and drag a color swatch out from the well. Drop this swatch inside the bottom rectangle of your robot (the hips).

You can drag and drop any color from the Color Mixer onto any element in your document.

You can drag and drop a color inside any of the closed shapes in your drawing to apply a basic (solid) fill. If the stroke changes instead of the fill, you dropped the swatch on the stroke; choose Edit > Undo and try again.

tip   *It is often easier to drop color inside a small shape if you first zoom in on the element.*

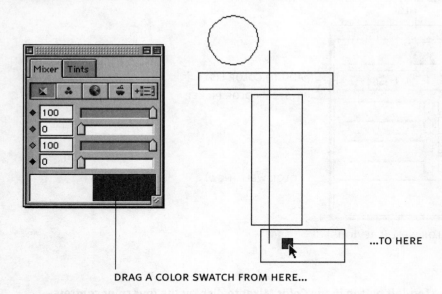

DRAG A COLOR SWATCH FROM HERE...

...TO HERE

tip   *Power Tip: Hold the Shift key when you release the mouse to force the swatch to apply to the fill, regardless of where on the object the swatch lands.*

You will use drag-and-drop techniques to fill the remaining shapes in the robot.

4] Fill the torso rectangle and the head with the same color as the hips.

Next you will create and apply a screen, or tint, of a color to the shoulder rectangle.

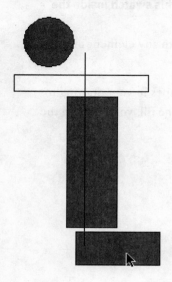

5] Click the Tints tab at the top of the Color Mixer panel group to display the Tints panel and then select Black from the pop-up menu in the Tints panel.

The Tints panel displays a strip of tints, in small squares called swatches, in 10 percent increments of the base color—in this case, black. This panel also provides a custom tint control (with an entry field and slider) for creating other tint values.

The Color List menu in the Tints panel enables you to directly select any color that currently exists in the Color List panel as a base color for a tint.

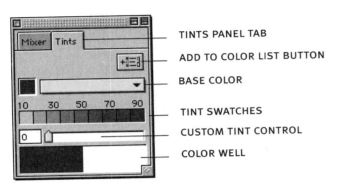

TINTS PANEL TAB

ADD TO COLOR LIST BUTTON

BASE COLOR

TINT SWATCHES

CUSTOM TINT CONTROL

COLOR WELL

6] Drag the 30 percent swatch and drop it inside the shoulder rectangle of your robot.

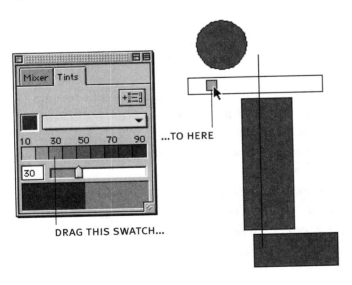

...TO HERE

DRAG THIS SWATCH...

> **tip** *If the stroke color changes instead of the fill, use Edit > Undo and try again. Zooming in closer will often make filling small objects easier. You can also hold the Shift key when you release the mouse to force the swatch to apply to the fill.*

Next you will change the thickness of the robot's spine.

7] Select the spine line with the Pointer tool. Select the Stroke Inspector by choosing Window › Inspectors › Stroke or Modify › Stroke. Alternatively, you can select the Stroke Inspector by clicking the Inspector button on the toolbar and then clicking the Stroke tab.

The Stroke Inspector appears. With this Inspector, you can control the stroke (line) characteristics of the selected object.

STROKE TAB

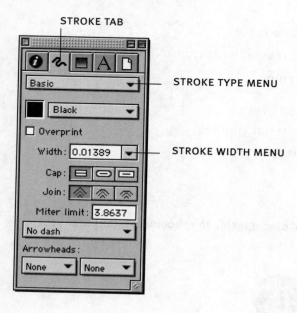

STROKE TYPE MENU

STROKE WIDTH MENU

8] At the top of the panel, make sure that the Basic and Black stroke options are selected. Change the width to 4 points either by entering 4 pt in the Width field and pressing Enter or selecting 4 from the adjacent menu.

The selected line should now appear thicker, representing the increased stroke width.

tip *Because you set the unit of measure for this document to inches earlier, you must type pt after the value in the width field so FreeHand will properly apply a 4-point stroke. Entering a 4 without the pt and pressing Enter will result in a stroke that is 4 inches wide! (The Stroke Width menu is always displayed in points for convenience.)*

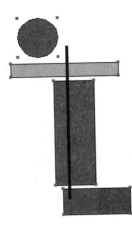

9] Select the torso with the Pointer tool. Hold down the Shift key and click the head, shoulder, and hip elements. In the Stroke Inspector, change the stroke type to None on the Stroke Type menu. Then press the Tab key to deselect all elements.

You have now removed the outlines from the robot elements.

You can add to a selection by holding down the Shift key and clicking additional objects. Selecting the four elements together enabled you to change the stroke for all four at once.

You can apply a thick or thin stroke to any selected graphic, or you can remove the stroke altogether.

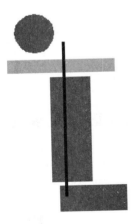

tip   *To deselect all objects, press the Tab key. You can also deselect all objects by clicking the Pointer tool on an empty part of the page or pasteboard. Windows users: if a panel is active, you must first activate the document window by clicking it before you can use the Tab key to deselect all objects.*

APPLYING GRADIENT FILLS

You will now change the fill inside two of the elements from a solid shade, called a basic fill, to one that changes from one shade to another, called a gradient fill. FreeHand enables you to define your own gradient fills or to select from a library of predefined styles.

1] Display the Styles panel by choosing Window › Panels › Styles.

Styles are collections of visual characteristics for graphics or text that can save you time and help you achieve design consistency by letting you apply or edit attributes for several objects in one quick step. As you will see in upcoming lessons, you can also use the Styles panel to apply your own fill and stroke settings to objects or to apply paragraph formatting (font, size, leading, and so on) to text quickly and easily throughout your documents.

The Styles panel initially displays two default styles—one each for text and objects. FreeHand also provides a collection, or library, of gradient presets that make it as easy to apply a complex gradient fill to an element as it is to apply a solid-color fill with the Color Mixer.

2] Choose CMYK Styles from the Options menu at the top of the Styles panel. Select the gradient style named Reds by clicking it. Then click Import.

This style now appears in the Styles panel. In this display of styles, you can see the style name plus an icon for each style that indicates the style type: object or text.

tip *Since these style presets can be customized, this specific style may not be available on your system. If Reds is not available, select another that you like and use it instead.*

3] Choose Options › Hide Names in the Styles panel.

Now the Styles panel displays icons for each style that show the visual characteristics of the individual styles.

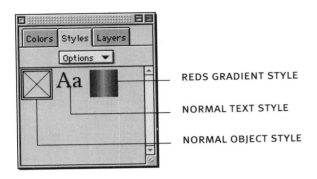

REDS GRADIENT STYLE

NORMAL TEXT STYLE

NORMAL OBJECT STYLE

4] Drag the Reds gradient swatch from the Styles panel and drop it inside the torso rectangle.

The gradient fill is immediately applied to the rectangle.

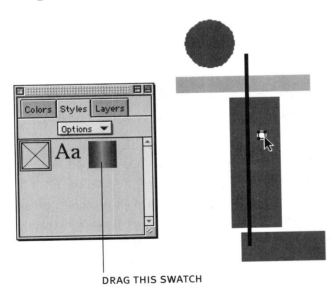

DRAG THIS SWATCH

To modify this gradient slightly, you will use the Fill Inspector.

5] With the Pointer tool, select the torso rectangle. Click the Fill tab in the Inspector panel group to display the Fill Inspector. Alternatively, you can choose Window › Inspectors › Fill or Modify › Fill.

The Fill Inspector appears. With this Inspector, you can control the characteristics of the fill inside an element. Notice that the Fill type menu at the top of the Fill Inspector indicates that this element already has a Gradient fill.

A sample of the gradient is displayed in a color ramp on the left side of the Inspector. There are seven color swatches defining this gradient. These appear as swatches attached to the right edge of the color ramp: the starting color for the gradient appears at the top of the color ramp, the ending color appears at the bottom, and the five other colors appear in between. Gradient fills can contain up to 32 color swatches anywhere along the color ramp.

Two types of gradient are available, and you can change from one to the other by clicking the Graduated or Radial button in the Inspector panel. A graduated fill changes color in a straight line across the graphic. The direction of this color change is determined by the Direction control at the bottom of the panel. A radial fill changes color from a center point outward in all directions. When you click the Radial button, the options in the Fill Inspector change to enable you to reposition the center point of the radial fill.

6] Change the direction of this linear gradient by dragging the Direction control at the bottom of the Inspector to point down and to the right.
You can also adjust the direction by typing a value in the Direction Angle field.

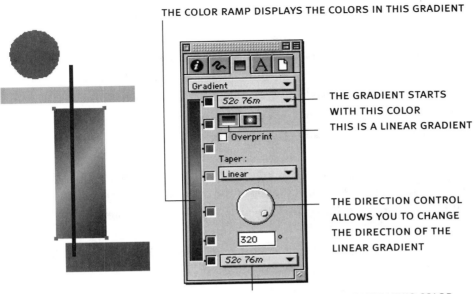

THE COLOR RAMP DISPLAYS THE COLORS IN THIS GRADIENT

THE GRADIENT STARTS
WITH THIS COLOR

THIS IS A LINEAR GRADIENT

THE DIRECTION CONTROL
ALLOWS YOU TO CHANGE
THE DIRECTION OF THE
LINEAR GRADIENT

THE GRADIENT ENDS WITH THIS COLOR

Next you will define your own gradient for the robot's head.

7] Select the circle and change the fill type from Basic to Gradient in the Fill Inspector. Then click the Radial button in the Fill Inspector. Move the center of the radial fill up and to the right by dragging the center point in the Fill Inspector.

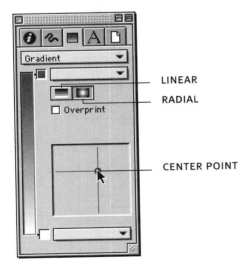

LINEAR

RADIAL

CENTER POINT

43

The circle is now filled with a radial fill, which helps create the appearance that the robot's head is a sphere instead of a flat circle.

Next you will make the robot's head a bit more colorful by changing the colors in the gradient to the same ones used in the gradient style you applied to the torso rectangle. The colors in this gradient style were automatically added to the Color List when you imported the style from the library. These colors were given names that describe their cyan, magenta, yellow, and black components.

8] Change the starting color of this gradient to dark red by choosing 52c 76m 69y 18k in the starting color menu at the top of the color ramp. Now change the ending color to orange by choosing 0c 26m 76y 0k in the ending color menu at the bottom of the color ramp.

The robot's head is now filled with a radial gradient that radiates out from the center point from orange to dark red.

9] Display the Color List by clicking its button on the main toolbar. Drag an orange swatch, 1c 57m 83y 0k, from the Color List and drop it anywhere on the color ramp in the Fill Inspector to add a new color to this gradient.

You can drag the swatch up and down along the ramp to reposition it in the gradient. If you want to remove a color from the gradient, simply drag the swatch to the right away from the color ramp and release the mouse.

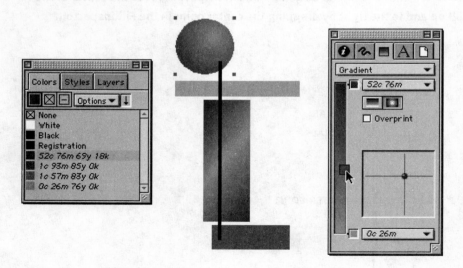

10] Save your document with File › Save.

tip   *Remember to save frequently as you work.*

ARRANGING, ALIGNING, AND GROUPING ELEMENTS

FreeHand arranges elements on the page in the order that they are created, which is why the spine of the robot is in front of the other body parts. You will rearrange the elements to make the robot look better.

1] Select the spine with the Pointer tool and choose Modify › Arrange › Send to Back.
The spine is now behind all of the other elements. The Arrange submenu offers four commands you can use in different situations. Use Send to Back or Bring to Front to move an object behind or in front of all of the other elements. Move Forward and Move Backward move a selected object forward or backward one element at a time.

Next get all the elements in your robot into proper alignment so the body looks symmetrical.

2] Select all of the elements by choosing Edit › Select › All. Choose Window › Panels › Align or Modify › Align.
The Align panel appears. This panel provides several choices for both horizontal and vertical alignment.

45

tip Alternatively, click the Align button on the main toolbar.

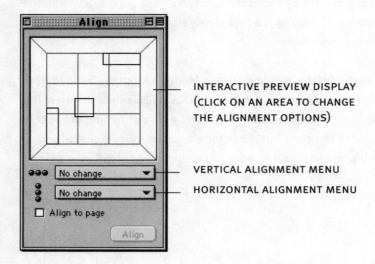

INTERACTIVE PREVIEW DISPLAY
(CLICK ON AN AREA TO CHANGE
THE ALIGNMENT OPTIONS)

VERTICAL ALIGNMENT MENU

HORIZONTAL ALIGNMENT MENU

3] On the upper (Vertical Alignment) menu, select No Change. On the lower (Horizontal Alignment) menu, select Align Center.

The preview display in the Align panel should show the desired results: elements centered left and right and not aligned up or down.

4] Click Align to Page in the Align panel to turn on this option.

The elements will now be centered horizontally on the page as well as centered horizontally on one another. (Because Vertical Alignment is set to No Change, the elements will not be adjusted vertically on the page.)

5] Click the button at the bottom of the Align panel to align your elements.

All five elements are now aligned accurately and centered horizontally on the page. To keep them aligned to one another and prevent accidental changes, you can group the elements.

6] With all five elements still selected, choose Modify › Group (Windows Ctrl+G, Macintosh Command+G).

This ties all the selected elements together into one group. One set of selection boxes now appears around the group, instead of individual selection boxes appearing around each element. Now you can move, resize, and modify all of these elements as one.

7] Save your work.

ADDING OTHER ELEMENTS

Next you will add arms and legs to complete the robot. The two arms are identical, so you can create one and make a copy for the second. The legs are identical also, but the feet point in opposite directions. For this effect, you will create a mirror image of the leg.

First you will create an arm. Then you will perform a simple copy-and-paste operation to create the second arm.

1] Choose the Ellipse tool and position the cursor about halfway up the left edge of the shoulder. Hold the Alt (Windows) or Option (Macintosh) key and the Shift key and draw a circle just a bit larger than the height of the shoulder box. Fill the circle with 50 percent black using the Tints panel and set the stroke to None in the Stroke Inspector. Holding Shift creates a perfect circle. Holding Alt or Option draws an object from the center. Notice that the cursor changes from the standard crosshair to a crosshair in a circle to indicate that you are drawing the circle from the center. These keys work the same way with the Rectangle tool.

Remember that you can choose Undo if you don't like your first attempt. Also, once the ellipse is on the page, you can use the Pointer tool with Shift and the Alt or Option key to resize the circle from the center.

2] Draw a vertical line from the middle of the circle downward to form the arm. Using the Stroke Inspector, change the width of this line to 8 points.

For this robot, the arm should not reach as low as the hips.

Remember to return to the Pointer tool.

3] Bring the circle to the front by selecting the circle and choosing Modify › Arrange › Bring to Front (Windows Ctrl+F, Macintosh Command+F).

The arm is almost ready to be duplicated, but it would be easier to work with if the two elements were grouped together.

4] Select the circle and the line at the same time by clicking either element with the Pointer tool and then holding down the Shift key and clicking the other element.

Holding down Shift and clicking additional elements allows you to select multiple objects. Shift-clicking a selected item deselects it while leaving all other selected elements selected.

5] Group the selected elements by choosing Modify › Group.

Now you can work with the arm as if it were a single element.

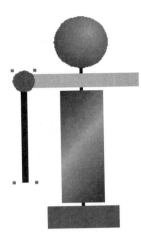

6] With the arm still selected, choose Edit › Copy.

This puts an electronic copy of the selected artwork onto the clipboard.

7] Choose Edit › Paste to paste a second copy of the arm on the page.

FreeHand will paste the duplicate arm on the page in the center of your screen.

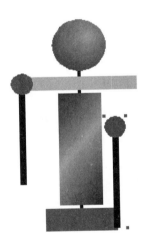

You now need to move the duplicate arm into position.

8] Use the pointer to move the second arm into position on the other shoulder. Then select both arm groups and use the Align panel to align both arms vertically.

In the Align panel, select Top from the Vertical Alignment menu, select No Change from the Horizontal Alignment menu, and turn off Align to Page. Choose Edit > Undo if something goes wrong.

9] Repeat steps 1 through 3 to create one leg by drawing a circle and a line. Fill the circle with any fill and set the stroke of the line to 8 points.
You will add a foot in the next task before duplicating this leg.

10] Save your work.

CUSTOMIZING TOOL SETTINGS

The robot's feet are rounded rectangles, which you can draw after making an adjustment to the way the Rectangle tool works. Notice that the Rectangle tool in the toolbox is one of several tools that has a small mark in the upper-right corner. This mark indicates that preferences can be set for this tool. Double-clicking these tools displays a dialog box where you can change the settings.

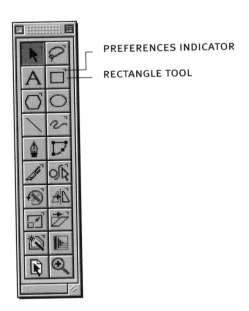

PREFERENCES INDICATOR

RECTANGLE TOOL

1] Double-click the Rectangle tool in the toolbox.

A dialog box appears where you can specify a radius for rounded corners. By default, the Rectangle tool uses a radius of zero, which draws rectangles with sharp, right-angle corners and no rounding.

2] Set the radius to 9 points by typing 9pt in the radius field. Then click OK.

The radius value determines how rounded the corners of your rectangle will be. A radius value of zero creates rectangles with angled corners; increasing the value creates larger curves at each corner of the rectangle. If you specify a value greater than half the length of any of the sides of your rectangle, those entire sides will be curved.

51

Dragging the slider in this dialog box also enables you to adjust this radius value. Since the unit of measure for this document is set to inches, the radius values are displayed in inches rather than points if you drag the slider.

3] Draw a small rounded rectangle at the bottom of the robot's leg. Fill it with any tint of black and remove the stroke.

Notice the rounded corners on the rectangle. Reposition the foot as needed with the Pointer tool.

4] Complete the leg by selecting all three pieces and grouping them together with Modify › Group.

Remember that you can select several elements at the same time by holding down the Shift key.

5] Save your work.

The robot is nearly complete.

CREATING A MIRROR IMAGE OF AN ELEMENT

Duplicating the leg is a bit more challenging than duplicating the arm because the new leg must face the opposite direction. You will use the Mirror tool, which is one of FreeHand's Xtra tools. Xtras are plug-in software extensions that enhance FreeHand's capabilities. Some Xtras are provided with FreeHand, but you can purchase many others from third parties. (Go to www.macromedia.com/software/xtras/ for more details.) Each Xtra adds a specific feature or group of features. Xtras providing additional tools are located in the Xtra Tools panel.

1] Choose Window › Toolbars › Xtra Tools to display the Xtra Tools panel.

This toolbar contains additional drawing, manipulation, and special-effect tools.

A wide variety of Xtras are included with FreeHand and are installed when you install the program. Your Xtra Tools toolbar may look slightly different, depending on which Xtras you are loading with FreeHand.

2] With the grouped leg still selected, click once on the Mirror tool in the Xtra Tools toolbar.

By default, this tool will create a mirror image of a selected object.

3] Position the cursor on the spine of the robot and then click the mouse.

A mirrored duplicate is positioned on the other side of the body, so your robot now has two legs.

Clicking the spine with the Mirror tool sets a vertical reflection axis at that point. This reflection axis works like a mirror, reflecting a selected item an equal distance on the opposite side of the axis.

tip *The robot's spine is in the exact center of the figure. Clicking the Mirror tool on this center line ensures that the new leg is the same distance from the spine as the old leg.*

ROTATING AN ELEMENT ON THE PAGE

The robot is so happy to have all of its parts—now help it kick up its heels.

1] With the Pointer tool, double-click the new leg.

A new set of transform handles appears around the selected item, and the center of transformation appears as a hollow circle in the center of these transform handles. Double-clicking an element in the workspace enables you to rotate, scale, skew, and transform elements without having to switch to the specific transformation tools. As you rotate this element, it will revolve around the center of transformation.

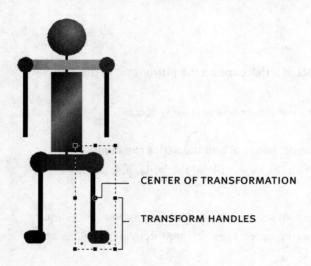

CENTER OF TRANSFORMATION

TRANSFORM HANDLES

2] Move the center of transformation by dragging the hollow circle in the center of the transformation handles to visually center the hollow circle on the circle at the top of the leg.

54

Next you will rotate the leg around this center point.

3] Position the mouse outside the transform handles surrounding the leg and drag out to the right and up slightly until the leg is rotated as shown here.

As you move the mouse over and around the control handles, the cursor will give you feedback to indicate what type of transformations you can apply, such as the rotation you applied to this element.

4] Double-click the leg again to hide the transform handles.

You can access these transform handles at any time by double-clicking an object or group on the page. When the transformation is complete, double-click the object again to hide the controls.

FreeHand also offers tools to perform specific transformations, including the Rotate, Reflect, Scale, and Skew tools in the toolbox, which you will explore in upcoming lessons.

The last step in creating this robot is to group all of its pieces together so they can't accidentally be disturbed.

5] Choose Edit › Select › All. Then choose Modify › Group or click the Group button on the main toolbar. Save your document.

Congratulations. You have just created your first piece of original art with FreeHand.

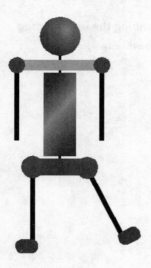

GETTING HELP

There will be times when you just cannot remember a specific technique and need a quick and easy resource for more information. In addition to the manuals that come with the application, FreeHand offers a comprehensive online help system for quick reference while you're working. For assistance in FreeHand, choose Help > FreeHand Help. A map of FreeHand's help system appears, providing you with point-and-click navigation to help you find the answers you need.

Experiment with the help system by looking up some topics in the help index or searching for help on a particular command or feature. Explore the Focus On topics, which present easy access to information on five dynamic focus areas within FreeHand: text, web graphics, drawing, printing, and layout.

The help system offers several additional features designed to help you get the most out of FreeHand. These include movie clips demonstrating hard-to-describe features and Tell Me How guides that provide step-by-step information on how to perform specific tasks. Take a look at these features—they're like having an instructor inside your computer.

If you have an Internet connection and a Web Browser, you can also find up-to-the-minute technical information at the Macromedia Web site (http://www.macromedia.com/support).

ON YOUR OWN

Create a companion for your robot using techniques you have learned in this lesson. Move the existing robot to one side of the page or onto the pasteboard to make room for the companion. You can create your own robot, or open a sample document and re-create the companion robot to match the sample. To see this example, choose File > Open and open Robot2.fh9 in the Complete folder within the Lesson01 folder.

WHAT YOU HAVE LEARNED

In this lesson you have:

- Opened FreeHand and created a new document [pages 8–9]
- Explored FreeHand's tools, toolbars, Inspectors, and panels [pages 10–20]
- Customized your workspace by connecting panels [pages 21-23]
- Created, duplicated, moved, and deleted elements [pages 24–27]
- Changed your view of your FreeHand document [pages 27–29]
- Created basic shapes with the Rectangle, Ellipse, and Line tools [pages 30–33]
- Applied basic and graduated fills and adjusted stroke width [pages 34–44]
- Arranged, aligned and grouped elements [pages 45–50]
- Customized application and tool preferences [pages 14, 51–52]
- Used one of FreeHand's Xtra tools to create a mirror image of a selection [pages 52–53]
- Rotated an element [pages 54–55]
- Learned how to get help [page 56]

and graphics

combining text

One of the most common uses for a vector program like FreeHand is designing corporate identity packages. FreeHand is uniquely qualified to handle such a task because it allows you to combine multiple pages of different sizes within the same document. This means you can quickly experiment with the look of a letterhead, business card, and envelope on accurately sized pages without switching windows. Updating graphic elements can be accomplished much more efficiently. In this lesson

This stationary was created from scratch using FreeHand's drawing and text tools.

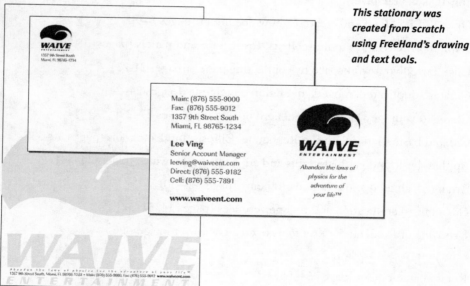

Designed by Tony Roame of Illustrated Concepts

you will set up a document with multiple pages, then combine graphic elements with text for a compelling corporate identity package.

If you would like to review the final result of this lesson, open Waive.fh9 in the Complete folder within the Lesson02 folder.

WHAT YOU WILL LEARN

In this lesson you will:

- Add pages to a document
- Arrange pages on the pasteboard
- Set a custom page size
- Specify measurement units
- Design the layout for printing with two ink colors
- Import a vector EPS file created elsewhere
- Change the appearance of objects
- Practice aligning elements
- Import text from an outside file
- Enter and format text

APPROXIMATE TIME

It usually takes about 1 hour to complete this lesson.

LESSON FILES

Media Files:

Lesson02\Media\WELogo.eps
Lesson02\Media\P2text.rtf

Starting Files:

None

Completed Project:

Lesson02\Complete\Waive.fh9
Lesson02\Complete\WaivePlus.fh9

Bonus Files:

Lesson02\Bonus\Bonus2.pdf
Lesson02\Bonus\Bonus2Done.fh9
Lesson02\Bonus\CropMarks.mov
Lesson02\Bonus\StepCards.mov

CREATING A NEW DOCUMENT WITH A CUSTOM PAGE SIZE

In this lesson you will assemble the letterhead, business cards, and envelope design for Waive Entertainment, a virtual-reality entertainment company. You will create the letterhead for an Executive-size page, which measures 7.25 by 10.5 inches. Your first task is to create a page with these dimensions.

1] Choose File › New to create a new document (Windows Ctrl+N, Macintosh Command+N).

A new document window will appear containing one page on the pasteboard.

2] Change the unit of measure for this document to Inches using the Units menu at the bottom of the document window.

This menu defines the unit of measure used throughout the document (except for the type size, which is always measured in points).

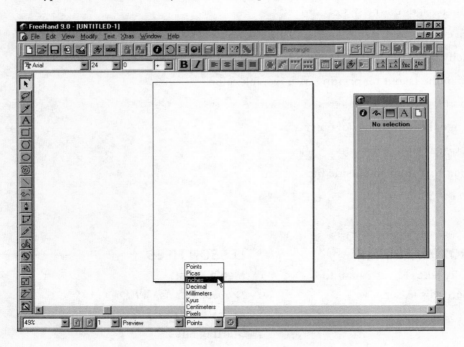

The only visible indication that the units have changed is that the Units menu now displays Inches instead of Points.

3] Choose Window › Inspectors › Document to display the Document Inspector.

The Document Inspector contains controls that enable you to change the size, orientation, and number of pages within your document.

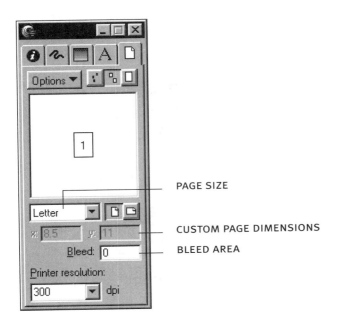

PAGE SIZE

CUSTOM PAGE DIMENSIONS

BLEED AREA

4] Use the Page Size menu in the Document Inspector to change from Letter to Custom.

Now you will be able to edit the page dimensions to change the page size to match the size of an Executive page.

You will also need to specify the bleed area, the amount of space that elements will print beyond the edges of the layout. On a printing press, layouts that require color extending to the edge of the page must be printed on larger sheets of paper than the document requires, and the color must extend beyond the boundaries of the layout. When the oversized sheets are cut to the correct page size, the color will extend beyond the cut. This will prevent strips of paper color showing at the edge of the page, even if the ink is not placed in the exact same position on each sheet due to paper shifting slightly on the press.

You can set the size of the bleed area in the Document Inspector, which defines the distance around the page that FreeHand will print. The default value is zero, which means nothing beyond the edge of the page will print. Your letterhead includes elements that extend to the edge of the layout, so you need to specify a bleed area.

5] Select the value in the x field and type a new width of 7.25. Press the Tab key to highlight the y field and type a height of 10.5. Press Tab again to highlight the Bleed field and type a value of 0.125. Press Enter to apply these changes.

This will change the page to the size of an Executive page and give the document a bleed area of one-eighth inch all around. (One-eighth inch is the standard bleed size

61

used by most printers.) The new page size is now displayed in the document window. The gray line surrounding the page indicates the bleed area.

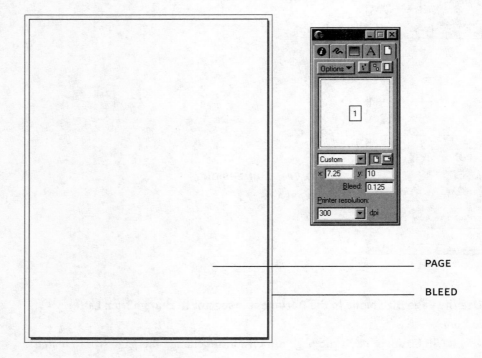

PAGE

BLEED

6] Save your document as MyWaive in your MyWork folder on your hard drive.
Remember to save frequently as you work!

ADDING CUSTOM PAGES AND
ARRANGING PAGES ON THE PASTEBOARD

FreeHand gives you the ability to create pages of different sizes within the same document. You are going to create one new page for the business card, 2 inches by 3.5 inches, and one new page for a commercial sized envelope, 9.5 inches by 4.125 inches. You will arrange these pages on the pasteboard so they are close to each other, which makes viewing and editing more convenient.

1] Go to the Document Inspector and click on the Options pop-up menu and select Duplicate.
This is one way to create an identical copy of an existing page. The duplicate page will be located about one inch to the right of the existing page.

2] Select the Page tool and click on the second page.

When you click on the second page you will see handles appear on the corners and sides.

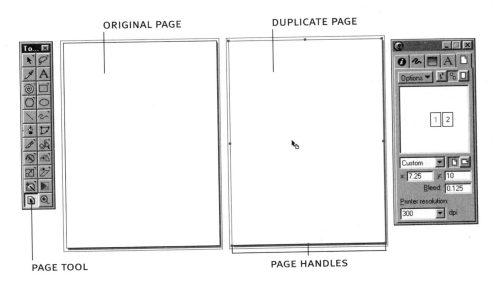

ORIGINAL PAGE

DUPLICATE PAGE

PAGE TOOL

PAGE HANDLES

3] Position the Page tool icon over the lower right corner of the page, then click and drag up and to the left until the page is approximately the size of a business card.

Earlier you set the page dimensions by typing in the Document Inspector. You can also change page dimensions visually when you click and drag on the page handles. In this particular case, however, you need specific page dimensions. For precise measurements, it is best to enter page dimensions in the Document Inspector.

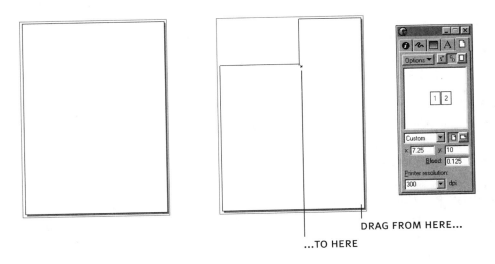

DRAG FROM HERE...

...TO HERE

63

4] In the Document Inspector, select the value in the x field and type a width of 3.5. Press the Tab key to highlight the y field and type a height of 2. Press Tab again to highlight the Bleed field and type a value of 0. Press Enter to apply these changes.

Now your second page is the exact size of a standard business card. Since the business card will not have any objects extending off the edge of the page, you do not need a bleed area.

5] Position the Page tool over the second page. Then hold down Alt (Windows) or Option (Macintosh) and click and drag down approximately eight inches.

This is the second way to create an identical copy of an existing page. The new page will be located wherever you drop it. Using the Page tool is a more flexible way of duplicating pages, since you can position the new pages exactly where you want them.

USING THE PAGE TOOL, HOLD DOWN ALT (WINDOWS) OR OPTION (MACINTOSH) AND DRAG FROM HERE...

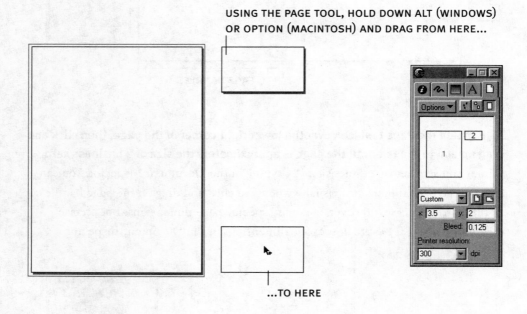

...TO HERE

tip   *Pages in FreeHand cannot overlap each other, so make sure the duplicate page you are dragging does not touch an existing page when you release the mouse button. If you attempt to move a duplicate page where it will overlap an existing page, the selected page will spring back to its previous position and no duplicate will be created.*

◎ POWER TIP   *It is possible to duplicate multiple pages at one time using the Page tool method. Hold down the shift key and click with the Page tool on each of the pages you want to duplicate, then hold down Alt (Windows) or Option (Macintosh) and drag the duplicate pages to a new location.*

6] Click on the third page with the Page tool. In the Document Inspector, select the value in the x field and type a width of 9.5. Press the Tab key to highlight the y field and type a height of 4.125. Press Enter to apply these changes.

Now your third page is the size of a #10 commercial envelope.

7] Use the Page tool to click on the business card page and drag it so that the top of the page is at the same height as the top of the first page. Then drag the envelope page so it is just below the business card page.

The easiest way to reposition pages on the pasteboard is by dragging them with the Page tool. If you want to move pages a long distance, such as the opposite side of the pasteboard, you can also drag the outline of the page in the Document Inspector.

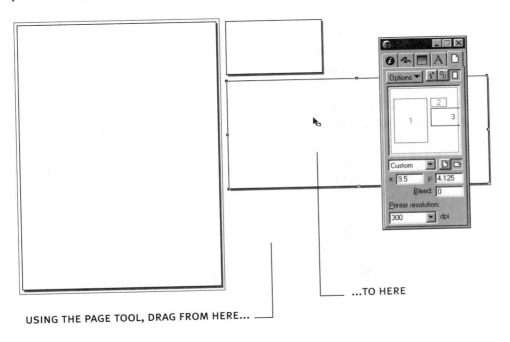

USING THE PAGE TOOL, DRAG FROM HERE...

...TO HERE

tip   *If you attempt to move a page where it will overlap an existing page, the selected page will spring back to its previous position and the page will not be moved. Pages can touch edges, but they can not overlap.*

tip   *You can delete unwanted pages by simply clicking on the page with the Page tool and pressing the Delete key.*

8] Save your document.

65

CREATING AND EDITING RULER GUIDES

You will use a ruler guide to help you position the logo in the correct distance from the top of the page. Ruler guides are nonprinting lines you can use in your documents to help you position elements accurately. One way to add ruler guides to your page is to drag them from the vertical or horizontal rulers on your page.

1] Display the page rulers by choosing View › Page Rulers › Show (Windows Ctrl+Atl+M, Macintosh Command+Option+M). Choose View › Fit All to see all three pages in the document window (Windows Ctrl+Alt+0, Macintosh Command+Option+0).

The rulers will help you position the elements on the page. On each ruler there is a location where the numbers start with zero. The place where those zeros intersect on the page is called the zero point (by default it is the lower left corner of the page). Notice that when you click on each page with the pointer tool, the zero point changes. That is because the rulers reflect the zero point of the active page.

2] Pull a ruler guide onto page 1 by pointing to the horizontal page ruler at the top of the page and dragging the mouse downward. Release the mouse over page 1 (the letterhead page).

The ruler guide appears at the place where you release your mouse. If the guide does not appear, it may be that you released the mouse over the pasteboard. Try again and be careful to release the mouse on page 1.

CLICK ON THE RULER AND DRAG FROM HERE...
...TO HERE

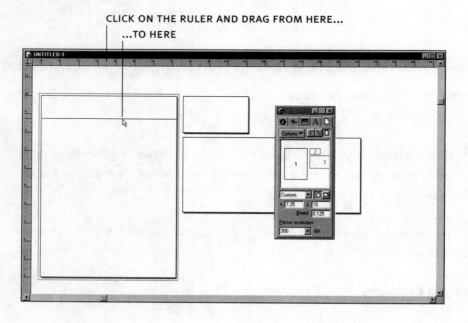

You can reposition the guide by clicking and dragging it to a new location. It is also possible to position guides precisely by entering numeric coordinates.

tip *To remove a ruler guide, drag it off the page and release the mouse.*

3] Double-click on the ruler guide you just placed on the page, then click Edit in the dialog box that appears. Type 10 in the location field, then press Enter. Press OK (Windows) or Enter (Macintosh) again to close the dialog box and apply the changes. The Edit Guides dialog box appears, and you can select a guide to enter precise coordinates. Since you only have one guide on the page at this time, it is already selected. The number you enter is based on the zero point of the page. The default location of the zero point is at the bottom of the page, so entering 10 in the location field will place the guide one half-inch from the top of the page, which is 10.5 inches high.

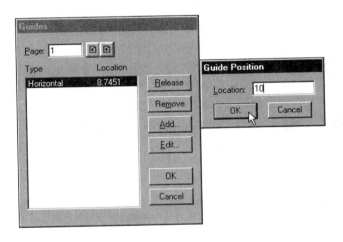

4] Pull a ruler guide onto page 2 (the business card page) by pointing to the vertical page ruler and dragging the mouse to the right. Release the mouse over page 2. Double-click on the ruler guide you just placed on page 2, then click Edit in the dialog box that appears. Type 3.25 in the location field, then press Enter. Press OK (Windows) or Enter (Macintosh) again to close the dialog box and apply the changes.

The ruler guide appears 0.25 inches from the right edge of the page.

CLICK ON THE RULER AND DRAG FROM HERE...

...TO HERE

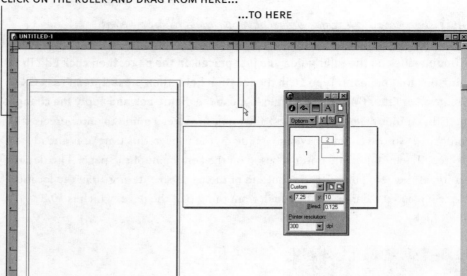

5] Choose View > Snap To Guides (Windows Ctrl+Atl+G, Macintosh Command+\).
Now when any element is moved within a few pixels of a ruler guide it will snap
into place.

IMPORTING A VECTOR GRAPHIC (EPS FORMAT)

Sometimes you will create artwork from scratch in FreeHand, and other times you
will import previously created art. Often this may be artwork supplied by a client,
such as a logo or other graphics. For this lesson you are going to import the logo for
Waive Entertainment, which was supplied on the CD. FreeHand can import vector
graphics in the EPS format, and it even has the ability to edit imported art.

**1] Choose File > Import (Windows Ctrl+R, Macintosh Command+R). Select
WELogo.eps from the Media folder within the Lesson02 folder and click Open.**

Your cursor will change to the import cursor, which represents the top left corner of the graphic.

IMPORT CURSOR

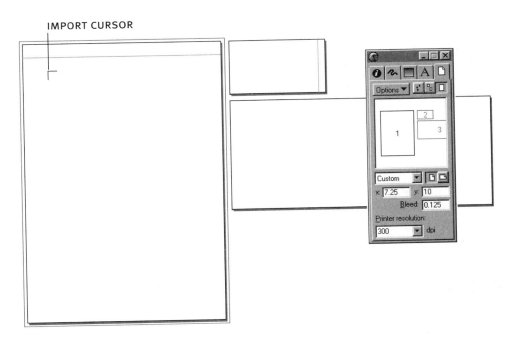

2] Position the cursor anywhere over the horizontal ruler guide on page 1 and click the mouse.

The graphic appears on the page in this position. It is already at the correct height, since you clicked on the ruler guide. If you clicked somewhere else, move the logo now so that the top edge of the logo snaps to the ruler guide. Next, we will make sure the logo is centered on the page.

tip *Be careful not to drag the mouse when clicking to position an imported graphic. When you click and drag with the import cursor, the graphic will scale itself to fit the size of the rectangle you drag. In most cases this is not the desired result.*

3] With the logo still selected, choose Modify › Align to display the Align panel. On the Horizontal Alignment menu, choose Align Center. The Vertical Alignment menu should be set to No Change. Make sure that Align to Page is turned on. Then click Apply (Windows) or Align (Macintosh).

Now you can be certain the logo is centered on the page horizontally.

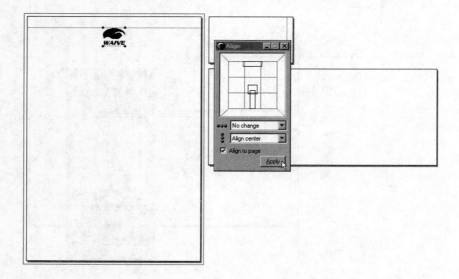

tip *In the Align panel, remember that the Vertical Alignment menu is the top menu and is identified by three spheres that are aligned vertically. The Horizontal Alignment menu is the bottom menu and is identified by three spheres that are aligned horizontally.*

4] Select the logo and choose Edit › Duplicate. Drag the duplicate logo to page 2 and position it so the right edge of the logo touches the vertical ruler guide on page 2. Now the logo on page 2 is 0.25 inches from the right edge of the page. The vertical position of this logo is not important right now. You will adjust that later in this lesson.

DUPLICATED LOGO   DRAG TO HERE

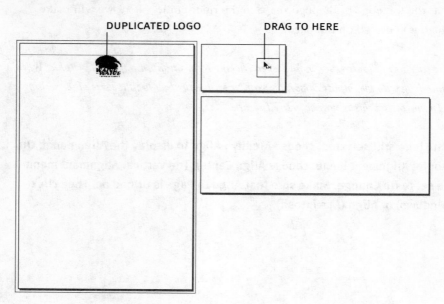

5] Select the logo on page 2 and choose Edit › Copy. Go to the page pop-up menu at the bottom of the screen and choose page 3 (the envelope page) to make it active, then choose Edit › Paste.

This time the logo lands in the middle of page 3. By default, pasted items land in the middle of the screen.

6] Move the logo so that it is touching the top and left side of the page.

If Snap to Guides is selected, the logo should snap into place when you get within a few pixels of the edge of the page.

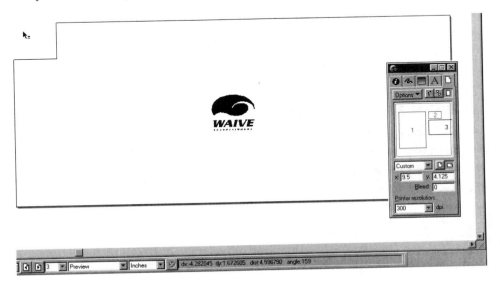

7] Choose Modify › Transform › Move to bring up the Transform panel. Click in the x field and type 0.25, then press Tab to move to the y field and type –0.25, then press Enter.

This moves the logo precisely 0.25 inches from the top and left side of the page. You can use the Transform panel any time you need to move an object a precise distance. Just remember that positive numbers in the x field move to the right, and positive

71

numbers in the y field move up. That is why you had to enter a negative number to move the logo down.

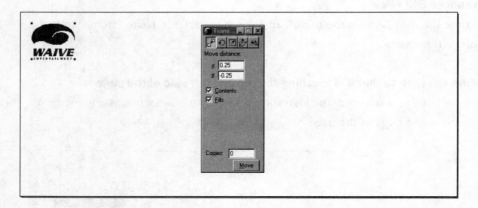

CLONING AND SCALING ELEMENTS

The logo is already the correct size for the top of the page where it is located, but now you need to put a larger version at the bottom of the page. Rather than using the Copy and Paste or Duplicate commands, you are going to Clone the logo to take advantage of its current position on the page.

1] Select the logo on page 1 and choose Edit › Clone.

This creates a duplicate logo directly on top of the original. The duplicate remains selected.

tip   *It may seem as if nothing happened, since there are no visual cues of a change in your document. If you want to verify that the command was executed, click on the Edit menu and observe that the Undo command says Undo Clone.*

2] Double-click the Scale tool in the Toolbox to display the Transform panel.

The Transform panel is displayed with the scale controls.

3] Make sure the pop-up menu shows Percent, then type 800 in the Scale % field and click Scale (Windows) or Apply (Macintosh).

The copy of the logo is enlarged to 800 percent of its original size.

If the Uniform box is checked when you scale an object, it keeps its proportions. If you turn uniform scaling off, you can scale the x and y values at different percentages, distorting the proportions as you scale the object. For this task, you want uniform scaling turned on.

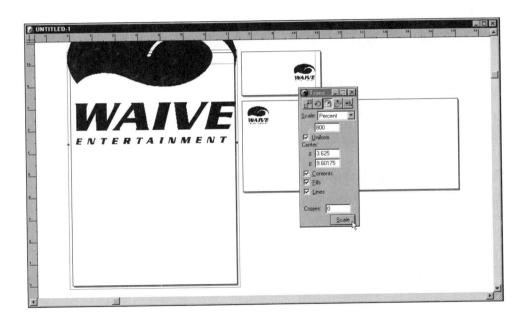

4] Close the Transform panel. Hold down the Shift key, and using the Pointer tool, move the large logo so that the word Entertainment is just above the bottom of the page. Release the mouse first, then release the Shift key.

Position the artwork similar to the example shown here. This artwork extends beyond the bleed area on the sides, but FreeHand will print only the portion that appears within the bleed area defined by the gray line that surrounds the page.

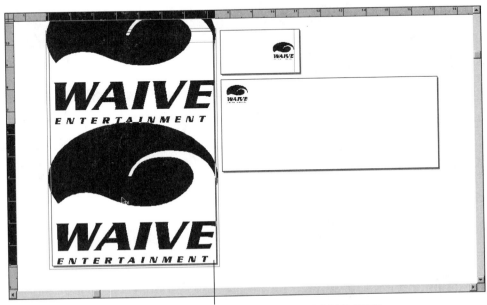

MOVE THE LARGE LOGO TO HERE

73

By keeping the Shift key pressed until you release the mouse, you force the logo to stay horizontally centered on the page, just as it was before you moved it. If you release the Shift key first, then the logo will land wherever the mouse is located instead of being in line with the original location of the logo.

5] Save your work.
Now you are ready to import colors for your layout.

IMPORTING AND CREATING COLORS AND TINTS

You will use two additional colors and a tint of one color in your layout. You will add these colors to the Color List.

1] Choose Window › Panels › Color List (or click the Color List button on the main toolbar) to display the Color List.
This panel displays the named colors currently available for this document. You need to add two colors to this list.

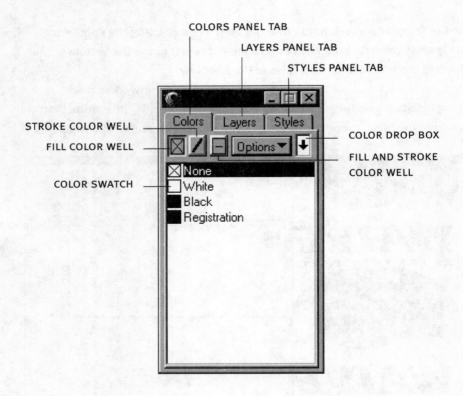

For projects that will be printed on a printing press, there are several industry-standard color selection systems for which printed swatch books of actual ink colors are available to help you choose colors accurately.

2] Select PANTONE® Coated from the Options menu at the top of the Color List.

This opens a color library containing the colors in the PANTONE Coated color-matching system. These colors are each identified by a unique number that corresponds with a number in the PANTONE Coated printed swatch book and a color of PANTONE ink.

FreeHand allows you to choose colors from PANTONE Coated and PANTONE Uncoated color libraries by using the Color List Options menu. The Uncoated color library shows the colors printed on standard (uncoated) paper. The Coated color library shows the same colors printed on coated paper, which has a thin coating of clay that has been polished to create a very smooth surface. Colors generally appear more brilliant on coated paper because the ink is not absorbed by the paper the way it is by uncoated paper. If you don't know what kind of paper your artwork will be printed on, your printer can advise you. For this lesson, it will not make any difference which of these two systems you choose.

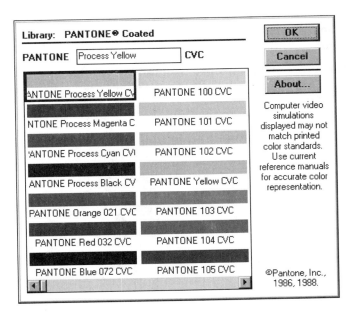

3] Type 286 to select PANTONE 286 and then click OK.

When the Add Color dialog box appears on your screen, the color name field is highlighted. If it is not, highlight the field and type 286. The color you type is displayed with a black border. When you click OK, the blue color, PANTONE 286 CVC, is added to the color list.

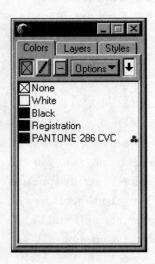

4] Select PANTONE Coated from the Options menu again and add PANTONE 425 to the color list.

The gray color, PANTONE 425 CVC, is added to the color list. You now have two PANTONE colors in the list.

76

5] Display the Tints panel by clicking the Color Mixer button on the main toolbar and clicking the Tints tab at the top of the panel group.

A tint is a lighter shade of a color expressed as a percentage of that color. The Tints panel displays a range of tints for the base color in 10 percent increments as well as a custom adjustment for creating tints at other values. You will use this panel to create a tint of one of the PANTONE colors in your document.

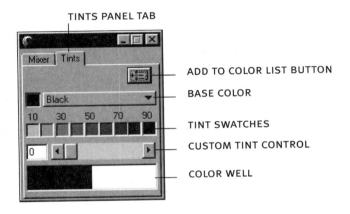

TINTS PANEL TAB

ADD TO COLOR LIST BUTTON

BASE COLOR

TINT SWATCHES

CUSTOM TINT CONTROL

COLOR WELL

6] Drag the color swatch next to PANTONE 286 in the Color List and drop it on the base color swatch at the top of the Tints panel.

Tints for that color now appear in the panel.

DRAG THIS SWATCH...

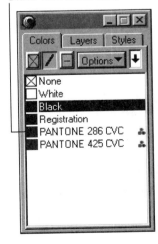

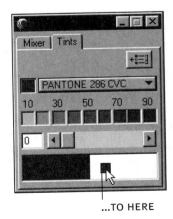

...TO HERE

7] Drag the 10 percent tint swatch from the Tints panel and drop it on the color drop box at the top of the Color List.

Dropping a swatch on the color drop box adds that color or tint to the Color List. You could also drop the swatch on an open spot in the color list, but be careful not to drop it on another color swatch or you will change that color to this tint.

The tint will be added to the Color List with the name 10% PANTONE 286.

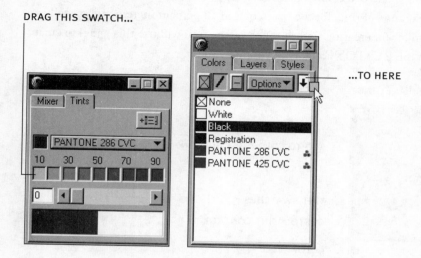

DRAG THIS SWATCH...

...TO HERE

The Color List will now have the colors and tints needed for this lesson.

tip *You could also use the "Add to Color List" button on the Color Mixer to add a tint to the Color List.*

8] Close the Tints panel. Save your work.

You just added the two colors and a tint that will be used for the elements of this document.

APPLYING COLOR TO OBJECTS

The Waive Entertainment logo was simply colored black when you imported it. Now that you have added colors to the Color List, you can apply those colors to elements on your page.

1] Choose View › Fit All (Windows Ctrl+Alt+0, Macintosh Command+Opt+0). Click on the logo at the top of page 1, then hold down the Shift key and click on the logo on page 2 and the logo on page 3.

All three logos are selected so you can apply color to them simultaneously.

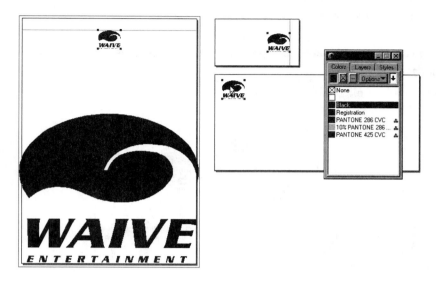

2] Make sure the Color List is displayed. Click on the fill well in the Color List, then click on the name of the blue color, Pantone 286.

When you click on the name of a color in the Color List, that color is applied to the selected objects' fill, stroke or both, depending on which color well is highlighted in the Color List. In this case you clicked on the fill well, so the blue color was only applied to the fills in the logos.

As you learned in Lesson 1, you can apply color by dragging a color swatch over an element. However, with this logo you would have to drag the swatch over each separate piece of the logo, and then repeat that for each of the other logos. In cases like this it is much faster to simply select all the objects and click on the name of the color you want to apply.

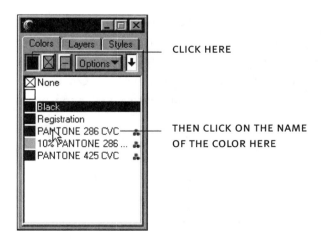

CLICK HERE

THEN CLICK ON THE NAME OF THE COLOR HERE

79

3] Click on the big logo at the bottom of page 1, then click on name of the blue tint, 10% Pantone 286.

The 10% blue tint is applied to the large logo.

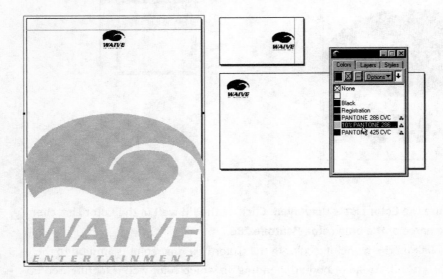

ADDING TEXT TO THE LAYOUT

FreeHand has a full array of features for entering, editing, and formatting text. In the next several tasks, you will use these features to position text in your layout and set the font and color. First, of course, you need to enter the text.

1] Select the Text tool from the toolbox and click once near the bottom of page 1 to begin a new text block.

You will see a blinking insertion point on your page where text typed on the keyboard will appear. The bar and arrows that appear above the blinking cursor are the Text Ruler, and they are used to set custom tabs for the type. These tabs provide formatting controls that are not necessary for this lesson. If desired, you can turn off the Text Rulers by choosing View > Text Rulers so that it is unchecked in the menu.

TEXT RULER

2] Type following address:

1357 9th Street South, Miami, FL 98765-1234 • Main: (876) 555-9000, Fax: (876) 555-9012 www.waiveent.com

You can enter the bullet between the ZIP code and main number by typing Alt 0149, with the NumLock on (Windows) or Option-8 (Macintosh). Enter two spaces between the fax number and the Web address.

3] Select the Pointer tool and click once on the words you just typed to select the entire block of text.

When the text block is selected with the Pointer tool, you can specify formatting that will apply to all of the text.

4] Choose View › Magnification › 100% to see the selected text at actual size.

When you change your view using the magnification commands, FreeHand automatically centers the view on the element (or elements) you have selected.

5] Using the controls on the text toolbar near the top of your screen, change the font to URWImperialT and the size to 10 points. Set the paragraph alignment to Center by clicking on the Center Alignment tab in the Text toolbar, or choose Text › Align › Center.

The URWImperialT font is on the included CD-ROM. If you don't have it installed, you can just use a font you already have installed.

The controls for changing the font, size, and alignment of the text can also be found on the Text menu and in the Text Inspector.

6] Select the Text tool again and click above the line you just entered, then type the following slogan: abandon the laws of physics for the adventure of your life™.
You can add the trademark symbol at the end by typing Alt 0153, with the NumLock on, (Windows) or Option-2 (Macintosh).

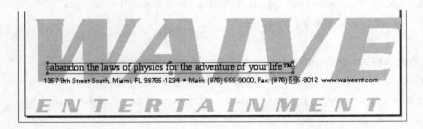

7] Using the same controls on the text toolbar near the top of your screen, change the font to URWImperialT, the style to Italic, and the size to 7 points. Choose Text › Convert Case › Sentence.
If you don't have the URWImperialT font, use the font you chose in step 5 and set the style to Italic.

> **tip** *To change the font to 7 points in the Text toolbar, type the number in the size field.*

The Convert Case commands enable you to change the capitalization of characters in selected text. The Sentence conversion changes all of the text to lowercase characters except the first letter at the beginning of a sentence.

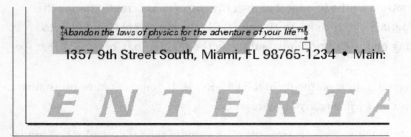

The top line of text may be displayed as a gray bar when you change the font size. This effect is called greek text, and it appears when the magnification level of the type is too low to render accurately on screen. You can control when greek text appears by choosing File > Preferences and changing the "Greek type below" field in the Redraw category. A smaller number will make FreeHand attempt to draw actual characters when type appears small on the screen. For instance, a 7 in this field would allow 7 point type to display actual characters when viewed at 100% magnification. The default setting of 8 in this field causes 7 point type viewed at 100% magnification to display as greek text.

82

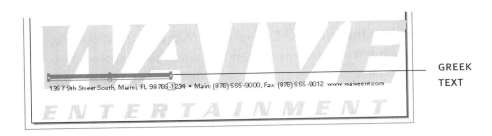

GREEK
TEXT

If you would like to see the actual characters of the text, you can simply zoom in to increase the magnification.

8] Bring up the Text Inspector by clicking on the Object Inspector icon on the toolbar and then clicking on the Text tab, or choose Window › Inspectors › Text. Click on the Character Inspector subset, which is the far left icon (abc).

This is where you can specify numeric controls for attributes of text, such as font, size, leading, baseline shift, range kerning and more.

9] Select the slogan text block with the Pointer tool, then type 74 in the Range kerning field. Press Enter to apply the changes.

This stretches the spacing of the characters in the slogan text block so they extend to a width that will match the address text block. If you used a different font than URWImperialT, then you may need to adjust the number in the Range kerning field so the text block is approximately the same width as the address text block.

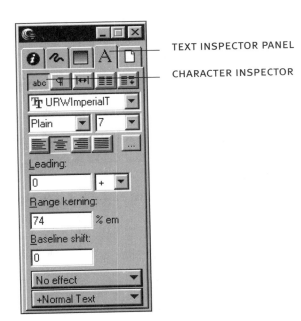

TEXT INSPECTOR PANEL

CHARACTER INSPECTOR

COMBINING TEXT AND GRAPHICS

10] **With the slogan text block still selected, hold the Shift key and click on the address text block with the pointer tool. Bring up the Align panel by clicking its icon in the toolbar or choose Window › Panels › Align. Make sure the first pop-up menu says No Change and the second pop-up menu says Align Center. Check the Align to Page box, then click Apply (Windows) or Align (Macintosh).**

These actions will select both text blocks and center them on the page from side to side.

11] **Deselect both text blocks by pressing the Tab key, then hold the Shift key and drag the address text block with the pointer tool until it is just above Entertainment. Release the mouse, then release the Shift key.**

By holding the Shift key you constrain movement on a vertical axis, which preserves the alignment action from the previous step. If necessary, use the up and down arrow keys to fine-tune the position of the text block.

12] **Deselect the address text block by pressing the Tab key, then hold the Shift key and drag the slogan text block with the pointer tool until it is just below Waive. Release the mouse, then release the Shift key.**

If necessary, use the up and down arrow keys to fine-tune the position of the text block.

Now your letterhead should match the example shown.

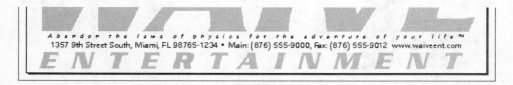

13] With the slogan text block still selected, choose Edit › Clone. Go to the Text Inspector and change the Range kerning back to zero. Then use the pointer tool to drag the cloned text block to page 2.

You may choose View > Fit All to make it easier to drag the slogan text block to page 2.

14] Click in the text block with the Text tool and press Enter to add line breaks in the desired locations.

Use the example shown as a guide and move the elements as necessary. If necessary, zoom in on the page by choosing Page 2 from the Page pop-up menu at the bottom of the screen.

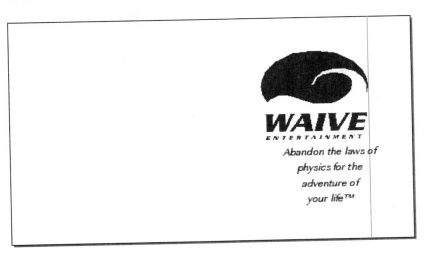

15] Use the pointer tool to click on the logo, then click the Lock icon in the Main toolbar or choose Modify › Lock.

This locks the logo in place so you can align objects to it. In FreeHand, a locked element can still be selected for purposes of alignment, but its position and attributes can not be changed.

16] With the logo still selected, hold the Shift key and click on the slogan. Go to the Align panel and uncheck the Align to Page option, then click Apply (Windows) or Align (Macintosh).

The alignment options from the previous Align command should still be selected. If they are not, make sure the first menu says "No Change," and the second menu says "Align Center." When you click Apply or Align the slogan will be centered under the logo on the business card page.

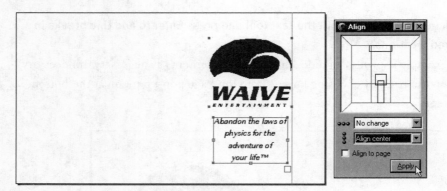

17] With both objects still selected, click the Unlock icon in the Main toolbar or choose Modify › Unlock.

This will unlock any objects in the current selection that are locked. It will have no effect on selected objects that are not locked.

18] Group the logo and the slogan by clicking on the Group icon in the toolbar or choose Modify › Group.

Grouping will make it easier to work with these elements later in the lesson. If the two elements do not group correctly, it may be because the logo is still locked. Make sure the logo is unlocked and both elements are selected, then try grouping again.

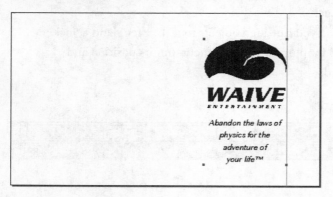

19] Save your work.

IMPORTING TEXT INTO A LAYOUT

Text created by an external source can be imported into a FreeHand document, which saves you the time of retyping it.

1] To make sure the business card page is visible, go to the page pop-up menu at the bottom of the screen and choose Page 2. Add a vertical ruler guide to Page 2, then double-click on the guide and set its position to 0.3125 inches.

Use the same techniques you learned when adding the previous ruler guides in this lesson. The guide you are adding now will be used for the imported text.

2] Choose File › Import (Windows Ctrl+R, Macintosh Command+R). Select P2text.rtf from the Media folder within the Lesson02 folder and click Open or press Enter.

Your cursor will change to the import cursor, which represents the top-left corner of the text block.

3] Move the import cursor over the ruler guide on the left side of the page and click.

The text for the business card is added to the page. The left edge of the text block should touch the ruler guide. If it does not, adjust the position of the text block now.

4] Select the text block with the pointer tool and change the font to URWImperialT and the size to 8.

Now the text matches the style of the letterhead. Next you will copy the address and add it to the envelope page.

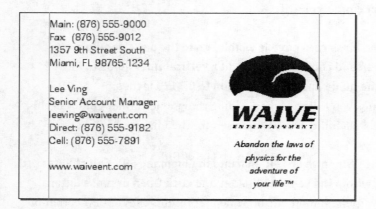

5] Hold the Shift key down and click with the pointer tool on the grouped logo and slogan.

Now the text and the logo group are selected.

6] Go to the Align panel and change the settings so that the first pop-up menu says Align Center and the second pop-up menu says No Change. Check the Align to Page box, then click Apply (Windows) or Align (Macintosh).

Now the text and the logo group are both centered on the page.

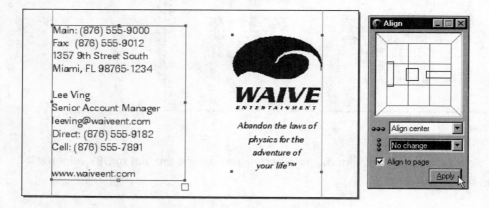

7] Double-click on the left text block with the pointer tool, then select the two lines of address text below the phone numbers. Choose Edit › Copy.

When you double-click on the body of a text block with the pointer tool, FreeHand recognizes that you want to edit the text and automatically switches you to the Text tool.

Main: (876) 555-9000
Fax: (876) 555-9012
1357 9th Street South
Miami, FL 98765-1234

Lee Ving
Senior Account Manager
leeving@waiveent.com
Direct: (876) 555-9182
Cell: (876) 555-7891

www.waiveent.com

Abandon the laws of
physics for the
adventure of
your life™

8] With the text tool still selected, click on page 3 below the logo and choose Edit ›
Paste. Position the address text block below the logo as shown.

All the text you need in this document has been entered. Now it is time to add some
color and extra emphasis to certain portions of text.

1357 9th Street South
Miami, FL 98765-1234

APPLYING A COLOR FILL TO TEXT

Now you will change the black fill of this text to something more subtle. You will
also select certain parts of the text block and change the font and color of the
selected text.

1] Choose View › Fit All, or Control+ Alt+0 (Windows) or Command+Option+0
(Macintosh). Select the pointer tool from the Toolbox. Hold Alt (Windows) or Option
(Macintosh) and click on the slogan below the logo on Page 2. Then hold the Shift
key down and click on each of the other text blocks in the document.

You are selecting all the text blocks so you can change their color all at one time. You must hold down the Alt or Option key to select the first text block because it is part of a group. This is called subselecting. You will use this technique in future lessons as well.

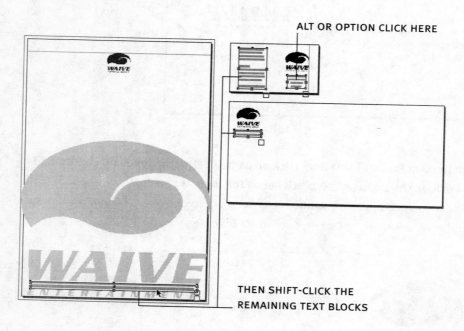

ALT OR OPTION CLICK HERE

THEN SHIFT-CLICK THE
REMAINING TEXT BLOCKS

2] With the text blocks selected, go to the Color List and drag the swatch of the gray color, Pantone 425, to the Fill well.

If the Color List is not visible, click on the main toolbar icon to bring it forward. When you release the swatch on the Fill well, the color is applied to all the selected text blocks.

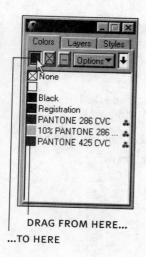

DRAG FROM HERE...

...TO HERE

3] Click on the Magnifying glass in the Toolbox, then drag a marquee selection around the bottom section of page 1.

The goal is to zoom in on the text at the bottom of the screen. You are going to highlight text to make changes.

4] Use the Text tool to highlight the Web site address. Change the font to URWImperialTExtBol.

If that font is not available on your system, choose another bold font.

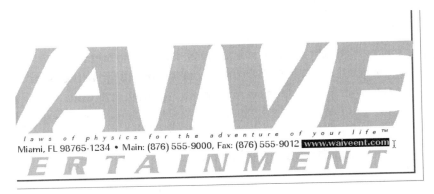

5] With the text still selected, go to the Color List and and drag the swatch of the blue color, Pantone 286, to the Fill well.

You can see that if part of the text block is highlighted, the color change only occurs in that portion of the text. You will repeat these steps on the business card.

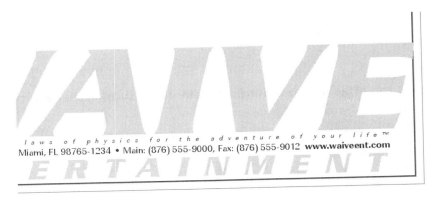

6] Click on the Next Page icon to move to page 2.

This is another way to move between pages. Now you should be looking at the business card.

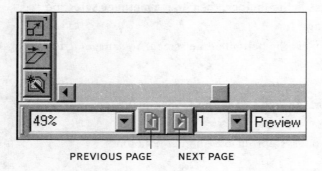

PREVIOUS PAGE   NEXT PAGE

7] Use the Text tool to highlight the Web site address. Change the font to URWImperialTExtBol and the size to 9. With the text still selected, go to the Color List and and drag the swatch of the blue color, Pantone 286, to the Fill well.

This emphasizes the Web site address on the business card, and now it matches the letterhead.

8] Highlight the name of the salesperson and change the font to URWImperialTExtBol and the size to 9. Leave the color of the name gray.

Now the name of the account manager gets more emphasis, and it helps visually separate the information on the card.

Main: (876) 555-9000
Fax: (876) 555-9012
1357 9th Street South
Miami, FL 98765-1234

Lee Ving I
Senior Account Manager
leeving@waiveent.com
Direct: (876) 555-9182
Cell: (876) 555-7891

www.waiveent.com

WAIVE
E N T E R T A I N M E N T

Abandon the laws of
physics for the
adventure of
your life™

Congratulations! Now you have designed a stationery package in FreeHand, complete with letterhead, business cards and envelopes.

ON YOUR OWN

Look on the CD to find an example of how you can use Lens fills to quickly arrange multiple business cards on one page for printing. For more information go to the Bonus folder in your Lesson02 folder and select the PDF file named Bonus2.PDF.

WHAT YOU HAVE LEARNED

In this lesson you have:

- Used the Document Inspector to set a custom page size and a bleed [pages 60–62]
- Used the Document Inspector and Page tool to duplicate, resize, and reposition pages [pages 62–65]
- Used ruler guides to align elements on the page [pages 66–68]
- Imported and placed an editable vector EPS graphic [pages 68–72]
- Used the Transform panel to position, clone, and scale elements on the page [pages 71–74]
- Used PANTONE colors and tints [pages 74–78]
- Practiced using the Fill Inspector, Stroke Inspector, Tints panel, and Color List panel to apply fills, strokes, and colors [pages 78–80]
- Entered text and changed the font, size, and other text formatting [pages 80–83]
- Used the Align panel to position elements on the page and relative to one another [pages 84–86]
- Imported text from another source into a layout [pages 87–89]
- Changed the color of specific characters in a text block [pages 89–92]

points and paths

working with

In this lesson, you will create illustrations that will be used in an advertisement. In the process, you will learn how to use the drawing and editing tools in FreeHand to work directly with **points** and **paths**.

Working with points and paths is at the heart of manipulating graphics in FreeHand. All graphics created in FreeHand consist of paths, which are lines defined by points. The span between two points, either straight or curved, is called a **path segment**. As you will see in this lesson, you can manipulate these paths, also known as **Beziér curves**, to create virtually any shape.

LESSON 3

The elements in this illustration were created by tracing patterns with FreeHand's drawing tools. Special text effects like the gradient fill and black outline can also be added. You will learn how to apply these techniques in this lesson.

Designed by Tony Roame of Illustrated Concepts.

In the first part of this lesson, you will experiment with basic shapes, the Freeform tool, and tracing templates to learn how to create and modify paths and points. Then you will apply these skills by tracing a template to create the car shown in the illustration.

If you would like to review the final result of this lesson, open CarAd.ft9 in the Complete folder within the Lesson03 folder.

WHAT YOU WILL LEARN

In this lesson you will:

- Manipulate basic shapes with the Freeform tool
- Learn the fundamental principles of points and paths
- Create and modify paths to create objects of any shape
- Copy artwork into existing documents
- Create gradient-filled text

APPROXIMATE TIME

This lesson takes approximately 2 hours to complete.

LESSON FILES

Media Files:

Demos\Movies\PenDemo.mov (optional)

Starting Files:

Lesson03\Start\Mountn1.ft9

Lesson03\Start\CarStart.ft9

Lesson03\Start\Road.ft9

*Lesson03\Start\Mountn2.ft9
(or saved file from Mountn1)*

Completed Project:

Lesson03\Complete\CarAd.ft9

Bonus Files:

Lesson03\Bonus\PenDemo.mov

MANIPULATING PATHS WITH THE FREEFORM TOOL

The Freeform tool enables you to avoid the complexity of working with individual points and paths, completely bypassing the Pen and Bezigon tools (which you will learn to use later in this lesson). Instead, you can interact directly with the path by pushing or pulling it into position. The Freeform tool is easy to learn and fun to use! The only drawback is that it is not quite as precise as the other tools. Depending on the type of artwork you're creating, that may or may not be a significant factor.

1] Open the document named Mountn1.ft9 in the Lesson03\Start folder.
 A custom-sized page appears containing the outline you will use to help you practice with the Freeform tool. You can see an irregular line across the page. This is the shape of the mountain profile you will create.

2] Select the Rectangle tool in the toolbox and draw a rectangle from the top-left corner of the page to the bottom-right edge of the line on the screen, as shown.
This is the starting point for your Freeform tool manipulations. The Freeform tool does not create paths; it can only modify paths that already exist. That's why you need to start with a basic shape like a rectangle or ellipse.

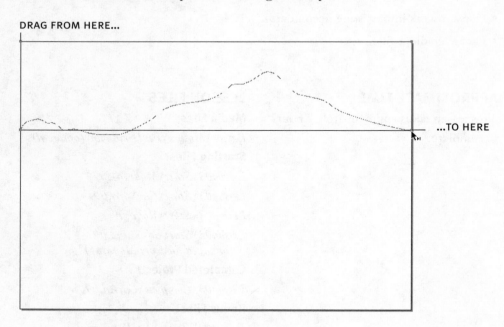

DRAG FROM HERE...

...TO HERE

3] Double-click the Freeform tool in the toolbox. Make sure the size is 50 and the precision is 5. Bend should be By Length, and Length should be 100.

These settings will make broad adjustments that bring the lower edge of the rectangle close to the shape of the tracing pattern.

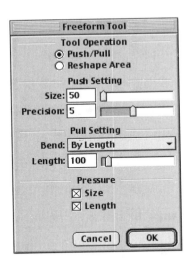

4] Move the cursor below the rectangle. Hold down the mouse button and drag up slowly until the cursor starts pushing the lower edge of the rectangle. Release the mouse when the edge of the cursor reaches the tracing template

The rectangle now has a large bulge where you pushed the Freeform tool against it. While the mouse button is held down, the cursor is surrounded by a circle that indicates the size of the Freeform tool. You can change the size of the Freeform tool while you are using it by pressing the arrow keys on the keyboard.

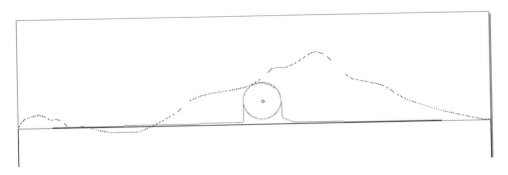

97

5] Continue pushing the path without releasing the mouse button until it loosely covers the template. Do not worry about being very accurate at this point.

The current settings on the Freeform tool are too big to be very accurate. Right now you are getting the line into position so that more precise settings can be used.

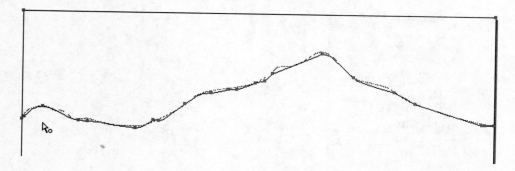

6] Double-click the Freeform tool in the toolbox and change the size to 10. Now zoom in to 200% on the left edge of the template.

These settings on the Freeform tool will enable you to make more precise adjustments.

Use the magnifying glass in the toolbox to zoom, or choose 200% from the magnification pop-up menu at the bottom of the window and scroll to the left edge of the template.

7] Move the cursor so that it is on top of the line. Drag the line so that it moves over the template.

Notice that when you move the cursor over the line, the "o" next to the hollow arrow changes to an "s." This indicates that you are going to pull the stroke rather than push it the way you did in the previous steps.

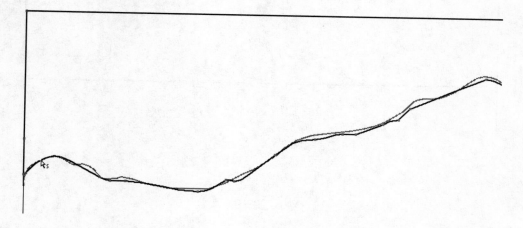

98

8] Use a combination of pushing and pulling with the Freeform tool to make the line conform to the template. Scroll the window as necessary to bring the next section of the template into view.

This is when you want to be as accurate as possible. If necessary, you can zoom in even further to move the line more precisely. When you are finished, your line should match the template closely, as in the figure shown here.

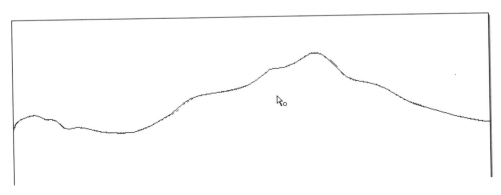

tip   *The Freeform tool moves the line the same distance regardless of the magnification. However, it can be difficult to tell exactly where you are moving the line at lower magnifications. You need to zoom in to see more detail and increase the accuracy of your alterations.*

9] Make the Color List visible, select the shape you have created, and assign the color 30c 6m 0y 0k that appears in the Color List. Set the path (stroke) color in the Color List to None.

Now your sky is blue and the profile of the mountains is clearly visible.

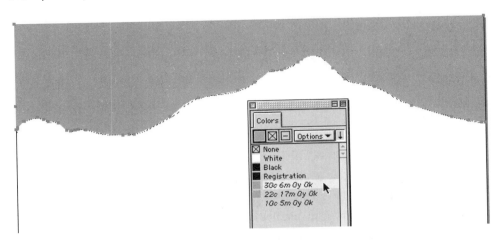

99

10] Save your work.

Now you will learn how to work with points and control handles to create vector paths. You will use the Freehand tool, Bezigon tool, and Pen tool.

IMPORTANT FOUNDATION INFORMATION

Please read this section carefully. Drawing paths and manipulating points is at the heart of creating artwork in FreeHand. While it is possible to create complex shapes in FreeHand by simply manipulating with the Freeform tool, almost all accurate path drawing is done by working with points and control handles. If you learn to draw paths correctly, you will save yourself hours of frustration and avoid potentially costly mistakes.

POINT PRINCIPLES

FreeHand uses three types of points: corner, curve, and connector. Each of these point types can have up to two control handles, one for each side of the point. A point may display both handles, one handle, or no handles at all. The most significant difference among the point types is the way they restrict the movement of control handles.

To change point types, select one or more points in your document and then click the desired point type icon in the Object Inspector. All points appear as solid squares until they are individually selected with the Pointer tool or Lasso tool.

Corner points turn into hollow squares when selected. Corner points offer the most flexibility of any point type. You can move either of the control handles in any direction. Each handle is completely independent. You create a corner point by simply clicking with the Pen tool or Bezigon tool.

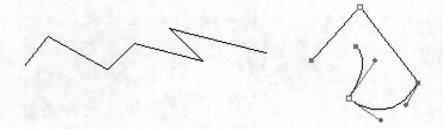

Curve points turn into hollow circles when selected. Curve points restrict the movement of control handles to one axis. That is, the two control handles are always on opposite sides of a point. The handles can move in and out independently, but as one handle rotates around the point, the other rotates in the opposite direction. The purpose of the curve point is to make it easier to create smooth curves in paths. You create a curve point by dragging with the Pen tool, or by clicking with the Bezigon tool while holding Alt (Windows) or Option (Macintosh).

Connector points turn into hollow triangles when selected. They are used less frequently than corner or curve points by many designers, but they can be quite useful. The purpose of connector points is to maintain a smooth transition between a straight line segment and a curved segment, even after one of the points is moved. Connector points restrict the movement of control handles to the same direction as the straight line segment—you can move the handle only in and out, not side to side. You create a connector point in Windows by holding the Alt key and clicking the right mouse button with the Pen or Bezigon tool; on a Macintosh you hold the Control key and click with the Pen or Bezigon tool.

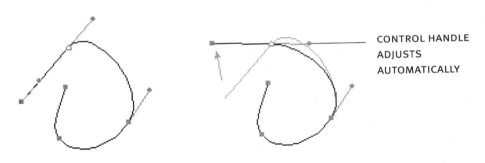

CONTROL HANDLE
ADJUSTS
AUTOMATICALLY

CONTROL HANDLE PRINCIPLES

There is more to control handles than meets the eye. Control handles can be retracted or revealed, they can be altered while you are still drawing with the Pen tool, and they can even be placed mathematically (using third-party plug-ins). Keep in mind that even if a point has control handles, the handles are hidden until the point is individually selected.

Extracting and retracting control handles:

Some points do not seem to have control handles—they are retracted. To pull a control handle out of a point, click the point with the Pointer tool; then hold Alt (Windows) or Option (Macintosh) and drag the point. As you do, the first control handle will be pulled out. You can repeat this step to get the other control handle. If you want to hide the control handles, select the point and go to the Object Inspector, where you can click the Retract button for the handle you wish to put away. If you click the wrong button, simply choose Edit > Undo and click the correct one.

Automatic control handles:

If you check the Automatic box in the Object Inspector, FreeHand will attempt to guess the ideal placement of control handles. In many cases, this option may give you the desired result. If you move the point to a new location, FreeHand will optimize the location of the handles. If you find the control handles are not in the right place, simply move them where you want them. As soon as one of the handles is adjusted manually, the Automatic box unchecks itself.

Determining exact point coordinates:

You can set the exact coordinates on the page for any point in FreeHand by clicking the point and going to the bottom of the Object Inspector and entering specific values in the x and y fields.

tip *The point coordinate fields are visible only if one point is selected. If more than one point is selected, the fields disappear completely.*

DRAWING WITH THE FREEHAND TOOL

The Freehand tool is the tool that most closely mimics traditional media, such as an ordinary pen or pencil. You click and drag to create lines. Once you release the mouse button, FreeHand converts the line you dragged into a vector path with points and control handles. You will use the Freehand tool to create some of the shapes that define the mountain in the illustration.

1] Open the document you saved in the first part of this section.
This is where you ended earlier in the lesson. You should see a blue sky and the profile of a mountain range. Nothing else is currently visible.

2] Open the Layers panel by choosing Windows > Panels > Layers. Click the text that says Dark. On the same layer, click the empty space to the left of the dark gray circle.

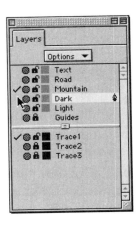

When you first click the layer name, that layer becomes the active layer. This is indicated by a pen icon that appears to the right of the layer name. When you clicked the blank space, a new check mark appeared for the layer named Dark, and the layer became visible.

You will learn more about layers in a future lesson. For now, you need to understand only that clicking the check mark toggles layer visibility, and the active layer is indicated by the pen icon on the right side of the panel.

The Dark layer already contains some objects. You are going to add objects to the Dark layer by drawing with the Freehand tool. But first you need to make the template for this portion visible.

3] In the Layers panel, click to make the check mark visible for Trace2 (located below the gray bar that divides the panel). Then close the Layers panel.

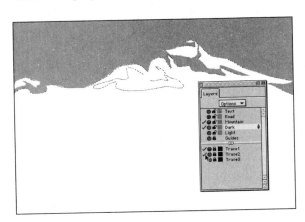

Now you can see where you are going to draw with the Freehand tool.

103

4] Zoom to at least 200% and move the middle of the mountain template into view.

Increasing the magnification improves your ability to trace accurately.

5] Double-click the Freehand tool in the Toolbox. Set the precision to 8.

As you move the cursor over the page, it changes to a plain crosshairs.

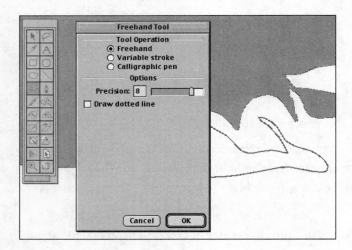

6] Move the crosshairs over the template and drag to start tracing. If you have to release the mouse button to scroll your window, be sure to start drawing at the endpoint where you left off. Stop when you have gone all the way around the template; your cursor displays a solid rectangle when it is over the starting point.

This is the most intuitive method of creating a freeform path (that is, not a basic shape such as a rectangle or ellipse).

If you don't like the way your freehand path is turning out, don't stop drawing! Keep the mouse button down and press Ctrl (Windows) or Command (Macintosh); then retrace your path. Sections of your path will be erased as you drag backward. When you have erased enough, release the keyboard key and resume dragging with the mouse to redraw the path.

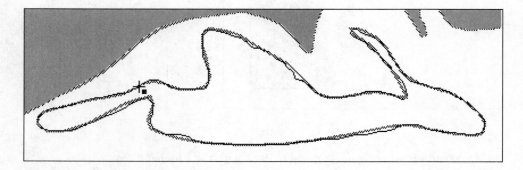

If you reach the starting point of your path and the solid rectangle does not appear next to the cursor, then your path probably contains multiple segments. To fix this, select the Arrow tool, hold the Shift key, and click the sections of your path that are not highlighted. Choose Modify > Join to merge the selected path segments.

7] Open the Color List. Select the shape you just drew and set the fill color to 22c 17m 0y 0k. Set the stroke color to None.

Now your new shape looks just like the existing shapes on the Dark layer.

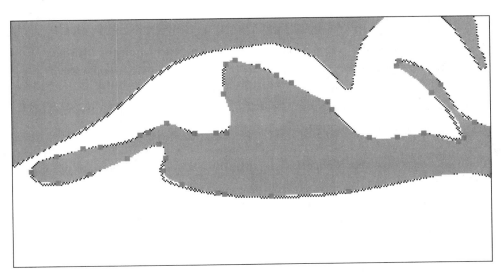

If you would like more practice with the Freehand tool, delete the preexisting shapes on the Dark layer and retrace the templates yourself. For additional practice with the Freehand or Freeform tool, uncheck the Trace2 layer and check the Trace3 layer to see templates for the light shapes. Then click the Light layer to activate it, make it visible, and delete those preexisting shapes, too.

8] Save your work.

In the next section, you will begin working with the Bezigon tool.

DIFFERENCES BETWEEN THE BEZIGON AND PEN TOOLS

The Bezigon and Pen tools are closely related; both use points and control handles to create paths, but they behave in slightly different ways. The choice between the two is a personal one. The next paragraphs provide a detailed analysis of the differences between these tools. This lesson will give you exposure to both tools so you can decide which one you prefer.

The Bezigon tool always places points with "automatic" control handles. You choose the type of point being placed by holding down different modifier keys. The control handles (and the path shape) change as you place the next point. If you go back and edit the path by dragging a point, the control handles will automatically adjust to what FreeHand considers an optimal curve. This may or may not be exactly what you are looking for. However, as always, you can edit the path as you please once it is drawn. With practice, you can accurately predict how control handles will be placed with the Bezigon tool. If you click and drag with the Bezigon tool, the point follows the movement of your cursor, and you will see the control handles adjust themselves as the point is repositioned.

The Pen tool allows more complete control over the control handles at the time the point is placed. Place corner points with the Pen tool by clicking, and place curve points by clicking and dragging with the mouse button down. While still holding down the mouse button, you can hold a modifier key to get even more control: holding Alt (Windows) or Option (Macintosh) while you drag locks the trailing control handle and allows you to independently position the leading control handle. Holding Control (Windows) or Command (Macintosh) freezes the position of the control handles and allows your dragging motion to reposition the point—all without the need to select a different tool and interrupt your concentration. (The CD that came with this book contains a QuickTime movie that demonstrates these techniques. Go to Bonus\Movies\PenDemo.mov.)

These Pen tool features make FreeHand's Pen tool the most elegant and refined tool of any vector drawing program currently available. With practice, you can draw virtually any path correctly the first time, without having to go back to edit control handles or alter points.

DRAWING WITH THE BEZIGON TOOL

In this section, you will use the Bezigon tool to create a car for placement in the ad you started in the previous sections.

1] Open the file CarStart.ft9 in the Lesson03\Start folder.

This is a new template file that will help you learn how to use the Bezigon tool. You will draw a car in five separate steps and then put the pieces together and export the finished illustration.

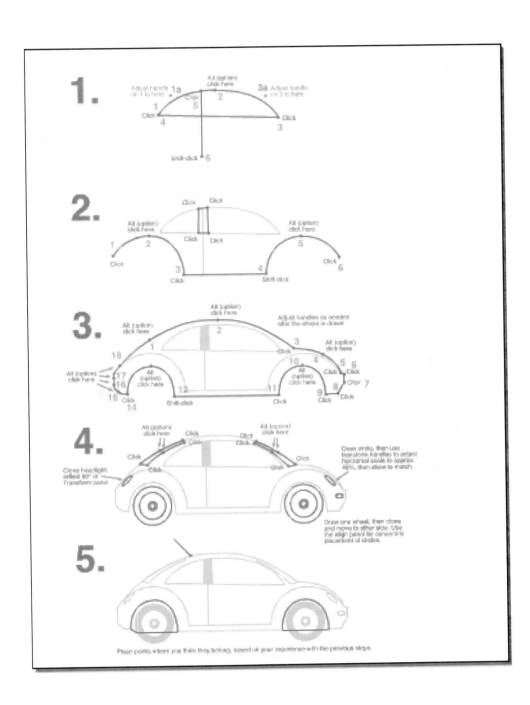

WORKING WITH POINTS AND PATHS

2] Zoom in to at least 200% and move Step 1 into view.

Now the tracing pattern is clearly visible. Next you will trace this pattern by placing corner and curve points with the Bezigon tool.

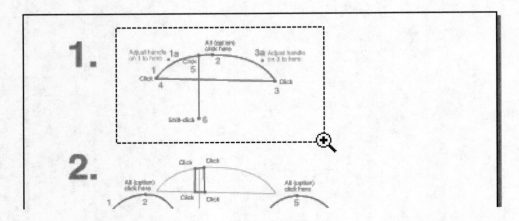

3] Select the Bezigon tool in the toolbox. Position the cursor on point 1 and click to create the first corner point. Move the cursor to point 2, and this time press the Alt (Windows) or Option (Macintosh) key while you click.

The second point has control handles that are displayed automatically. The path does not look like a curve yet, and the control handles are sticking out the wrong way. Don't make any adjustments yet—continue tracing the path. The handles will automatically adjust once the next point is in place.

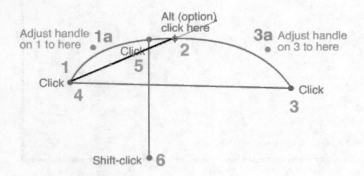

4] Move the cursor over point 3 and click. Since this is a corner point, no keys need to be pressed. Now close the path by clicking once more on the starting point.

Notice that when you click the third point, the control handles on the second point automatically adjust so that the curved segment is optimized. However, the optimized curve does not match the template provided, so some adjustments will need to be made.

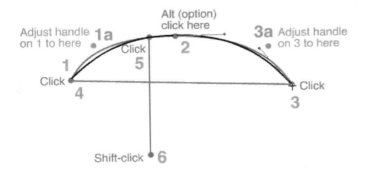

5] Click point 1 to highlight it. When the control handles appear, select the upper handle and move it into position 1a, as indicated on the template. Repeat this action for the opposite side of the shape, moving the upper handle to 3a.

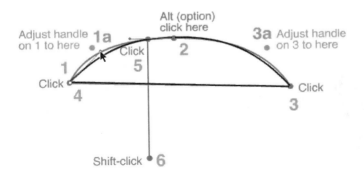

Now the shape you've drawn should match the template. This is the type of procedure that is typical when using the Bezigon or Pen tool to create paths. You have to set points where you think they belong and then adjust the placement of the points and control handles as necessary. With practice, it is possible to be quite efficient when drawing paths—so much so that you may be able to draw virtually any path correctly the first time, with little or no adjustment needed.

6] Assign a Transparent Lens fill of 75% black in the Fill Inspector. Press the Tab key to deselect all artwork.

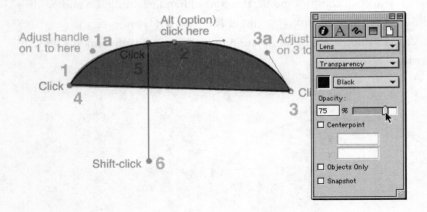

Now you are going to start drawing a new path, so you have to deactivate the first path. If the first path were still active when you clicked, you would add a point to the existing path rather than start a new one.

7] Click point 5; then hold down Shift and click point 6.

When you press the Shift key while clicking, you constrain the path to a straight line or a 45-degree angle. Remember to press the Shift key every time you want to draw a perfectly straight line.

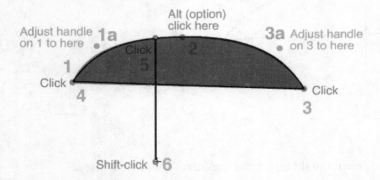

tip   *Watch the cursor as you create paths. The crosshairs cursor is displayed with an empty square beside it when FreeHand is ready to create a new path. The crosshairs appears with a small carat when you can add points to an active path. A solid square appears when the mouse is positioned over the first point in the path, so you know that clicking that point will close the path.*

8] Choose View › Custom › Step 2. Trace the shape on top first, simply clicking with the Bezigon tool until the path is closed. When the path is closed, go to the Color List and assign it a black fill and no stroke.

This will be the middle section of the car, between the front and rear windows.

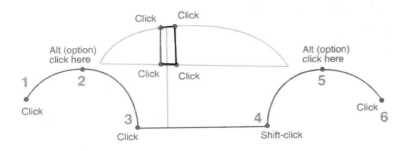

9] Now trace the lower shape in Step 2, following the directions in the template.

Make any adjustments you feel are necessary after completing the path. You can always tweak a control handle or the position of a point to more closely match the template.

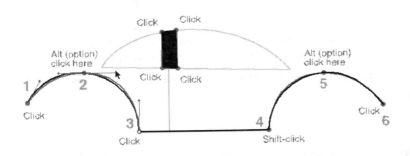

tip   *You can use the arrow keys to nudge a selected element or point in a small amount in any direction. For example, select a point on the last path—when selected, the point should appear as an outlined square. Now instead of using the mouse to move the point, press the right arrow key several times and watch the point move slowly to the right each time you press. This approach works the same way when you select a path, group, or block of type with the Pointer tool. The default movement is 1 point. You can change the default by choosing Modify > Cursor Distance and entering the desired amount.*

10] Select both elements in Step 2 and display the Transform panel by typing Ctrl+M (Windows) or Command+M (Macintosh). Enter *0* in the x field and *150* in the y field; then press Enter or click Move (Windows) or Apply (Macintosh).

The artwork from Step 2 is now in place over the artwork in Step 1.

11] Choose View > Custom > Step 3 to view the outline of the car. Trace it following the numbered steps on the template. Adjust control handles as necessary. When you are satisfied, fill the outline with 0c 10m 70y 0k.

In this step, you need to do some more significant editing. On both sides of each wheel, make sure the control handle goes straight up (pressing the Shift key is a great way to make that happen). Adjust other handles as necessary, such as those over the hood and trunk.

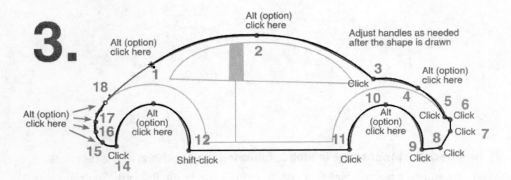

In the next step you will move this artwork into position at the top of the page.

12] Select the outline and choose Modify > Arrange > Send to Back. With the outline still selected, display the Transform panel by pressing Ctrl+M (Windows) or Command+M (Macintosh). Enter _0_ in the x field and _300_ in the y field; then press Enter or click Move (Windows) or Apply (Macintosh).

The artwork from Step 3 is now in place under the artwork in Step 1.

13] Choose View > Custom > Step 4 to view the next parts that need completion. Trace the front and rear windshield as indicated. Fill with a Lens fill set to 75% black transparency.

Use the same techniques you learned in the earlier steps. Don't forget to zoom in if you want to increase your accuracy. Next you will create the lights and wheels.

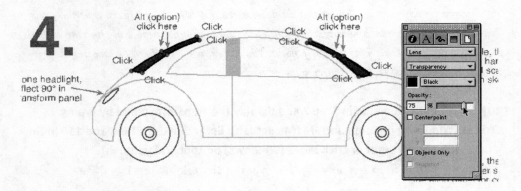

112

14] Select the Ellipse tool and draw a circle about 13.5 points in diameter. Check the size in the Object Inspector to make sure it is correct.

You are starting with a round object, and you are going to distort it so that it matches the ellipse shown in the template.

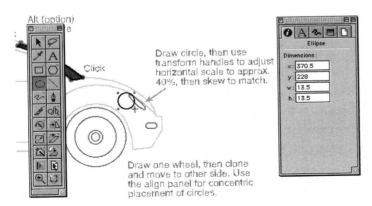

Alt (option)

Click

Draw circle, then use transform handles to adjust horizontal scale to approx. 40%, then skew to match.

Ellipse

Dimensions:
x: 370.5
y: 228
w: 13.5
h: 13.5

Draw one wheel, then clone and move to other side. Use the align panel for concentric placement of circles.

15] Double-click the circle to bring up the transform handles. Drag a side handle until the circle is slightly less than half its previous width. Move the ellipse so that it is centered on the headlight of the car.

You have the correct width, and now you are going to skew the circle so that it matches the desired shape. You need to have the circle in position so you know how far it needs to be skewed.

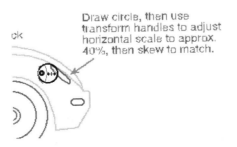

ck

Draw circle, then use transform handles to adjust horizontal scale to approx. 40%, then skew to match.

16] With the transform handles still active, move the cursor over the dotted line that runs between the transform handles. When the cursor changes to the skew icon, drag until the desired shape is reached. Give the skewed circle a white Fill.

The skew icon is visible only when you move the cursor right over the dotted-line part of the transform handles. If you are inside the dotted line, the cursor becomes a move icon; if you are outside, it becomes a rotate icon.

113

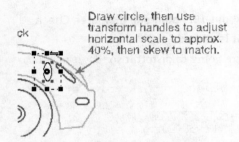

Draw circle, then use transform handles to adjust horizontal scale to approx. 40%, then skew to match.

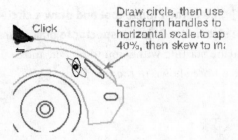

Draw circle, then use transform handles to horizontal scale to ap 40%, then skew to ma

Click

17] Copy the finished headlight and paste it over the tail light. Choose Modify › Transform › Reflect and enter *90* in the first field; then click Reflect (Windows) or Apply (Macintosh). Give the new tail light a red fill.

When you click Apply, the headlight flips and becomes a tail light. If the headlight is not pasted on top of the tail light, when reflect occurs it may seem to disappear because it is reflected with the xy axis and will be placed somewhere else on the page. Next you will draw a wheel, starting with the outer edge.

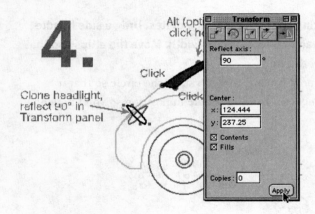

Clone headlight, reflect 90° in Transform panel

Click

Click

Alt (opti click he

18] Select the Ellipse tool and position it in the center of the wheel. Hold Alt (Windows) or Option (Macintosh); then click and start dragging. As you are dragging, also press the Shift key. Stop when the circle is the same size as the outside edge of the wheel.

The Alt or Option key draws the ellipse from the center outward, rather than drawing from an edge. The Shift key constrains the ellipse to a perfect circle.

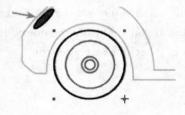

19] Select the first circle and choose Edit › Clone. Grab any corner with the Arrow tool and begin dragging inward. While the mouse button is down, press Alt (Windows) or Option (Macintosh) and the Shift key to keep the circle centered and constrained. Stop when you reach the next largest circle in the template.

This is the fastest and easiest method for creating concentric circles.

20] Repeat the previous technique to create the two inner circles on the wheel. Then select the second-largest circle and give it a 20% black fill. Give the largest circle a black fill. Select all pieces of the tire and group them.

The tire should now look like the following figure. Grouping the tire enables you to move it easily to the other side of the vehicle.

21] Select the grouped tire and clone it. Drag it over to the other wheel well while holding the Shift key to constrain movement to a straight line.

The Shift key keeps the tires level with each other.

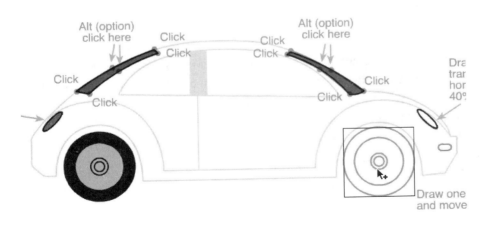

115

22] Select all the elements from Step 4 and display the Transform panel. Enter _0_ in the x field and _450_ in the y field; then press Enter or click Apply.

Now the artwork from Step 4 is in place over the other artwork.

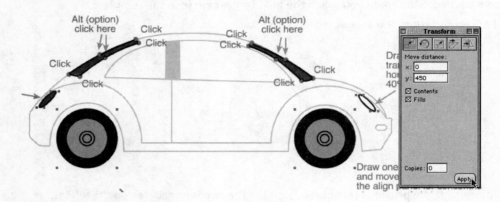

23] Choose the custom view for Step 5 and create the antenna, front blinker and wheel wells as shown. Give each of the wheel wells a black fill, and give the blinker an orange fill.

These are the last elements needed to finish the car.

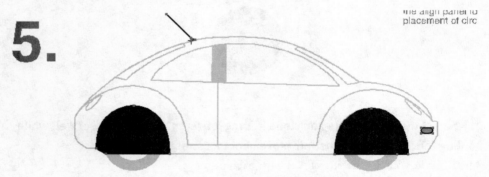

Place points where you think they belong, based on your experience with the previous steps.

24] Select the three elements in Step 5 and choose Modify › Arrange › Send to Back. With the objects still selected, display the Transform panel and enter _0_ in the x field and _600_ in the y field; then press Enter or click Move (Windows) or Apply (Macintosh).

Now your car is completely assembled. It should appear similar to the illustration shown here. To make it easier to work with the car as a single element, you should group it.

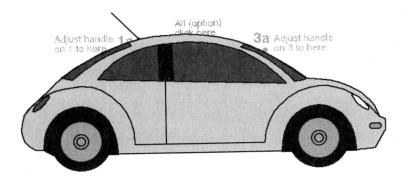

25] Choose Edit > Select > All and then Modify > Group.

Now your artwork is ready to be used in another document.

26] Save your changes.

Next you will use the Pen tool to create a path.

DRAWING WITH THE PEN TOOL

In this section, you will create the foreground and use the Pen tool draw the road for your car.

1] Open the file Road.ft9 in the Lesson03\Start folder.

This is a new template file that will introduce you to the Pen tool. You will draw the road and horizon in two steps and then bring these elements into your original document.

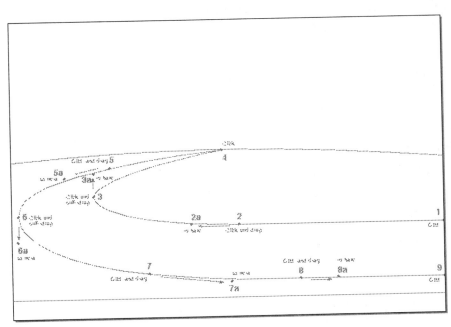

117

2] Select the Rectangle tool. Position the crosshairs at the bottom-left corner of the template and drag to the upper-right edge of the curved horizon line. With the rectangle still selected, choose Modify › Ungroup.

You need to ungroup the rectangle so you can access the individual points.

This rectangle is almost exactly what you need to create the first shape. All that remains is to make the top of the rectangle curved. To do this, you are going to learn a new way to bend and move path segments—without using drawing tools.

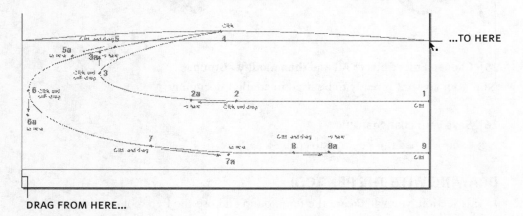

...TO HERE

DRAG FROM HERE...

3] Select the Pointer tool and position the cursor in the middle of the top line segment, as shown. Hold Alt (Windows) or Option (Macintosh); then drag upward slowly with the mouse. Press the Tab key to deselect the artwork.

Notice that the path pivots at the points on either side of this line segment. What you are actually doing is adjusting the control handles, as you can see. Release the mouse when you have the line segment in position over the template.

This is another way to manipulate path segments. In some ways, it is similar to using the Freeform tool, but you don't need a special tool.

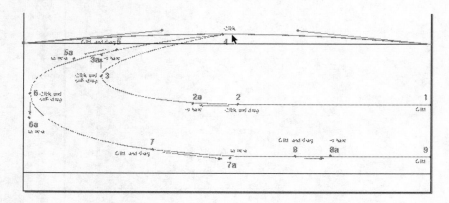

118

4] Select the Pen tool. Position the crosshairs over the first numbered point and click. Now move to the second point, but this time keep the mouse down when you click, and drag to the mark labeled 2a. Hold the Shift key to keep the control handle straight. Release the mouse before you release the Shift key.

Now you are experiencing one of the primary differences between the Pen tool and the Bezigon tool. Dragging with the Bezigon tool repositions the point before it lands, but dragging with the Pen tool creates curve points. The advantage to using the Pen tool to create curves is that you can define the control handles right away, taking the guesswork out of how they will be positioned.

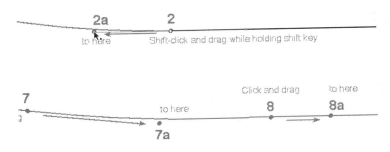

5] Continue with the Pen tool all the way around, following the numbered cues. Close the path by clicking once more on the first numbered point.

Now that the path is closed, you can assign a fill to it.

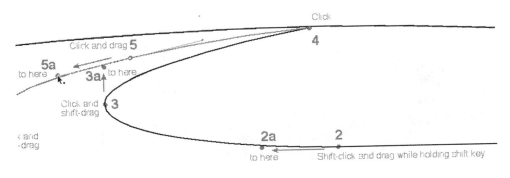

6] Go to the Color Mixer and create the color 0c 0m 0y 90k.

The dark gray color appears in the right side of the color well in the Color Mixer.

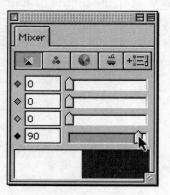

7] With the road still selected, go to the Fill Inspector and choose Gradient from the pop-up menu. Make the top color 0c 0m 0y 90k and the bottom color 0c 0m 0y 75k.

You will have to mix lighter gray in the Color Mixer before you can apply it. The road should now be darker at the top and lighter at the bottom, as shown here.

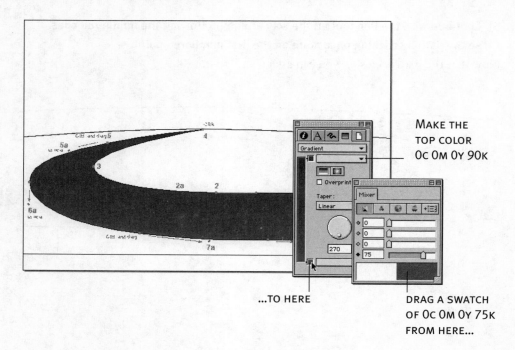

MAKE THE
TOP COLOR
0C 0M 0Y 90K

...TO HERE

DRAG A SWATCH
OF 0C 0M 0Y 75K
FROM HERE...

8] **Select the horizon shape by clicking somewhere on the stroke. Go to the Fill Inspector and choose Gradient from the pop-up menu. Click next to the top color swatch on the pop-up menu and choose the color 10c 5m 0y 0k from the list. Leave the bottom swatch white. Set the stroke to None.**

Now the horizon shape looks just like the illustration shown here.

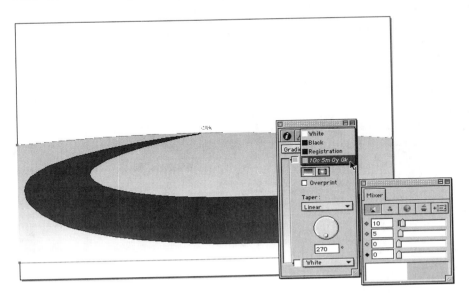

9] **Save your work.**

Your two shapes are ready to be added to the original document in this lesson.

10] **Select the two shapes and choose Edit › Copy. Then close this document.**

Now you will go back to your original document with the mountains and paste these elements.

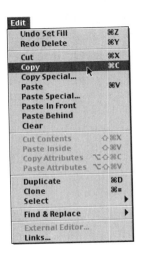

EXCHANGING ELEMENTS BETWEEN DOCUMENTS

In this section, you will take the elements that you have created in the previous two documents and add them to the first document with the mountains.

1] Open the mountain file you saved previously, or open the file Mountn2.ft9 in the Lesson03\Start folder. Choose View › Fit to Page to see the whole page on the screen. This is the way your document looked when you left it to work on the car. Now you are going to add elements created using the previous two templates to complete your ad.

2] Make the Layers panel visible by choosing Window › Panels › Layers. Make sure that all of the top layers are visible (check marks should be displayed); then click the name of the road layer to make that your target layer. The pen icon should be displayed to the right of the name, indicating that this is the active layer. Close the Layers panel. You are making sure the stacking order is correct by putting objects on separate layers.

3] Choose File › Paste. If nothing happens (or the wrong element lands on your page), Choose Edit › Undo, go back to the road file you created, select both filled objects, and copy them. Then return and paste again.

The pasted objects land in the middle of your window, and they are both selected. All you have to do now is move them into position.

4] Click the road and horizon objects with the Arrow tool and drag them into position. Hold the Shift key to constrain movement to a straight line.

When placed correctly, the top of the horizon should just cover the bottom edge of the lowest dark shape on the mountain, as shown.

5] Save your work. Then open the car file you created. Move the window on your screen so you can see the mountain file underneath. Click the car and drag it onto the portion of the mountain file that is visible; then release the mouse.

When you release the mouse button, a copy of the car is moved to the mountain file. Copying and pasting is an efficient way to move objects between FreeHand documents, but you can also drag and drop, bypassing the menu commands. Which method you use is up to you—both work well.

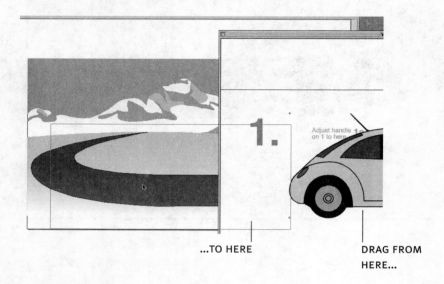

...TO HERE

DRAG FROM HERE...

6] Click the mountain file window to make it come to the front. Move the car into position at the bottom of the road, as shown. Press the Tab key to deselect all art.

Now all your illustration pieces are in place—you only need to add the text to complete the ad.

7] Make the Text layer active by clicking on it in the Layers panel. Make sure it is visible—you should see a checkmark to the left of the name.

When the text layer is visible, you will see a line of type appear below the car. You are going to add the headline next.

125

8] Select the Text tool from the toolbox and click in the upper-left corner of the page. Type *MOVE AHEAD!* Make the type size 60, make the font Helvetica Bold (or a similar font), and assign the same color as the body of the car.

The text should resemble the image shown here. Next you are going to give the text a fat stroke while keeping it editable as text.

9] Highlight all the text by dragging over it with the Text tool. Go to the Stroke Inspector and select Basic from the pop-up menu. Make the stroke width 6 points and set the Join option to Rounded (the middle button).

You need to select the text with the Text tool so that you can change the stroke width and Join option. If you only select the text with the Pointer tool, you won't have access to any other options in the Stroke Inspector.

126

This fat border is unacceptable by itself. The stroke cuts into the letter shapes and makes the text less readable. We will fix that in the next step.

10] Select the text block with the Arrow tool and choose Edit › Clone. With the clone selected, go to the Color List and set the stroke to None.

Now the letter shapes are clearly visible, but the thick, rounded border remains. Remember this technique—it is a standard method for creating a border around live text in FreeHand.

11] Save your work.

WHAT YOU HAVE LEARNED

In this lesson you have:

- Used the Freeform tool to edit basic shapes [pages 96–100]
- Created paths using the FreeHand tool [pages 102–105]
- Discovered the differences between the Bezigon and Pen tools [pages 105–106]
- Used the Bezigon tool to trace templates [pages 106–117]
- Created a path using the Pen tool [pages 117–122]
- Modified a path shape by Alt (Windows) or Option (Macintosh) -dragging a line with the Arrow tool [page 118]
- Combined artwork from different documents by copying and pasting [pages 122–125]
- Applied a custom stroke to live text [pages 125–127]

and styles

using layers

LESSON 4

Layers and styles are among FreeHand's most powerful features for organizing and simplifying your documents and making it easier to apply and modify the look of an element. **Layers** are transparent planes or overlays that help organize objects and control they way they stack upon each other in an illustration. A **style** is a set of graphic attributes such as color, fill, and stroke or a set of text attributes such as font, style, space before and after, indents and tabs, and alignment.

Creating a complex illustration, like this picture of a country sunset, is made easier by Freehand's ability to combine and manipulate different layers, as you will learn to do in this lesson.

Designed by Julia Siferf of Glasgow & Associates

You will apply these features to the creation of a stylized drawing of sunbeams radiating above a hillside. As you work, you will use the Pen tool, perform and duplicate transformations, work with layers and styles, apply path operations, and use the powerful Paste Inside command. You will also export your artwork so it can be imported into other applications.

If you would like to review the final result of this lesson, open Sunbeams.fh9 in the Complete folder within the Lesson04 folder.

WHAT YOU WILL LEARN

In this lesson you will:

- Import tracing patterns to help you accurately create paths and elements
- Organize a document into layers
- Create paths with the Pen tool
- Create and duplicate transformations
- Create an object style so you can easily apply and modify visual characteristics
- Trim unwanted portions from graphics
- Import another FreeHand document
- Export artwork for use in other applications

APPROXIMATE TIME

This lesson takes approximately 2 hours to complete.

LESSON FILES

Media Files:

Lesson04\Media\Pattern1.tif
Lesson04\Media\Pattern2.tif
Lesson04\Media\Pattern3.tif
Lesson04\Media\Frame.fh9

Starting Files:

None

Completed Project:

Lesson04\Complete\Sunbeams.fh9
Lesson04\Complete\Sunbeams.eps

CREATING A NEW CUSTOM-SIZE DOCUMENT

You will begin working on the artwork for this lesson in a new document.

1] Create a new document by choosing File › New (Windows Ctrl+N, Macintosh Command+N).

A blank page appears, which you will now adjust to the page size needed for this illustration.

2] Change the unit of measure to Inches using the Units menu at the bottom of the screen. Choose Window › Inspectors › Document to display the Document Inspector.

The Document Inspector shows the current page dimensions and orientation.

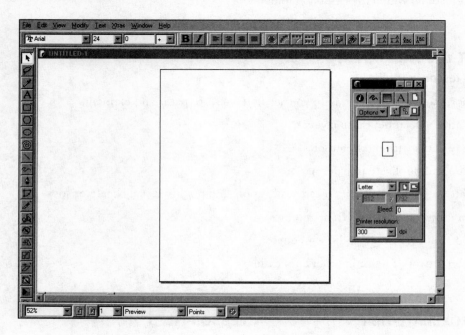

3] In the Document Inspector, select Custom on the Page Size menu, enter the dimensions *6.125* by *4.875* inches, and click the icon for Landscape orientation.

Landscape orientation displays the page so that the height is the smaller dimension and the length is the larger dimension.

Your page is now the correct size, but it appears small in the document window.

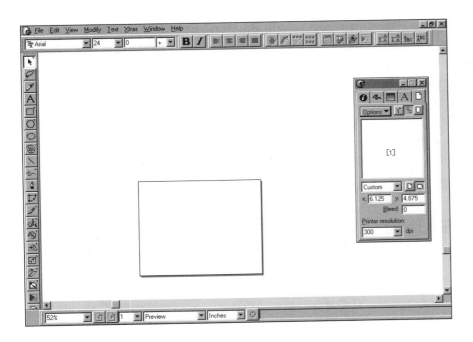

4] **Close the Document Inspector and choose View › Fit to Page (Windows Ctrl+Shift+W, Macintosh Command+Shift+W) to make the document larger in the window.**

5] **Save the document as *MySun* in your MyWork folder.**

The page is now ready for you to begin creating the illustration.

IMPORTING A TRACING PATTERN AND MOVING IT TO A BACKGROUND LAYER

As you learned in the last lesson, a good way to accurately create paths and elements is to trace an existing image of the desired layout or artwork. For example, you can use a scanned image of a pencil sketch or other printed source as a pattern for tracing in FreeHand.

In the last lesson, you opened a template containing a tracing pattern. Here you will import an image called Pattern1.tif to use as a tracing pattern in the drawing you will be creating. This pattern will become the basis for the sunbeams.

You will want this pattern in the background so you can trace over it, but you will not want it to print. You will accomplish this by using layers. By placing elements on layers, you can control the visibility and printing of individual elements.

1] Choose File › Import (Windows Ctrl+R, Macintosh Command+R). Select Pattern1.tif from the Media folder within the Lesson04 folder and click Open. Align the cursor with the top-left corner of the page and click the mouse to position the artwork accurately on the page.

An image of a rectangle enclosing a circle with one ray appears.

tip   *Be sure to just click when you place the template. If you click and drag when importing objects into FreeHand, the imported object will assume the dimensions of the selection you drag. While this can be desirable in certain situations, most of the time you will want to place objects at their original dimensions.*

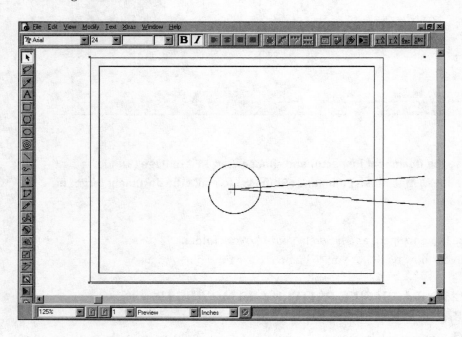

tip   *If the image does not look very clear on the page, you should check your preference settings. Choose File > Preferences to display the Preferences dialog box and click Redraw. Make sure that the High-Resolution Image Display option is turned on and then click OK. The imported image should now be displayed more clearly.*

Place this pattern on a layer so you can move it into the background.

2] Choose Window > Panels > Layers to display the Layers panel.

Foreground, Guides, and Background. These are preset layers in every FreeHand document. Notice that the Background layer appears below a separator line in the panel.

You can add additional layers in any FreeHand document, and you can use these layers to organize elements and control the visibility and printing of the elements on each particular layer. You can move graphic elements from one layer to another, except for the Guides layer, which holds all of the guides you use for aligning elements in your document. As you learned when you used guides in Lesson 2, the Guides layer does not print. Any other layer that appears above the separator line in the panel is a printing layer and is considered a foreground layer. Any layer appearing below the separator line is a nonprinting background layer.

In this first use of layers, you will move the pattern image into the background so it will be visible to trace over, but will not print.

3] With the image still selected, click the name Background in the Layers panel.

The lines in the image will dim, indicating that this artwork is now on a nonprinting background layer.

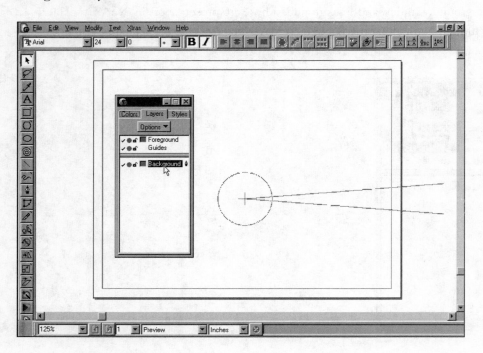

4] Lock the Background layer by clicking once on the lock icon next to the layer name in the panel.

This will prevent accidental changes to the layer as you work. It also prevents you from accidentally adding the next elements you create to the Background layer. Notice that the Foreground layer is selected in the panel. This indicates the current active layer, where the next elements will be added.

5] Save your work.

Creating the elements of the sky will be much easier now that the tracing pattern is in place.

6] Create a new layer by choosing New from the Options menu in the Layers panel. Double-click the name of the new layer, Layer-1, and type *Sky* as the new name for this layer. Press Enter to complete the name change.

You can see that the Sky layer is a foreground (printing) layer because it appears above the separator line in the Layers panel. This new layer is now the active layer, as indicated by the pen-tip icon on the right edge of the panel. The artwork you create next will be added to this layer.

135

7] Using the Rectangle tool, create a rectangle that matches the size and position of the large rectangle visible in the background.

This rectangle will define the edges of your picture and will appear behind all of the other artwork.

tip *The rectangle tool may still have the corner radius setting used in an earlier lesson. To reset the corner radius, double-click the rectangle tool and move the slider to 0.*

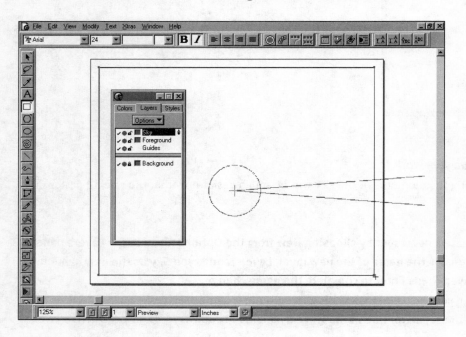

8] Save your work.

You will assign a gradient fill to this element, but first you need to import the colors you will use for this illustration.

DEFINING PROCESS COLORS

When defining colors in FreeHand, you must determine whether to create **spot colors** or **process colors**. Spot colors match the color of the specific ink that will be used on a printing press to print that color in a FreeHand illustration. For example, to use green and red in your document, you could use a green ink and a red ink. In that case, you would define the red and green colors in your document as spot colors. This is how you added colors for the letterhead elements in Lesson 2.

Alternatively, you could define every color you use as a process color, a combination of cyan, magenta, yellow, and black inks, as you did for the car and other elements in Lesson 3. The majority of full-color printed pieces you see use process color printing.

Why choose one rather than the other? If you have fewer than four colors in your document, printing with spot color can be cheaper, since it uses fewer inks. You can also match colors precisely with spot color and choose from a wider variety of colors than CMYK colors can reproduce. On the other hand, if your artwork contains many colors, it is much cheaper to use process color, which can create almost any color you need using the same four ink colors. (The exceptions are some very bright colors and specialty inks, such as fluorescents and metallics, which CMYK cannot reproduce.)

Without high-end color management software, it is unlikely that your computer monitor will represent colors as they will appear when printed on a printing press. For this reason, FreeHand includes libraries of spot and process colors for use in your artwork, including PANTONE for spot color (which you used in Lesson 2), PANTONE for process color, Trumatch, Focaltone, Toyo, and Munsell. By referring to the printed samples in a swatch book, you can more accurately predict how your artwork will appear when it is printed on a press. You will be importing colors from the PANTONE Matching System for process colors in this lesson.

1] Choose Window › Panels › Colors to display the Color List. Choose PANTONE Process from the Options menu in the Color List panel.
This displays the colors available in the PANTONE Process color library. You will select several colors from this library to import into your document.

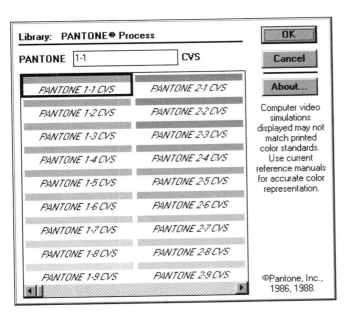

2] Click the color named 1-5. Then scroll to the right. Hold down the Ctrl (Windows) or Command (Macintosh) key and click 18-7 to add this to the selection. Continue to hold down the Ctrl or Command key while adding 31-5, 161-6, 221-5, and 289-1 to the selection. Then click OK.

This imports all six of these colors into the Color List panel.

tip *FreeHand displays the names of process colors in italic type, while the names of spot colors are displayed in roman characters.*

3] Display the Fill Inspector by choosing Window › Inspectors › Fill. Select the rectangle on your page with the Pointer tool (if it is not already selected). Change the fill to Gradient, with PANTONE 221-5 (light blue) at the top and PANTONE 1-5 (yellow) at the bottom.

The entire rectangle should be filled with a gradient from blue at the top to yellow at the bottom. Because the filled rectangle is on the topmost layer, no other elements are now visible.

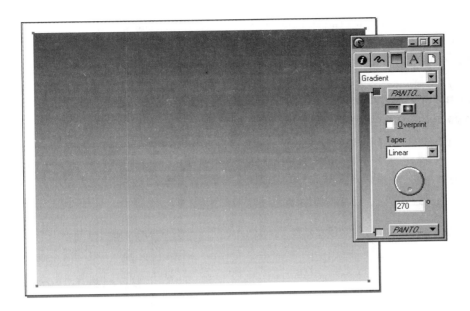

4] Display the Stroke Inspector by clicking the Stroke tab at the top of the Inspector panel group. On the Stroke Type menu, select None.

Another way to display the Stroke Inspector is to choose Window > Inspector > Stroke.

5] Press the Tab key to deselect all elements. Hide the Inspector and display the Layers panel.

6] Now create a new layer by choosing New from the Options menu in the Layers panel. Double-click the default name, type the new name *Sun*, and press Enter.

On this layer, you will trace the sun and sunbeams. However, the sky is blocking your view of the tracing pattern. To solve that problem, you will temporarily hide the artwork on the Sky layer while creating new elements on the Sun layer.

7] Hide the Sky layer by clicking the check mark to the left of the name Sky in the Layers panel. Then save the document.

You can use the check mark to display or hide the contents of any layer whenever it is helpful to do so. The Sun layer should be the active layer at this time, as indicated by the layer name Sun reversed out of a black bar in the Layers panel.

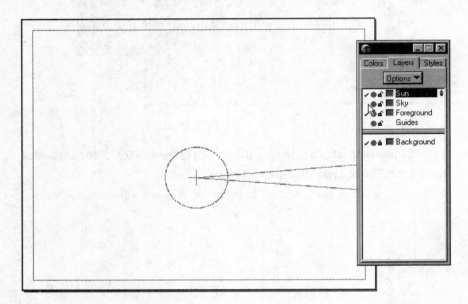

CREATING AN ELEMENT WITH THE PEN TOOL

In this task, you will trace the sunbeam displayed in the background by creating corner points with the Pen tool. Then you will duplicate that element to create a sky full of sunbeams radiating out from the sun.

1] Select the Pen tool by clicking it once in the Toolbox.

2] Position the Pen tool cursor at the center of the sun and click the mouse once. Move to the top-right corner of the sunbeam and click, and move to the bottom-right corner and click again. Now close the path by clicking once on the starting point.

It is important to close this path by clicking the starting point. You have created an empty triangular shape, which you will now fill.

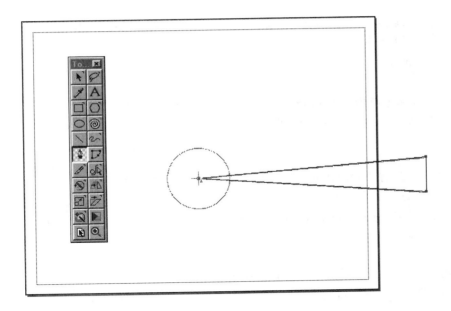

3] Display the Fill Inspector by choosing Window › Inspectors › Fill. Change the type of fill to Gradient and use the menus to change the top color to PANTONE 161-6 and the bottom color to PANTONE 1-5. Change the angle to 180 degrees.

You could also drag swatches of these colors from the Color List and drop them on the top and bottom swatches on the gradient in the Fill Inspector. Remember that you can change the angle by rotating the direction control or by typing a new value into the field just above the bottom color and pressing Enter. The angle of 180 degrees makes the gradient extend from the top color on the right to the bottom color on the left.

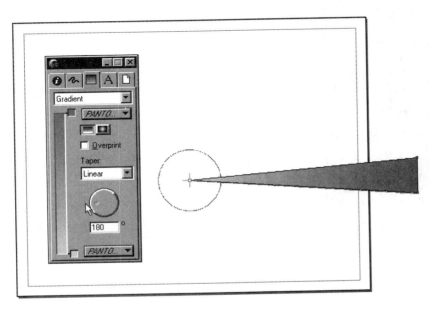

4] Click the Stroke tab in the Inspector panel group to display the Stroke Inspector. Change the type of stroke to None.

The first sunbeam is complete.

5] Press the Tab key to deselect the artwork. Then save your work.

Now you will create additional copies of this sunbeam rotating around the center of the sun.

ROTATING A COPY AND DUPLICATING THE TRANSFORMATION

You have used the transform handles to manually rotate elements into position. In this task, you will use the Transform panel to precisely control both the amount and center of rotation.

1] Go to the View menu and make sure that Snap to Point is checked.

This option will help ensure that your sunbeams rotate around the exact center of the circle.

2] Select the sunbeam with the Pointer tool. Double-click the Rotation tool in the Toolbox to display the Transform panel showing the rotation controls.

This panel allows you to enter specific information for transforming elements. The transformations include moving, rotating, scaling, skewing, and reflecting elements.

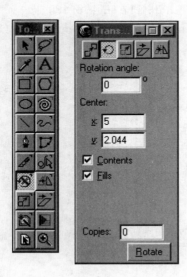

3] Click the Rotation tool once and release it at the center of the circle (on the left tip of the sunbeam) to specify the center of rotation.

This spot will now be the point the sunbeam rotates around. Because you have enabled the Snap to Point option, your cursor changes to an arrow when you are over the left tip of the sunbeam.

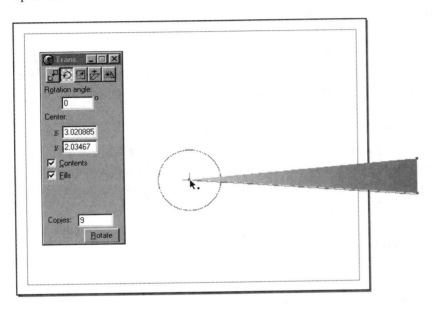

4] Enter a rotation angle of 20 degrees in the Transform panel and set the number of copies to 9; then click Rotate (Windows) or Apply (Macintosh).

All of the sunbeams now appear in position, each rotated 20 degrees counterclockwise from the one next to it.

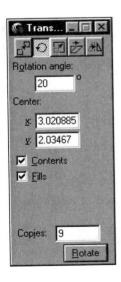

143

5] Close the Transform panel and save your work.

The sky is almost complete.

COMBINING ELEMENTS WITH PASTE INSIDE

Now that the sunbeams are complete, you will add the sun and use the **Paste Inside** feature to create **clipping paths** to limit the visible portion of the sunbeams to the area within the sky rectangle. To create a clipping path, you paste artwork inside a closed path using the Paste Inside command. Only the part of the artwork located inside the closed path will appear; the part of the artwork that extends outside of the clipping path will not be displayed or printed.

1] Select the Ellipse tool from the Toolbox. Position the cursor on the center of the circle in the tracing pattern, hold down Shift to create a perfect circle and Alt (Windows) or Option (Macintosh) to draw the circle from the center, and drag downward and to the right. Release the mouse when your circle is the same size as the circle in the tracing pattern.

To ensure that the new ellipse you create remains a perfect circle, always release the mouse before you release the Shift and Alt or Option keys.

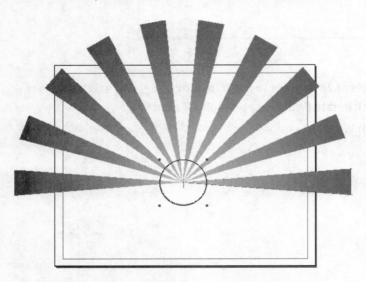

2] Fill the sun with PANTONE 1-5 and set the stroke to None. Choose Edit › Select › All to select all of the sunbeams and the sun (Windows Ctrl+A, Macintosh Command+A). Choose Modify › Group to group these elements together (Windows Ctrl+G, Macintosh Command+G).

Grouping these elements will make it easier to select all of the elements at once so you can work with them later.

3] Display the Layers panel and click the space to the left of the Sky layer in the column where a check mark appears for the other layers.

The Sky layer should now be visible (indicated by the check mark) and should appear behind the sunbeams, since the Sky layer is below the Sun layer in the Layers panel.

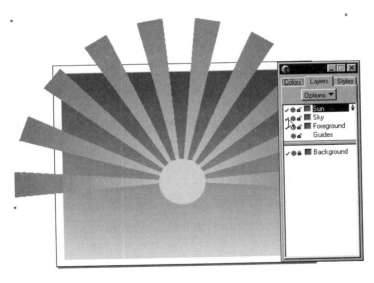

4] With the sunbeam group still selected, click the Sky layer in the Layers panel to move the sunbeam artwork to the Sky layer.

Clicking a layer name in the Layers panel moves the selected elements to that layer.

tip *You can check to see which layer any element is on by selecting the element. The layer containing the selected element will be selected in the Layers panel. If you have artwork selected on several layers at once, the name of each layer with a selected element will be highlighted in the Layers panel.*

Next you will use the sky rectangle to mask the unwanted portions of the sunbeams using FreeHand's Paste Inside command.

5] With the sunbeam group selected, choose Edit › Cut. Then click the sky rectangle and choose Edit › Paste Inside.
The sunbeam artwork was in the desired position over the sky when you cut the artwork. The cut operation removed the artwork from the page. After you select the sky rectangle and choose Paste Inside, only the portion of the sunbeam artwork that appears within the edges of the sky rectangle appears on the page. This makes the sky a clipping path that hides the portions of the sunbeams that extend beyond the rectangle.

146

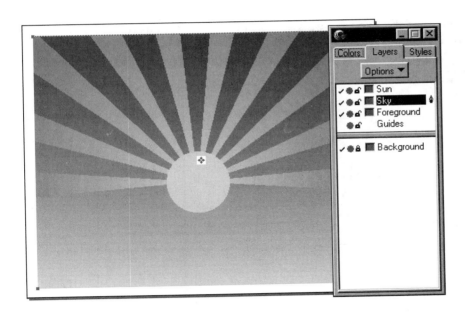

tip
The Paste Inside feature can save a great deal of time. Instead of having to trace each sunbeam individually and trying to match the edges of the sky rectangle for each one, one sunbeam was created that extended well beyond the edge of the rectangle. All of the other sunbeams were copied and rotated from that first one—each one extending beyond the edge of the rectangle. Paste Inside clips all the elements to the desired border in one step, saving you time in creating the elements and ensuring that the edges of all elements are perfectly aligned.

6] Save your work.
Now that the sky is complete, you will begin working on the hills.

CHANGING YOUR VIEW OF THE ARTWORK

FreeHand offers various ways for you to view artwork on your monitor, using the View menu at the bottom of the document window. Preview is the fully rendered view you have been working in; it displays the highest quality view. Fast Preview enables you to sacrifice some display quality for speed while still displaying the fills and strokes. Faster still is the Keyline mode, which displays the elements without fills and strokes. The quickest display mode is Fast Keyline, which displays only those elements that define the basic layout of your artwork.

1] Use the View menu at the bottom of the document window to change the view from Preview to Keyline.

Keyline mode enables you to clearly see all of the paths in your artwork, even if some are behind other elements.

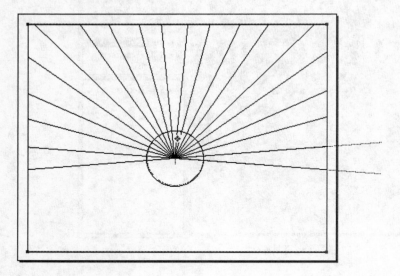

2] Use the same menu to change the view to Fast Keyline.

The elements that you pasted inside the sky rectangle are no longer displayed.

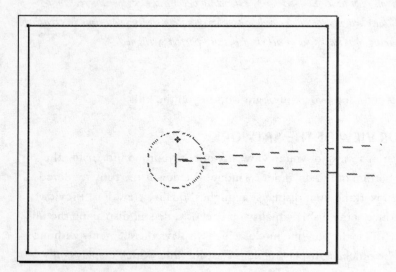

The two keyline views provide an excellent way to see through elements as you work. And although you can apply fills and strokes in the keyline views, don't forget to change back to one of the two preview modes to see the results!

3] Change the view to Fast Preview mode.

This mode provides lower-quality display of fills and strokes, but with faster screen redrawing than Preview mode. This lower quality is especially apparent in Gradient fills, which are displayed as bands of color rather than smooth color transitions.

4] Change back to the Preview mode.

The speed difference between the Fast Preview and Preview modes will be more apparent as the complexity of the artwork increases.

CREATING OTHER FOREGROUND LAYERS

You will use a different tracing pattern to create the next elements.

1] Press the Tab key to make sure that no elements are selected. Hide the Sky layer by clicking the check mark to the left of the layer name in the Layers panel. Rename the Sun layer by double-clicking the name, typing *Pattern 2*, and pressing Enter.

An advantage of using layers is that you can hide layers that are not currently being used. Remember that clicking a layer name when elements are selected moves those elements to that layer. Pressing the Tab key deselects all elements so no elements will change layers when you rename this layer.

2] **Create a new layer by choosing New from the Options menu in the Layers panel. Double-click the default name of the new layer, type *Hills*, and press Enter.**

This is the layer where you will create the hills artwork.

3] **Point to the name of the Pattern 2 layer in the Layers panel. Hold down the mouse button, drag the layer down below the Background layer, and then release the mouse.**

150

Moving this layer below the separator line in the Layers panel makes Pattern 2 a background layer. Any artwork you put on this layer will be visible as a tracing pattern but will not print.

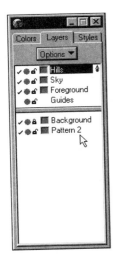

4] Hide the artwork on the Background layer by clicking the check mark to the left of the layer named Background in the Layers panel.

Since Background is above Pattern 2 in the Layers panel, the artwork on the Background layer will cover up the artwork you will put on the Pattern 2 layer in the next step. Hiding the Background layer will allow you to see the Pattern 2 layer.

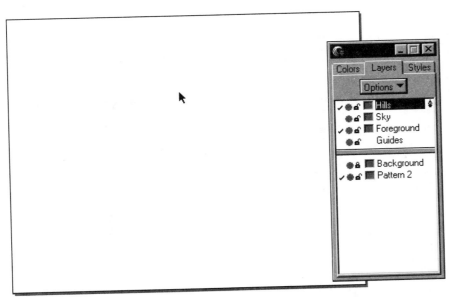

5] Choose File › Import, select Pattern2.tif from the Media folder within the Lesson04 folder, and click Open. Align the cursor with the top-left corner of the page and click the mouse to position the artwork accurately on the page.

This image extends below the bottom edge of the page.

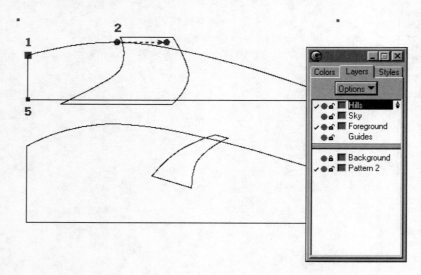

6] With this image selected, click once on the Pattern 2 layer in the Layers panel to send the artwork to that layer. Click the lock icon to the left of the Pattern 2 layer to lock the layer and prevent accidental changes.

The Hills layer should be the active layer, ready for you to begin tracing the shapes.

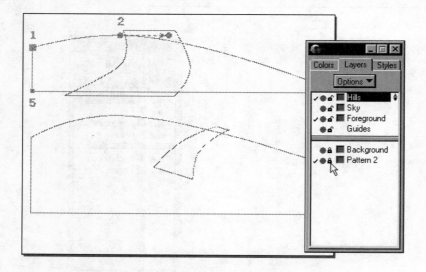

7] Save your work. You can hide the Layers panel if you wish.

CREATING CURVED PATHS WITH THE PEN TOOL

You need to create three hills for this illustration, each with its own road. You will use the Pen tool to create these features.

1] Using the Pen tool, click once on the top-left corner of the top pattern (point 1) to start the path.

This first pattern has the point positions identified. You will create this path by adding the points in order, from 1 to 5, and then clicking again on point 1 to close the path. Clicking point 1 adds a corner point in this position.

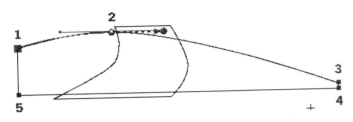

2] Position the cursor on point 2 at the top of the curve. Drag to the right to pull out the control handles until the first segment of the path matches the pattern (which will occur when the cursor is positioned over the red dot in the pattern). Then release the mouse button.

When you drag with the Pen tool, you create a curve point.

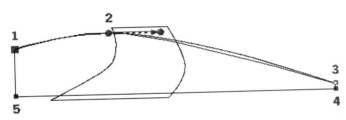

3] Click once on point 3 to add a corner point.

The top-right segment may not match the pattern exactly, but don't stop to make adjustments until you have completed and closed the path. It will be much easier to make the adjustments after all of the points have been created.

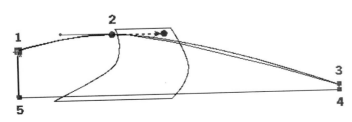

153

4] **Hold down the Shift key and click point 4 and then point 5. Then click the original point (point 1) to close the path.**

Holding down Shift when adding additional points ensures that the segment being added will be vertical, horizontal, or at a 45-degree angle to the previous point.

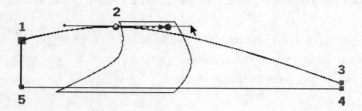

5] **Using the Pointer tool, click the curve point (2) to display the control handles. Drag the right handle out farther to the right until the curve matches the pattern. Save your work.**

Try to drag directly to the right to avoid changing the segment to the left of the curve point, which already matches the pattern.

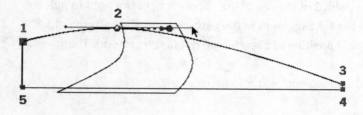

tip *If the pattern for the road is not visible, it's probably because your hill shape has a fill. If so, change the fill to None in the Fill Inspector.*

6] **Press the Tab key to deselect the hill path. Trace the road that overlaps this hill shape by clicking the Pen tool at the upper-right corner of the road pattern to create a corner point.**

The road will extend beyond the edges of the hill; you will trim off the excess later.

7] Add a curve point at the outermost part of the curve on the right side by holding the mouse and dragging downward to pull out control handles. Release the mouse and then trace around the rest of the pattern, adding corner and curve points as needed. Finally, click the original point to close the path.

tip *Always work around a path, and trace the entire path before making adjustments with the Pointer tool.*

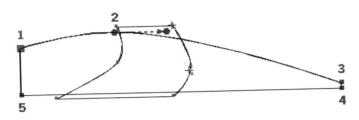

8] Display the Color List by choosing Window › Panels › Color List. Drag the swatch next to PANTONE 18-7 and drop it inside the road you just created. Drag the swatch next to None and drop it on the edge of the path to change the stroke to None.

You can also make these changes using the Fill and Stroke Inspectors.

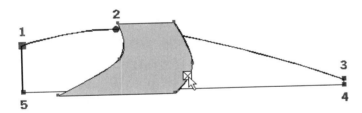

9] Press the Tab key to deselect the road. Fill the hill with PANTONE 289-1 and set the stroke to None.

Drag color swatches from the Color List or use the Fill and Stroke Inspectors to make these changes.

tip *Windows users should remember that the document window must be active for Tab to deselect elements. If the Color List is active, for instance, simply click the page or pasteboard to activate the document window.*

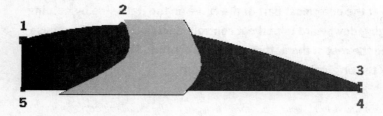

10] Save your work.

Next you will define object styles for these two elements.

DEFINING AND APPLYING OBJECT STYLES

You can record the visual characteristics of an element as an object style to make it easier to apply the same characteristics to other elements in the future. In addition, when you change a style definition, all of the elements that have been assigned that style will automatically be updated to reflect the changes.

You will create two styles for filling the hills and roads in your illustration.

1] Display the Styles panel by choosing Window › Panels › Styles.

FreeHand offers two types of styles: object and paragraph. **Object styles**, which you are using in this task, record the stroke and fill characteristics of a selected element. **Paragraph styles** record character and paragraph formatting for text. Two default styles—a Normal style for objects and a Normal style for text—are already displayed in the Styles panel.

> **tip** *The styles panel may still show the graphic view used in Lesson 1. To change the styles panel to list view, select Show names from the Options pop-up menu.*

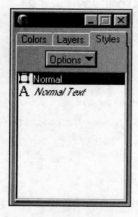

In the first lesson, you learned how to import a style from a library. Next you will create styles of your own.

2] Select the hill element with the Pointer tool. Choose New from the Options menu in the Styles panel to define a new style based on the fill and stroke of the selected element.

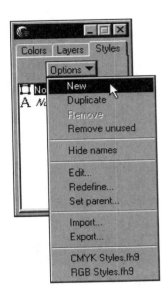

A new object style, named Style-1, appears in the Styles panel. The artwork does not visibly change, but it is now connected to this style.

3] Double-click the name Style-1, type *Hill*, and press Enter to change the name of this style.

The Hill style is defined as a basic PANTONE 289-1 fill with no stroke—the current style of the selected object.

4] Select the road element with the Pointer tool and create another new style by choosing New from the Options menu in the Styles panel. Double-click the default new style name and change it to *Road*.

The Road style is defined as a basic PANTONE 18-7 fill with no stroke.

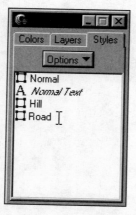

5] Save your work.

Next you will trim off the excess portion of the road to match the edges of the hill.

COMBINING ELEMENTS WITH PATH OPERATIONS

In an earlier task, you used the Paste Inside feature to make the sunbeams visible only within the sky rectangle. In this task, you will use the **Intersect** command to trim off the excess portions of the road to match the edges of the hill.

When you are dealing with an individual element that you will not need to move later, you can use Intersect and the other path operations to permanently clip off unwanted portions of selected elements, simplifying the document. Paste Inside, although it would work here as well, is more useful when there are multiple elements, or when you may wish to move the artwork in the future; no matter how you arrange the elements later, the clipping path will always define the visible edges of the artwork.

tip *If you have multiple elements or may need to move elements later, it is usually best to use Paste Inside. Otherwise, you can use Intersect, Union, and the other path operations to easily create complex and accurate paths.*

1] Select the hill with the Pointer tool and choose Edit › Clone to make a duplicate of the hill in the same position, on top of the existing artwork. The clone of the hill is already selected, so now add the road to the selection by holding down Shift and clicking the edge of the road that is visible.

Do not use the Select All command, since that would select both copies of the hill.

158

2] Choose Modify › Combine › Intersect.

The two individual shapes are replaced by the shape defined by the intersection, or overlap, of the two selected shapes: the trimmed road. You cloned the hill before creating the intersection, so the trimmed road now sits in front of the original hill.

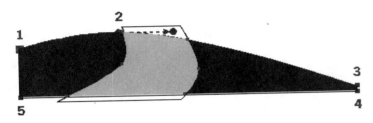

3] The trimmed road is already selected. Add the hill to the selection by Shift+clicking it with the Pointer tool. Then group the hill and road together by choosing Modify › Group.

Grouping the elements will prevent you from accidentally moving either the road or the hill without the other element.

4] Save your work.

CREATING OTHER ELEMENTS

Now you will trace the other two hills and roads.

1] Press the Tab key to make sure that no elements are selected. Click Normal in the Styles panel so that the next items you create will have a black stroke and no fill.

The active style when no elements are selected determines the style that is assigned automatically to the next elements. Using Normal while tracing the shapes will make it easier to see the patterns, since Normal specifies a black stroke and no fill.

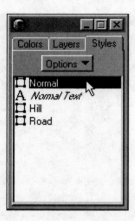

2] Use the Pen tool to trace the next hill pattern in the same manner as the first, clicking to position corner points and dragging to pull out control handles for curve points.

Remember to trace around the entire shape and to click the starting point to close the path.

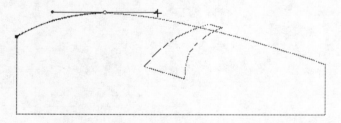

tip *To trace the remaining elements, you can use either the Pen or Bezigon tool, as you prefer.*

3] Trace the road for this second hill.

160

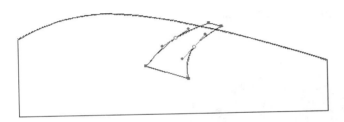

4] Apply the Road style to this element by clicking Road in the Styles panel. Select the hill element and apply the Hill style.

You can also apply a style by dragging the icon to the left of the style name in the Styles panel and dropping it on the desired object.

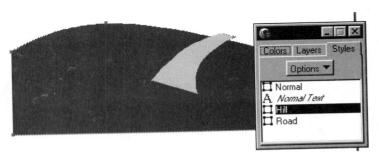

Next you will trim off the excess portion of the road with the Intersect command.

5] With the hill path selected, choose Edit › Clone. Hold down the Shift key and click a visible portion of the road to select it along with the clone of the hill. Choose Modify › Combine › Intersect.

The road is trimmed to match the edges of the hill.

tip *Zoom in closer if you have difficulty selecting the road and the hill at the same time.*

6] Select the hill and road and choose Modify › Group.

The second hill is now complete—only one more hill to go!

7] Repeat steps 1 through 6 for the third hill pattern and its road.

This third pattern is visible below the page, so you may need to scroll down to see it clearly.

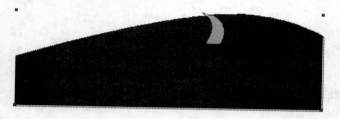

8] Save your work.

ALIGNING ELEMENTS

The three groups that make up the hillsides in this illustration need to be aligned to one another so the road appears to be continuous. To align the three individual hill groups, you will select them together and use the Align panel.

1] Choose Edit › Select › All in Document to select all three hill groups.

Note that the Select All command selects only the items on the page, not those on the pasteboard. Select All in Document selects all of the elements in the document, on all pages and the pasteboard, in any unlocked and visible layers.

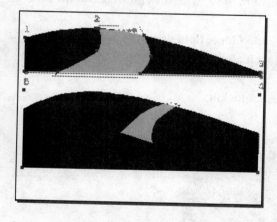

2] Choose Window › Panels › Align to display the Align panel. Click the bottom-middle square on the Align panel grid to set the panel to center the groups horizontally and align the bottom edges.

You can set the alignment by clicking the grid or by choosing from either menu at the bottom of the Align panel.

3] Click Apply (Windows) or Align (Macintosh).

All three hills are now aligned to one another, but they are stacked up in the wrong order. The road should be visible going over all of the hills.

4] Press the Tab key to deselect all elements. Click the visible road with the Pointer tool to select the hill in front and choose Modify › Arrange › Send to Back.

163

The most distant road segment is now on the bottom of the stack, and the middle segment is in front of the others, hiding the closest segment.

5] Press the Tab key to deselect all elements and click the middle (larger) road with the Pointer tool. This element must be moved only one item back, rather than all the way to the back, so choose Modify › Arrange › Move Backward.
Send to Back and Bring to Front move selected items to the very back or front within the current layer. Move Backward and Move Forward move selected elements one item backward or forward. If more than one element is on top of the element you want to move forward, you select this command again until the element is placed correctly.

Now group the hills in their correct positions.

6] Choose Edit › Select › All in Document to select all three hill groups and then choose Modify › Group. Save your work
The hills are ready to be positioned on the page.

POSITIONING ARTWORK AND EDITING STYLES

Now turn on the Sky layer so you can see how the Hill layer looks with it and make any modifications to the styles.

1] In the Layers panel, hide the Pattern 2 layer and show the Sky layer by turning their check marks off and on, respectively. Use the Pointer tool to move the hills into position so that the bottom and sides of the hills slightly overlap the edges of the sky rectangle.

164

You will use the Paste Inside feature to trim these hills the same way you did with the sunbeams earlier. Before you do this, though, you will change the style definitions to change the appearance of the hills.

2] Display the Tints panel (Window › Panels › Tints). Select PANTONE 289-1 as the base color from the menu at the top. Click the 40 percent swatch to display it in the color well at the bottom of the panel and then click the Add to Color List button. In the dialog box that appears, accept the default name for this tint by clicking the Add button.

This will add 40 percent PANTONE 289-1 to the Color List.

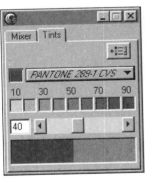

3] Display the Styles panel (Window › Panels › Styles) and press the Tab key to make sure that no elements are selected in your document. Click the Hill style once in the panel and choose Edit from the Options menu in the Styles panel.

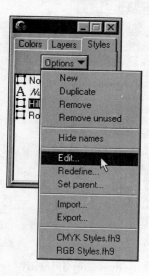

This displays the Edit Style dialog box, where you can change the characteristics of elements that have this style assigned.

4] Change the fill to Gradient, with PANTONE 289-1 at the top and the 40 percent tint of that color at the bottom. Then change the angle to 90 degrees and press Enter.

The fill settings appear on the left side of the dialog box. You can change the angle by entering a new value in the field just above the bottom color in the gradient strip or by rotating the angle dial just above the angle field.

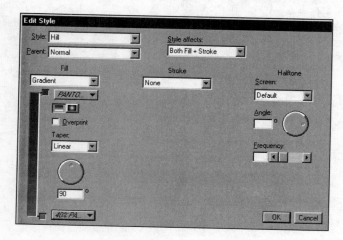

5] Click OK to apply the changes and return to the artwork.

Changing the style definition automatically changes the style of all elements that have this style applied.

6] Edit the Road style by selecting that style in the Styles panel and choosing Edit from the Options menu in the panel. Change the fill to Gradient, with PANTONE 18-7 at the top and PANTONE 31-5 at the bottom, with an angle of 270 degrees.

In both the hill and road elements, the gradients will flow from a lighter color on the top to a darker color at the bottom.

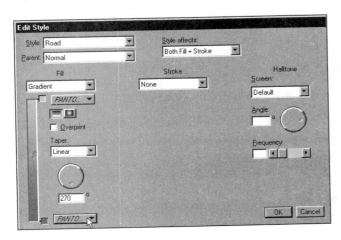

7] Click OK to see the results. Click Normal in the Style panel. Then save your work.

The hills and roads are now filled with gradient fills. Notice how the gradients give the impression of sunlight highlights on the hilltops.

167

tip *This is a simple demonstration of the power that object styles can offer. Imagine that you had created a state map and made all interstate highways 2 points wide and blue by defining and applying a style. If your client then decides that these highways should all be 4 points wide and red, you can simply edit the style definition to update every highway on the map.*

ADDING ELEMENTS TO THE CLIPPING PATH

You will hide the parts of the hills that extend beyond the edges of the sky rectangle by adding the hill group to the clipping path you created earlier.

1] The hills are in the correct position, so select the hill group and choose Edit › Cut.
The hills disappear from the page.

2] Select the sky rectangle and choose Edit › Paste Inside.
The hills are added to the sunbeam artwork inside the sky rectangle, and the edges of the artwork are defined by the rectangle.

The hills have been removed from the Hills layer and pasted into the Sky layer. Notice how the edges of the hills now perfectly match the edges of the sky graphic.

3] Save your work.

SCALING AND REFLECTING ARTWORK

You still need to create the trees in the illustration. The artwork for the four trees is identical, so you can create one tree and then scale and reflect copies into position.

1] Hide the Sky layer. Use the Options menu in the Layers panel to create a new layer and change the name of that layer to *Trees*. Rename the Hills layer *Pattern 3*. Move the Pattern 3 layer below the separator line to make it a background layer.

Remember that the check mark next to a layer name allows you to control the visibility of the individual layers. Also remember that you rename layers by double-clicking the layer name and entering a new one.

tip *In this case, you renamed the empty Hills layer to use it for a new purpose. When you no longer need a particular layer in your document, you can also use the Options > Remove command in the Layers panel to delete the selected layer.*

Now open the tracing pattern for the trees.

2] Choose File › Import, select Pattern3.tif from the Media folder within the Lesson04 folder, and click Open. Position your cursor at the top-left corner of the page and click the mouse.

The image of four trees appears on the Pattern 3 layer, because it is the active layer, as indicated by the pen tip symbol on the right edge of the panel.

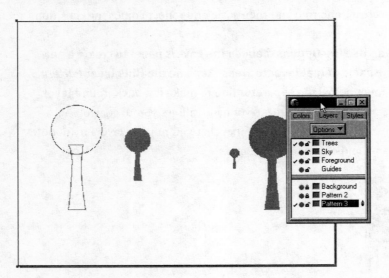

tip *If the image does not appear on the Pattern 3 layer, move it to that layer by clicking that layer in the Layers panel when the image is selected.*

3] Press the Tab key to deselect the image. Lock the Pattern 3 layer and click the Trees layer to make it the active layer. Save your work.

You are now ready to begin creating a tree.

4] Zoom in to clearly see the tree pattern on the left. Trace the tree trunk using the Pen or Bezigon tool.

Make sure to close the path so it can be filled in.

5] Fill the tree trunk path with PANTONE 31-5 and change the stroke to None.

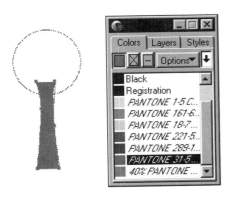

The next element to trace is a circle. You can make it easier to create a circle that will accurately match the pattern by using nonprinting ruler guides.

6] Choose View › Page Rulers › Show to display the rulers at the top and left edges of the document window (Windows Ctrl+Alt+M, Macintosh Command+Option+M). Position your cursor on the numbers in the top ruler and drag a nonprinting ruler guide down to the top of the circle pattern. Drag a ruler guide from the left ruler and position it at the left edge of the circle pattern.

171

These guides will make it easier to trace the circle pattern.

7] Select the Ellipse tool and position the cursor at the intersection of the two ruler guides. Hold down the Shift key to create a perfect circle and drag downward and to the right until the circle you are drawing matches the pattern.

Use ruler guides any time you need assistance in positioning or aligning elements.

8] Using the Fill Inspector, change the type of fill to Gradient. Click Radial Fill and change the top color to PANTONE 18-7. Change the bottom color to 40% PANTONE 289-1. Then drag the PANTONE 289-1 color swatch from the Color List and drop it in the middle of the color ramp to add a third color to the gradient. Move the centerpoint up and to the left by dragging the centerpoint control in the Fill Inspector.

172

The color ramp can be used to create a gradient fill combining up to 32 colors. Your Fill Inspector settings should look similar to the ones shown here.

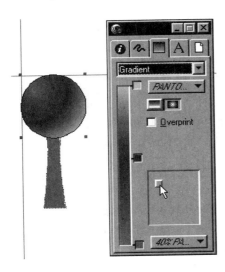

9] Change the stroke around the circle to None. Then select both the circle and the trunk and group them together to complete the tree. Save your work.

The first tree is finished.

10] Choose Edit › Duplicate to create another copy of the tree. Move this tree just to the right of the second tree pattern from the left, so its trunk bottom aligns with the trunk bottom of the pattern tree.

This second tree is much too large.

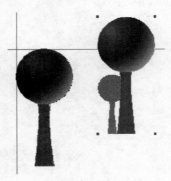

11] Hold down the Shift key and use the Pointer tool to drag the upper-right selection handle downward and to the left until the height of the tree matches the pattern. Then move the tree to position it to match the pattern.

tip *Holding the Shift key prevents the object proportions from changing.*

Two trees have been created, and there are only two more trees to go. However, you want the side of the trees with the lighted lower edge to face the sun, so the trees on the right must be reflections of the trees on the left.

12] Select both trees and choose Edit › Clone. Using the Reflection tool, position your cursor somewhere in the center of the page, between the center two trees. Hold down the Shift key and drag the mouse downward to reflect the trees around a vertical axis. Press the Tab key to deselect the new trees.

The two trees on the right now have the lighted lower edge on the left, facing the sun. The line that appears when you reflect an object is the reflection axis. By holding down the Shift key, you constrain the reflection axis vertically, horizontally, or to a 45-degree angle.

13] Resize and position the two trees on the right to match the pattern.
Remember to hold down Shift while resizing so you do not accidentally distort the trees.

USING LAYERS AND STYLES

14] Display the Sky layer to see your trees in position on the rest of the artwork you have created. Save your work.

If you do not see the trees in front of your sky and hills, make sure that your layers are in the right order.

Your work in this lesson is almost complete.

IMPORTING A PICTURE FRAME

Layers make it easy to add optional elements to your documents, allowing you to show or hide the artwork as needed. Organize your documents into layers when this will make it easier to select, modify, or view the elements.

In this task, you will import a frame to surround your illustration. By placing this frame on a layer by itself, you will be able to easily view and print the artwork with or without the picture frame.

1] Create a new layer and rename it *Frame*.

The Frame layer will now be the active layer, where the artwork you are about to import will appear.

2] Import Frame.fh8 from the Media folder within the Lesson04 folder. Position your cursor at the top-left corner of the page and click.

This picture frame graphic was created to fit this page; positioning the import cursor at the top-left corner of the page imports the artwork in the correct position. Reposition the frame if necessary so it fits on the page.

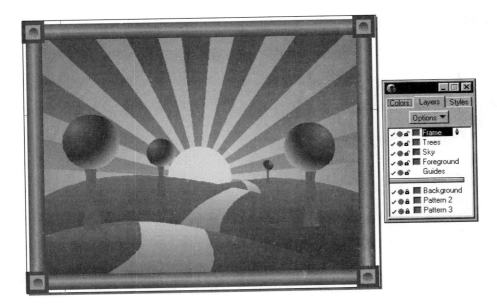

3] Save your work.

OTHER LAYER PANEL CONTROLS

You can change the colors of the selection boxes that appear on different layers so you can more easily identify the layer you are using, and you can use the Keyline view to see your artwork without fills or strokes.

Experiment with changing the color of selection boxes.

1] Select one of the trees on your page.

Notice that the selection boxes appear in a light blue—the same blue that appears next to the name of the Trees layer where that artwork is located. You can change these colors so the colors of the selection boxes indicate the layer on which the selected artwork is located.

2] Display the Color Mixer and create a bright red or magenta color. Drag the new color from the color well in the Mixer and drop it on the color swatch next to the Trees layer.

The selection boxes of the selected tree should now be displayed in this new color, which also appears next to Trees in the Layers panel. Items on the Trees layer now display red selection boxes when selected.

tip One of the preference settings you specified in Lesson 1 made this feature available. If your selection boxes do not match the color of the swatch, choose File > Preferences > General and turn on the Smoother Editing option.

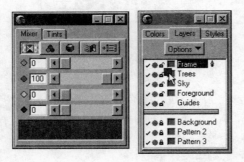

3] Click the small gray circle next to Trees in the Layers panel.

This changes the display of this layer from Preview to Keyline. Preview shows the printing image, whereas Keyline shows the paths without the fills and strokes. The Keyline view can be useful when you need to see the position of elements on another layer but do not want that other layer to obstruct a background image. Clicking the circle again turns the Preview for this layer back on.

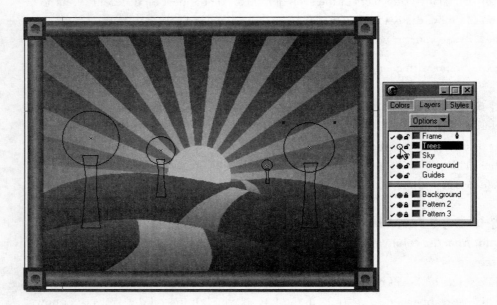

4] You do not need to save these changes, so choose File › Revert.

The Revert command restores the document to the last saved version. This command is useful only if you save frequently as you work.

EXPORTING ARTWORK FOR USE IN OTHER PROGRAMS

FreeHand 9 files are the same on both the Macintosh and Windows platforms, so no special preparation is needed to switch your files from one system to another. Simply save your file as you would normally, and you can open the file directly using FreeHand on either computer platform.

tip *Macintosh users can add the .fh9 to Filenames so that Windows users can open the files by double-clicking.*

To use your FreeHand artwork in other applications, you will need to use the Export command.

1] Choose File > Export.

A dialog box appears where you can identify a location for the new file, type a name for the file, and choose a file format.

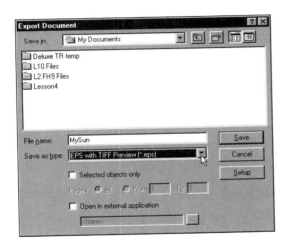

By default, FreeHand artwork is exported as an EPS, or Encapsulated PostScript, file. This is the best format to use for print production, because it delivers the same quality as the original FreeHand artwork, maintaining the high quality and resolution independence that you count on with FreeHand when the artwork is printed to a PostScript printer or output device.

The EPS format can be imported into the leading page layout applications, including QuarkXPress and Adobe PageMaker. FreeHand provides EPS formats for both platforms, so you can easily prepare artwork for both computer systems.

2] Hold down the mouse on the Format menu to see the wide range of file formats FreeHand exports.

The formats available enable you to create files ready to use in your own print, multimedia, and Internet projects. FreeHand also supports several other formats so you can prepare artwork for other specific applications.

```
   Adobe Illustrator 1.1™
   Adobe Illustrator 88™
   Adobe Illustrator® 3
   Adobe Illustrator™ 5.5
   Adobe Illustrator™ 7.x
   ASCII text
   BMP
   DCS2 EPS
   FreeHand 5.x document
   FreeHand 7 document
   FreeHand 8 document
   Generic EPS
   GIF
   JPEG
✓  Macintosh EPS
   Macromedia Flash (SWF)
   MS-DOS EPS
   PDF
   Photoshop™ 3 EPS
   Photoshop™ 4/5 RGB EPS
   Photoshop™ 5
   PICT
   PICT (Paths)
   PICT2 (Paths)
   PNG
   QuarkXPress™ EPS
   RTF text
   Targa
   TIFF
```

For situations where you will be printing to a non-PostScript printer, the TIFF format is available. TIFF is a bitmap image format that supports both color and grayscale images at high or low resolutions, according to your specific needs.

To save a file for a multimedia project, you select Formats > BMP (Windows) or Formats > PICT (Macintosh). To use your FreeHand files in multimedia applications such as Macromedia Director and Authorware, you select the bitmap format appropriate for the platform where you are developing the multimedia project.

To prepare a graphic for use on a Web page, you choose Formats and then GIF, JPEG, or PNG. These are the most popular bitmap formats for the World Wide Web. In Lesson 9, you will also create an animation in FreeHand and export it in the SWF format, which allows you to add high-resolution, animated vector graphics to your Web pages as an alternative to the bitmap formats described here.

3] Choose GIF from the Format menu. Click Setup (Windows) or Options (Macintosh) to display specific controls for this file format. Then click More to see other options.

Although these buttons are not available for every format, you will be able to choose your own settings for the graphics you create in formats that do offer choices. For example, many of the bitmap image formats give you control over the pixel resolution of the exported image. The GIF format, for instance, offers you Transparent and Interlaced options.

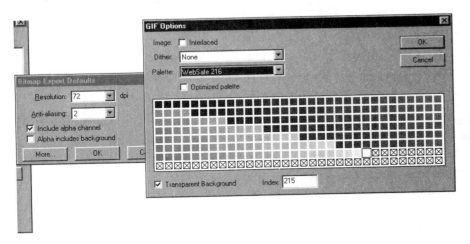

4] Click Cancel twice to return to the Export dialog box.

Several formats are available for preparing graphics for specific applications.

5] Select Formats › Photoshop 4/5 RGB EPS.

Adobe Photoshop users can easily transfer their FreeHand artwork to Photoshop by selecting either the Photoshop 3 or Photoshop 4/5 EPS format. The Photoshop EPS formats save the file differently than FreeHand's default EPS format and deliver better results when files are transferred to Photoshop.

You can also export artwork in the QuarkXPress EPS format for graphics that will be imported into QuarkXPress. There is actually no output quality difference between FreeHand's default EPS format and the QuarkXPress EPS format; however, the QuarkXPress EPS format has a color TIFF preview (instead of a PICT preview). This makes it easier to view the file in QuarkXPress and also makes this a good choice for cross-platform work. (The Windows platform always uses TIFF previews for EPS files, but user testing has indicated that many users find it easier to choose the correct export format if the name of the destination application is available as an option.)

Other application-specific formats allow you to prepare artwork as files for previous versions of FreeHand, as Adobe Illustrator files, or as PDF files for viewing in Adobe Acrobat.

6] Select Formats › EPS with TIFF preview (Windows) or Macintosh EPS (Macintosh). Choose your MyWork folder as the location in which to save this file and click Export.

This creates a new file with the specified format. By default, FreeHand also saves the FreeHand document information in the EPS file so you can open it to make changes in FreeHand at a later time.

As you can see, because FreeHand offers such a wide variety of export formats, it works equally well whether you're designing for print, multimedia, or the Internet. It also enables you to use your artwork in all three of these types of projects simply by exporting the same artwork to different formats.

tip *At times, you may need to make changes to your artwork after you have exported the file. Remember that the Save command saves only the FreeHand document—it does not update the exported file. In this situation, after making the desired changes and saving the FreeHand file, choose File > Export Again to update the exported file with the changes.*

ON YOUR OWN

Experiment with these techniques in a new document by creating another sunset image. This time, select your own colors and use a circle as the clipping path that defines the outer edge of your sunset image.

WHAT YOU HAVE LEARNED

In this lesson you have:

- Practiced creating a custom-size page [pages 130–131]
- Imported tracing patterns into nonprinting background layers [pages 131–133]
- Locked tracing pattern layers so they cannot be accidentally changed [page 134]
- Created and named multiple foreground and background layers to organize elements [pages 135–136]
- Learned when to use spot color and when to use process color [pages 136–137]
- Practiced importing colors into the Color List [pages 137–138]
- Activated and repositioned layers to organize your document [pages 139–140]
- Created paths with the Pen tool [pages 140–142]
- Rotated elements around a point and duplicated that transformation [pages 142–144]
- Created clipping paths with the Paste Inside command [pages 144–147]
- Experimented with the Preview and Keyline views [pages 147–149]
- Defined and modified object styles [pages 156–158]
- Trimmed artwork using the Intersect command [pages 158–159]
- Scaled objects proportionately using the Shift key [pages 169–174]
- Practiced reflecting objects around a central axis [pages 174–176]
- Imported another FreeHand document onto a new layer [page 176]
- Color-coded layers so that the object selection boxes show which layer the object is on [pages 176–178]
- Exported your illustration as an EPS file [pages 179–182]

creating more complex art

LESSON 5

In the previous lessons, you learned how to create artwork with the basic drawing tools, such as the Rectangle and Ellipse, as well as with the Bezigon tool, Pen tool, and Freeform tool. However, it is not always practical or most efficient to draw each path from scratch. Sometimes you can use the path operations, such as Punch and Union, to help you create more complex paths quickly and easily.

In addition to creating new artwork, there are times when you will want to manipulate or distort existing artwork to create perspective or conform to specific dimensions. FreeHand has special features to help you in these areas, including the Perspective Grid and envelopes. You will learn how to use these features in this lesson.

Designed by Tony Roame of Illustrated Concepts.

This advertising piece was created in FreeHand using the program's sophisticated tools for creating complex objects and distorting artwork. In this lesson, you will learn how to use the Perspective Grid, create and save envelopes for distortion effects, and more.

If you would like to review the final result of this lesson, open the JavaZone.fh9 file and the JavaMug.fh9 file in the Complete folder within the Lesson05 folder.

WHAT YOU WILL LEARN

In this lesson you will:

- Use Xtra path operations, including Union, Punch, and Inset Path
- Use FreeHand to perform math calculations in panel fields
- Assign graphic styles to objects
- Attach text to paths
- Blend gradient fills
- Attach blends to paths
- Import artwork from other FreeHand files
- Set up the Perspective Grid options
- Manipulate the Perspective Grid on your page
- Apply artwork to the Perspective Grid
- Automatically trace imported images
- Use the envelope feature to distort artwork

APPROXIMATE TIME

This lesson takes approximately 1 hour and 45 minutes to complete.

LESSON FILES

Media Files:

Lesson05\Media\CloudySky.TIF

Starting Files:

LogoStart.ft9

RibbonStart.ft9

MainPage.ft9

Completed Project:

Lesson05\Completed\JavaZone.fh9

Lesson05\Completed\JavaMug.fh9

Bonus Files:

Lesson05\Bonus\Thingie.fh9

Lesson05\Bonus\PerspDemo1.mov

Lesson05\Bonus\PerspDemo2.mov

Lesson05\Bonus\EnvDemo.mov

CREATING ILLUSTRATIONS WITH PATH OPERATIONS

Many complex shapes are really just a combination of simple rectangles and ellipses. If you break artwork down into components, very often you can reconstruct the pieces in FreeHand with simple shapes and path operations. In the next steps, you will build a coffee mug from scratch using simple shapes and path operations.

1] Open a new document in FreeHand. In the center of the page, create an ellipse that is 19p0 wide and 5p0 high.

Use the Object Inspector to set the numeric values, or watch the Info toolbar as you draw, if that toolbar is displayed.

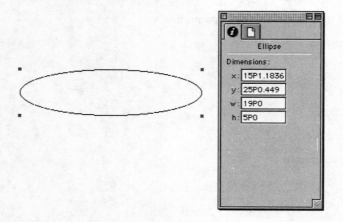

2] Clone the ellipse (Edit > Clone) and move it down about 15 picas.

You can drag the ellipse down and watch the page rulers, or you can watch the values displayed in the Info toolbar. To move the ellipse numerically, you can use the Transform panel.

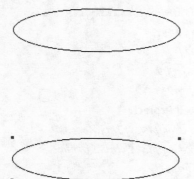

3] Make sure Snap to Point is enabled. (View › Snap to Point).

This is essential for the next few steps to be executed accurately.

4] Select the Rectangle tool and position your mouse over the left edge of the upper circle until it snaps to the point. Drag from that point until your mouse snaps at the right edge of the lower circle.

Your cursor changes shape when it snaps to a point. Here you are drawing a rectangle the exact width of the ellipses, and the ends are perfectly centered on the ellipse at each end.

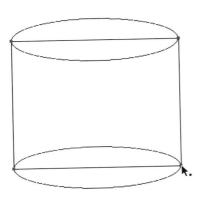

5] Select the rectangle and the lower circle and choose Modify › Combine › Union, or click the Union icon in the Xtras Operations panel.

Here you used Union to round out the bottom of the rectangle to form the body of the mug. You could have drawn the same shape with the Bezigon or Pen tool, but this is faster and much more precise.

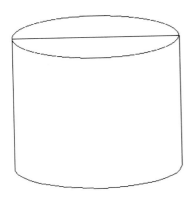

187

6] With the rectangle path still selected, display the Styles panel and click Mug Outside. Send this shape to the back (Modify › Arrange › Send to Back).

You created and used Styles to define the trees in the previous lesson. Here, the styles are already defined, and you simply applied them.

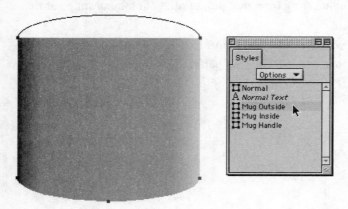

7] Select the top circle and fill it with the lightest color, 15% 13c 32m 55y 10k. Set the stroke to None.

Your drawing is already starting to look pretty good, but the mug really needs a rim and a different fill to indicate depth. You are going to take care of that in the next step.

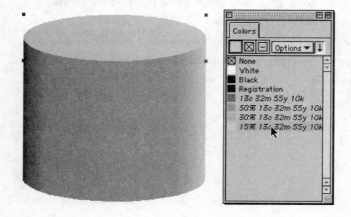

8] Clone the circle. Click the Inset Path button on the Xtra operations toolbar or choose Modify › Alter Path › Inset Path. In the dialog box that pops up, set the number of steps to 1 and the inset value to 0p2.5.

Inset Path is a great way to evenly expand or contract a path. If you had wanted to expand the path rather than inset it, you would have entered a negative number.

You cloned the path before the Inset operation because you want to keep the large path as the rim of the mug. This shape will be the inside piece.

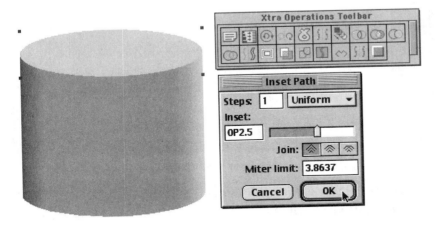

9] With the inset path selected, assign it the style Mug Inside.

Now it really looks like a convincing mug, but it needs a handle. You are going to construct a handle in the next steps.

10] Create a circle that is 14p0 by 14p0.

Use the Object Inspector to set the numeric values, or watch the Info toolbar as you draw.

Next you will make another circle half this size.

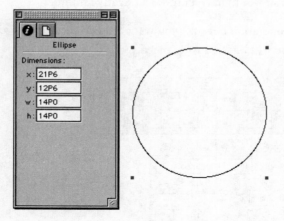

11] Clone the circle you just drew. With the clone selected, display the Object Inspector. Type /2 after the number in the w field; then click after the number in the h field and type /2 here as well. Press Enter.

You needed to make a smaller version of this circle that was half the size of the original. Rather than scale it at 50%, you let FreeHand do the math for you in the Object Inspector fields by entering */2*, which means "divide by two"—so FreeHand read 14 divided by 2 and returned a value of 7.

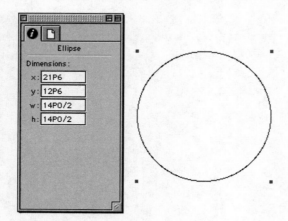

In this case, it would have been easy enough to perform the calculation on your own, but often you will have numbers with three or four decimal places. FreeHand's ability to perform calculations comes in very handy then.

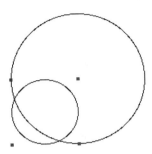

tip *You can also add, subtract, and multiply as well as divide in any number field. Just add a +, −, /, or * between numbers, and FreeHand will make the necessary calculations for you. You can even mix measurement systems when adding. For instance, you can enter a Move distance of 2i + 3p0 in the Transform panel, and FreeHand will correctly move the object 2.5 inches.*

12] Display the Align panel and center the two circles.
Click the center of the Align panel grid to select this option quickly.

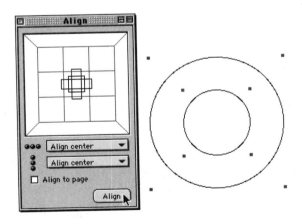

13] Choose Modify › Join or Ctrl + J (Windows) or Command + J (Macintosh) to join the two circles to form a composite path.

A composite path has four selection handles at the corners of the bounding box, just like a group. However, a composite path has only one fill and stroke shared by all the paths. You are going to punch this path in the next step, turning it back into an ordinary path.

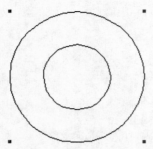

14] Employing the Snap to Point technique you used earlier, use the Rectangle tool to draw from the top center of the large circle down and to the right until the rectangle is completely below and to the right of the circle.

Move the mouse in the top center area of the large circle until the cursor changes to indicate the snap is taking place.

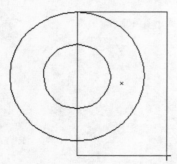

15] Select both the rectangle and the composite path; then choose Modify › Combine › Punch, or click the Punch icon in the Xtra Operations toolbar.

The top path always punches through all selected objects beneath it. You drew the rectangle last, so it was on top, and it punched through the half of the circles that it covered. By default, the path that is used to punch will delete itself in the operation, so the rectangle disappears along with the rest of the punched elements.

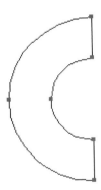

16] In the Styles panel, assign the style Mug Handle to the handle.

Your handle is looking better, but it needs a little help on the ends.

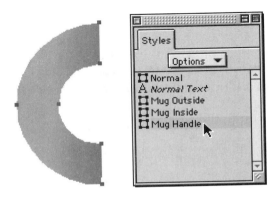

17] Use the Pointer tool to select all four points on the right side of the handle. Display the Object Inspector; then click the Corner point icon. Press Tab to deselect the handle.

You can Shift+click each point individually, but you may find it easier to drag a selection marquee around the four points all at once.

You can change point types for multiple points at one time. In this case, changing to a corner point allows you to position the control handles for each point independently of the existing control handles.

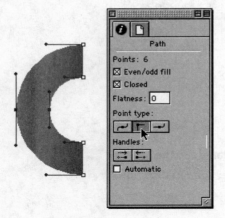

18] Click the top point; then hold Alt (Windows) or Option (Macintosh) and drag from the center of the point, moving down and to the right until you have a rounded end, similar to the figure shown here.

This is the technique you need to use when you need to get a control handle out of a point that is not currently displaying one.

19] Select the second point up from the bottom and repeat the previous step, dragging the other control handle out from the center of the point and positioning it as desired.

Now the handle has a much more three-dimensional appearance. Notice how little it can take to make something appear to have more depth. A few curves, a little help with gradient fills, and you are well on your way to better artwork.

20] Move the handle into place on the mug. Select all the artwork; then group it (Modify › Group).

You mug is finished now. You will apply a logo to it at the end of this lesson, using the live envelopes feature in FreeHand.

21] Save your work.

195

CREATING MORE COMPLEX ART

ADDING TEXT TO A PATH

Text is great in paragraphs and headlines, but sometimes you need to take it a little further. Text in FreeHand can be attached to paths, which means it can break away from the normal restriction of a straight baseline and be free to follow curves and circles. You are going to attach text to a circle in the next steps.

1] Open the document named RibbonStart in the Start folder within the Lesson05 folder.

The artwork for the ribbon has already been assembled on page 1. All you will need to do is add the text that identifies what the ribbon is for.

note *You may recognize the many simple shapes that make up this ribbon. It was created using the same techniques you learned when you created the mug. If you would like more practice with these techniques, go to page 2 in this document and create your own ribbon, following the steps indicated in the illustrations.*

2] Select the circle with the radial fill and clone it.

Remember that cloning places an exact copy of the original in the identical location. Since the selection handles don't change, it's easy to think that nothing happened. It did work—just check the Undo menu item if you're not sure. If the Undo menu item says Undo Clone, then your previous operation was successful.

3] Display the Transform panel by double-clicking the Scale tool in the Toolbox. Set the Scale to 70% and press Enter or click Scale (Windows) or Apply (Macintosh).

The Transform panel automatically resizes objects from their center. When this is the desired result, the Transform panel is often an ideal way to scale objects.

196

4] Click with the Text tool on an empty portion of the window and type *HIGHEST RATED* in all capital letters. Use the text toolbar to change the text to 14-point News Gothic T Bold.

You could also change these settings in the Text Inspector or by selecting items from the Text menu. If you don't have the News Gothic T Bold font available, you can just use a font that you already have installed.

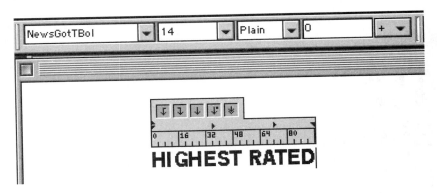

5] Select the text and the circle you cloned and click the text toolbar button for Attach to Path or choose Text > Attach to Path.

Your text appears at the top of the circle, and it is centered automatically.

tip *If you are joining text to an open path and it attaches to the wrong side of the path, you need to change the path direction. Choose Edit > Undo to detach the text and then select the path and choose Modify > Alter Path > Reverse Direction. Attach the text again, and it will flow the way you want.*

6] Select all the text and change the color to white.

You can select the text by highlighting it with the Text tool, or you can simply click the text with the Pointer tool.

7] Click with the Text tool at the end of the word *RATED*. Press Return and type *COFFEE SHOP* all in capital letters.

FreeHand is unique in the way it handles this type of text on a path. All you have to do to move text to the opposite side of a closed path is press Return. Not only is all the text on the second line applied to the opposite side of the path, but it is also automatically attached at the ascenders (tops of the letters).

tip *You can control how the text is situated on a path. To access these controls, select the text on a path; then display the Object Inspector. Here you can set the text to skew and rotate along the path, control what part of the text is attached to the path, and more. For the purposes of this ribbon, the default settings are fine.*

8] Select all the artwork for the ribbon and group it.
Grouping the ribbon will make it easier to select and copy when you need it later in this lesson.

9] Save the file as *MyRibbon* in your MyWork folder.

ADDING BLENDS TO A PATH

In the same way that you attach text to a path, you can attach blends of objects to a path. This can open the door for some excellent creative possibilities. Keep these capabilities of FreeHand in mind when you are designing artwork of your own.

1] Open the document LogoStart in the Start folder within the Lesson05 folder

The JavaZone logo has already been started. All you need to do is create a special effect for the *O* in *Zone*.

2] Double-click the Spiral tool in the Toolbox. Change the settings so that the first spiral type is selected, Draw By is set to Rotations, the number of rotations is 2, Draw From is set to Edge, and the left option is for Direction.

Like the other tools that have changeable settings, the Spiral tool has a small mark in the upper-right corner.

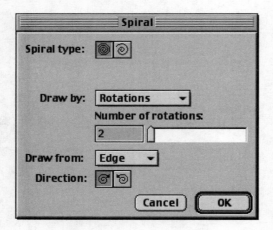

3] Click just to the left of the bottom of the letter *Z* and drag up until the spiral evenly fills the space available.

Leave a small cushion of space around the spiral for the blend that will be attached to it.

CLICK HERE AND DRAG

**4] Select the two gradient rectangles below the logo and choose Modify ›
Combine › Blend.**

The two rectangles have already been created and given the correct fill. FreeHand
picks the number of blend steps based on the resolution setting in the Document
Inspector. You will change this setting in the next step.

**5] With the blend selected, display the Object Inspector and set the number of
steps to 99.**

This is enough steps to provide the right effect once the blend is attached to the spiral.

6] Select both the blend and the spiral and choose Modify › Combine › Join Blend to Path.

Just as when you attached text to a path, all you have to do is select the two elements and perform a single command.

tip *Unlike for text on a path, FreeHand has no specific command to remove a blend from a path. You need to choose Modify > Split to detach the blend from the path.*

7] In the Object Inspector, uncheck Rotate on Path.

Just as with text on a path, the Object Inspector holds additional options. Here, you achieve a radically different look when the Rotate on Path option is not checked.

8] Select the entire logo, including the spiral, and group it (Modify › Group).

Grouping the logo makes it easier to work with when you move it to other documents.

9] Copy the logo and save this file as *MyLogo* in your MyWork folder.

In the next task, you will paste this logo on the main page.

COPYING ELEMENTS FROM OTHER DOCUMENTS

Often it is necessary to bring artwork from one FreeHand file into another. In this lesson, you are working with a very common situation: a logo from one document needs to be added to another document. There are many ways to share artwork between FreeHand files. The most frequently used method is copy and paste, as you will do here, but you can also drag the artwork from one FreeHand document window into another, or import an entire FreeHand document by choosing File > Import.

1] Open the document named MainPage.ft9 located in the Start folder within the Lesson05 folder.

This document already contains elements of 2D artwork for a store front view and side view, a parking lot, and a sidewalk. These elements are all on the pasteboard. Lower down on the pasteboard is an empty page.

2] Choose View › Custom › Front & Center to view the middle of the store front.

This may already be the view you are looking at. You used custom views in Lesson 3 when you switched between steps while drawing the car.

3] **Paste the logo you created in the previous task. If necessary, reopen the document and copy the logo again; then return and paste it. Position the logo so that it is visually centered above the doors and between the wavy lines.**

You will enlarge the logo in the next step. Here you are positioning it to make resizing with the transform handles a more intuitive process.

4] **Double-click the logo to activate the transform handles. Hold the Control key (Windows and Macintosh) and begin dragging a corner of the transform handles. With the mouse button still down, also press the Shift key to keep the dimensions of the logo proportional. Drag until the logo is large enough; then release the mouse button and then release the modifier keys.**

Holding down the Control key before you start dragging a transform handle makes the object expand out from the center.

5] **Zoom out so you can see then entire store front. Select all the elements that make up the store front, including the logo, and group them.**

The store front needs to be grouped so you can apply it to the Perspective Grid later in this lesson.

6] **Save this document as *MyMain*.**

SETTING UP THE PERSPECTIVE GRID

Normally perspective drawing requires a rather technical process of defining a horizon line, calculating vanishing points, establishing convergence lines, and planning intersections. This is a daunting task for the uninitiated, and it can be time consuming even for the experienced.

The Perspective Grid in FreeHand is a new approach to design for vector illustration. It allows you to define one-, two-, or three-point perspective, complete with vanishing points, a horizon line, and grid lines for each plane, with ease and efficiency. You get immediate feedback for each change you make to the grid, and you can save grids for later use (only one grid can appear on a page at a time). The next steps take you through the process of setting up the Perspective Grid for this project.

The CD that came with this book contains a Quicktime movie which demonstrates how to set up the Perspective Grid. Go to Lesson05\Bonus\PerspDemo1.mov.

1] **Make the page in the document you saved (MyMain) visible by choosing Fit Page from the Magnification pop-up menu at the bottom of the window.**

You can also choose the same command from the View menu or use the keyboard shortcut Ctrl-Shift-W (Windows) or Command-Shift-W (Macintosh).

2] **Display the Document Inspector, set the page size to 6 inches by 9 inches, and click the Landscape Page button.**

While it's possible to resize the page with the Page tool, it's usually faster and more accurate to use the Document Inspector when you have specific measurements in mind.

> **tip**   *Remember, you can use the letter i to specify inches regardless of your current unit of measure.*

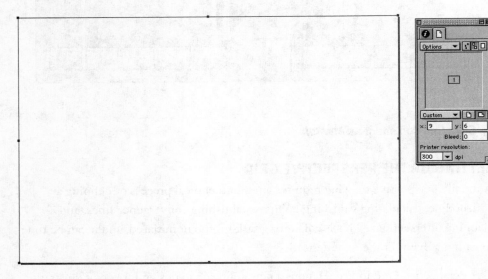

3] Make the Perspective Grid visible by choosing View › Perspective Grid › Show.

It looks cool all by itself, but you will learn in the next steps how to arrange the grid so it can give you the professional results you are looking for.

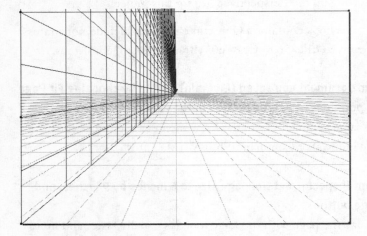

4] Define a two-point grid by choosing View › Perspective Grid › Define Grid. Set the number of vanishing points to 2; then click OK.

You can define one-, two-, or three-point perspective with the Perspective Grid in FreeHand. You can save multiple grids in your document and switch between active grids at any time.

note *You can have only one grid active at a time, and the grid is visible on only one page at a time. Each page in your document is assigned the active grid. If you are planning to work with multiple grids on multiple pages, be sure to save and name your Perspective Grids in a clear and concise way.*

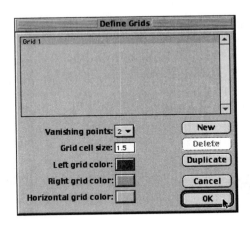

When you click OK, the Perspective Grid with two-point perspective appears on the page. By default, the grid planes are centered on the page. You are going to reposition the planes so that they fit the requirements of this project.

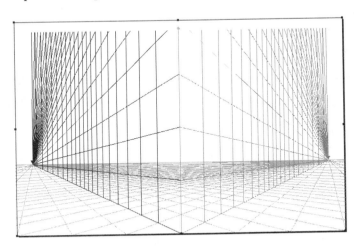

5] Make the page rulers visible by choosing View › Page Rulers. Make sure the unit of measure is set to Picas at the bottom of the screen.

You will need the page rulers visible so you can tell where to position the Perspective Grid.

207

6] Select the Perspective Grid tool from the Toolbox and position it at the bottom edge of the page. Drag the grid from the bottom of the page up to approximately 3p6 on the vertical ruler.

Notice that the grid is still visible in its former location as you drag it to a new position. This gives you a good idea of how much change is taking place between moves.

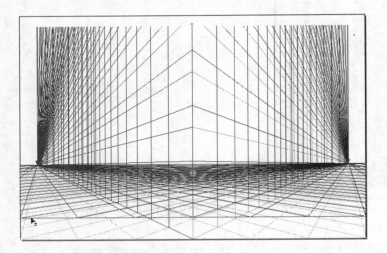

7] Position the Perspective Grid tool over the horizon line and drag it down to the 10-pica mark on the vertical ruler.

The horizon line is possibly the single most important setting in a perspective drawing, because every other angle depends on it.

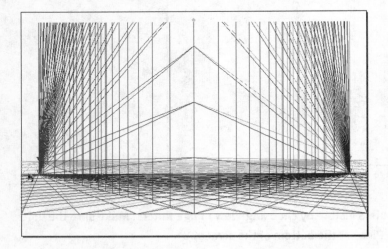

8] Position the Perspective Grid tool over the place where the vertical grids meet at the center of your page. Click and drag to the left to 14p0 on the horizontal ruler.

Where these planes meet is always the front corner of your artwork in a perspective drawing. In this case, you want the front corner of the building to be on the left side of the page. You will move the right plane to this location next.

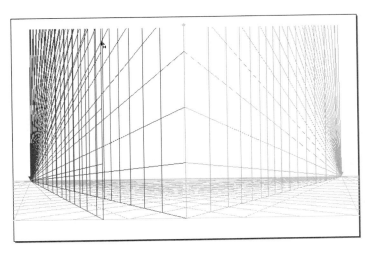

9] Position the Perspective Grid tool over the front edge of the right vertical grid at the center of your page and drag it to the 14p0 mark on the horizontal ruler. Release the mouse when the grid snaps into place.

In this step, you moved the right plane over to meet the left plane. Notice that it snaps into place when you get close enough.

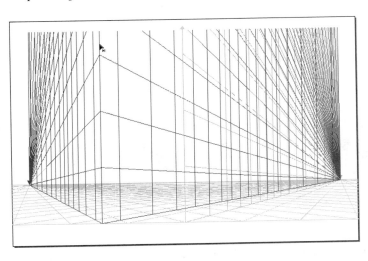

209

10] Position the Perspective Grid tool over the left vanishing point and drag this vanishing point off the left edge of the page to -12p0 on the horizontal ruler.

Sometimes in perspective drawing, the vanishing points will not appear on the page, as is the case here.

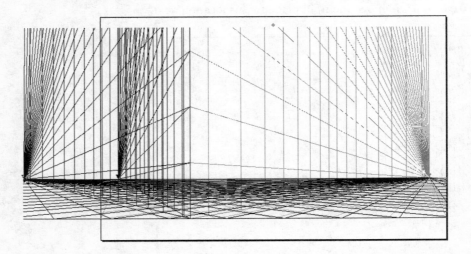

11] Position the Perspective Grid tool over the right vanishing point and drag it off the right edge of the page to 60p0 on the horizontal ruler.

The right vanishing point also falls off the edge of the page. Scroll your window view, if necessary, to move the vanishing point into position.

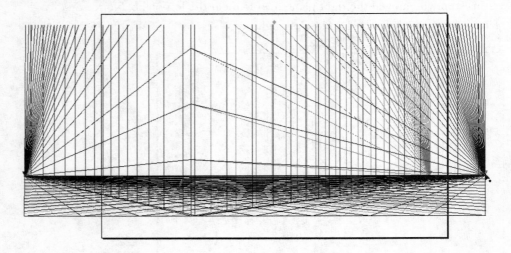

Now your Perspective Grid is established, and you are ready to begin creating perspective artwork.

12] Save your work.

"PERSPECTIFYING" ARTWORK ON VERTICAL PLANES

Even if you could only use the Perspective Grid as a reference to draw your own artwork, it would be invaluable. However, FreeHand allows you to actually "apply" artwork to the grid, making it functional as an actual tool, in addition to being a reference guide.

Applying artwork to the Perspective Grid affects your ability to work with the artwork. Objects that are applied to the Perspective Grid are put in an envelope, which allows them to be distorted to fit the grid. An object that has been applied to the Perspective Grid is called **perspectified** artwork. When an object is perspectified, you can no longer subselect or modify the content of the artwork (until it is released). However, you can use the Perspective Grid tool to move the artwork anywhere on the grid, and it will change in size and amount of distortion to correspond with the grid location. The term **perspectify** was coined to describe this change. In the next steps you will learn how to perspectify artwork on the vertical planes of the Perspective Grid.

The CD that came with this book contains a Quicktime movie which demonstrates how to use the Perspective tool. Go to Lesson05\Bonus\PerspDemo2.mov.

1] Choose View › Custom › Flat Art. Select the store front and copy it.

This view shows you all the art that will be applied to the Perspective Grid. You grouped the store front earlier, so it's easy to copy now.

2] View the page again by choosing Fit Page from the pop-up menu at the bottom of the document window. Paste the store front.

Notice that the Perspective Grid appears in front of your artwork, so the grid is always visible.

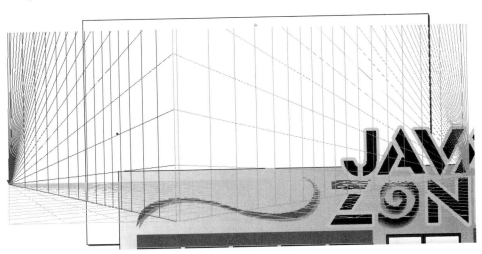

211

3] Select the Perspective Grid tool and start dragging the store front to the left. As you drag, press the right arrow key on your keyboard. Move the store front on the grid so that the bottom-left corner touches the intersection of the three grids.

This is the process used to apply objects to the grid: start dragging with the Perspective Grid tool and then press an arrow key; the art will then be applied to the grid.

tip   *If you get art on the wrong grid, just keep pressing different arrow keys while you're dragging the object until you find the option you want.*

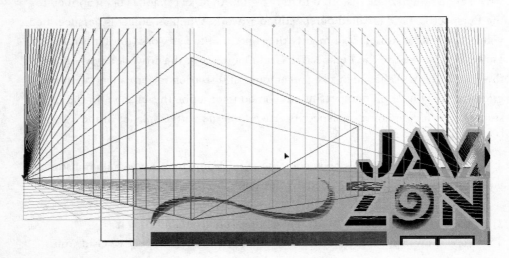

4] Zoom in on the lower-left corner at least 400% and use the Perspective Grid tool to position the lower-left corner so that it is exactly at the intersection of the grids.

The magnification is necessary so you can see exactly where your artwork is landing. You will get a considerably better view as you zoom in. It is nearly impossible to correctly position an item on the Perspective Grid when you are in the 100% or Fit Page view.

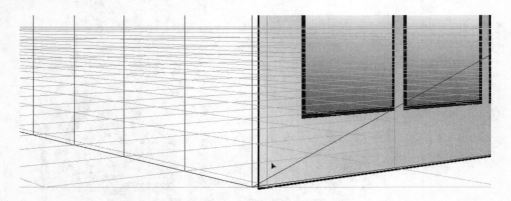

5] Return to the Flat Art view. Select all the elements that make up the store side and group them. Copy the grouped store side.

You can select only one object at a time with the Perspective Grid tool, so only one object at a time can be applied to the grid. Therefore, you need to group everything that will appear on the grid together.

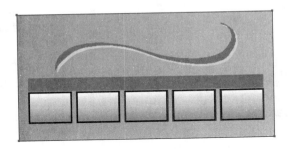

6] Choose View › Fit to Page or Select Fit page from the pop-up menu to view the page again. Paste the store side.

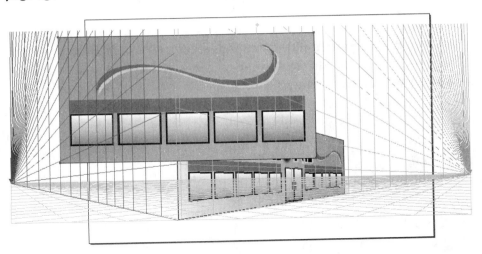

7] Select the Perspective Grid tool and start dragging the store side to the left. As you drag, press the left arrow key on your keyboard. Move the store side on the grid so that the bottom-right corner touches the intersection of the three grids.

Pressing the left arrow while you are dragging applies objects to the left grid plane.

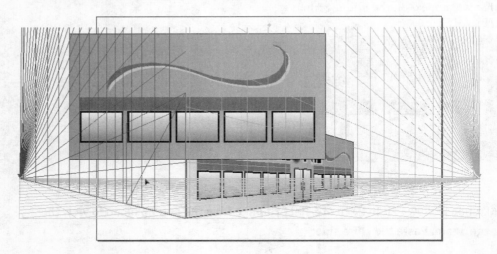

8] Zoom in on the intersection of the three grids at least 800% and use the Perspective Grid tool to position the lower-right corner of the left side so that it is exactly at the intersection of the grids.

Make sure there are no gaps between the store side and the store front, and make sure the bottom edge rests on the bottom of the grid.

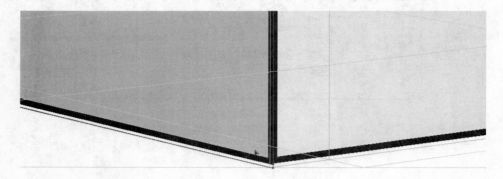

9] Choose View › Fit Selection or press Ctrl+0 (Windows) or Command+0 (Macintosh).

Look at how the store side and the store front match at the top. Notice that even though you positioned the grid perfectly, the alignment is off at the top. Fortunately, you can fix that easily.

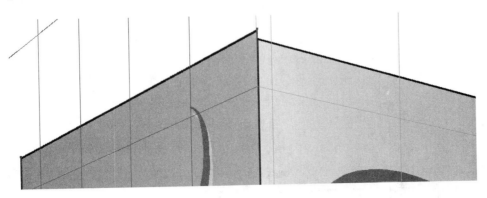

10] Zoom in on the top of the store side, so that you can see both top corners.

11] Use the Pointer tool to click the top-left corner point; then Shift+click the top-right corner point. Click the top-right corner point and drag it down until it matches the corner of the store front.

If necessary, zoom in even further on the top-right corner to get a better view.

The Perspective Grid is much like the live envelopes, which you will learn about later in this lesson. The corner points can be moved for individual control over the perspective effect.

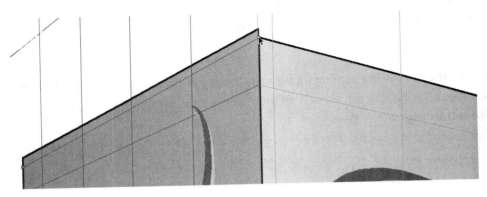

note *When you manually modify objects on the Perspective Grid, they become detached from the grid. In this case, you are done moving the artwork, so it doesn't matter.*

215

12] Choose Fit Page from the View menu; then temporarily turn off the Perspective Grid so you can view your progress. Turn the Perspective Grid back on when you are done.

Now you have a convincing store set up in perspective, and it took considerably less effort than would have been required in any other illustration program.

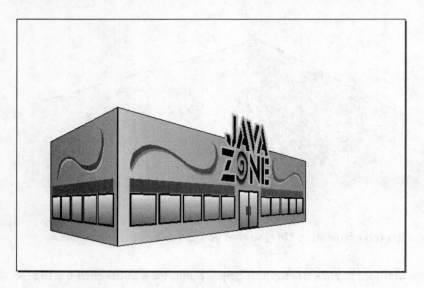

13] Save your work.

There is more artwork to apply to the grid; you will work on that in the next task.

"PERSPECTIFYING" ARTWORK ON THE GROUND PLANE

In the previous steps you perspectified artwork on the vertical planes of the Perspective Grid. In this section you will perspectify objects on both sides of the ground plane, which will complete the perspective effect and help establish the context of the vertical artwork.

1] Select and copy the parking lot from the top of the document. Return to the page and Paste the parking lot. Move it off the lower edge of the page so that you can see the bottom edge of the store front.

You need to make enough room so you can see the other artwork on the page as you are moving this object on the Perspective Grid.

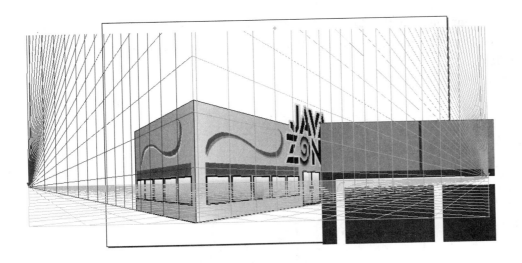

2] Select the Perspective Grid tool and start dragging the parking lot. As you drag, press the down arrow key on your keyboard. Move the parking lot on the grid so that the left edges touches the lower edge of the store front.

Be sure not to leave any gaps in the artwork; err on the side of overlapping objects. Send the parking lot to the back (Modify > Arrange > Send to Back) if necessary.

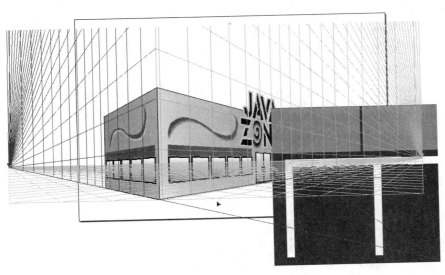

3] Select and copy the sidewalk from the top of the document. Return to the page and paste the sidewalk. Move it so that you can see the lower edge of the store side.

Again, make sure there is enough room so you can place the sidewalk in context as you move it on the grid.

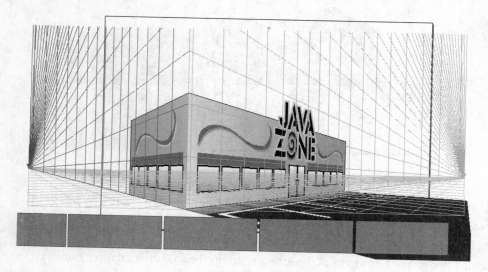

4] Select the Perspective Grid tool and start dragging the sidewalk. As you drag, press the up arrow key on your keyboard. Move the sidewalk on the grid so that the top edge touches the bottom edge of the store side and the right edge meets the edge of the sidewalk from the parking lot, as shown here.

Make sure there are no gaps between the objects. If necessary, send the sidewalk to the back.

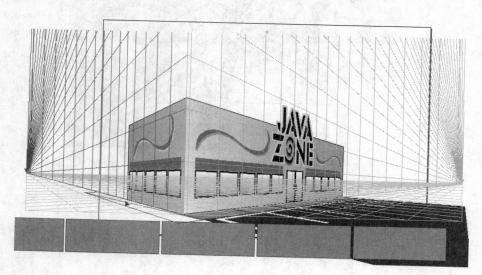

5] Zoom in on the corner where the sidewalk turns and adjust the position of the sidewalk with the Perspective Grid tool so that it lines up correctly.

Zooming to 800% is a good rule of thumb, but you get even better accuracy if you zoom in further than that.

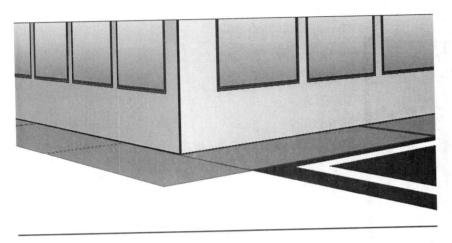

6] Press Tab to deselect all artwork; then choose Fit Page. Save your work.

Now all the artwork for the Perspective Grid is in place. The rest of the background and foreground elements still need to be imported or created, though.

TRACING IMPORTED ARTWORK

Sometimes you don't need to start from scratch to create vector artwork in FreeHand. The Trace tool allows you to convert an imported bitmap image into vector objects. It offers an extensive array of options and is capable of producing highly accurate traces which meet or exceed the quality of standalone tracing programs. You can use it to convert hand drawn line art into vector paths that can be filled, or you can trace color photographs and other bitmap images to produce a unique vector version of the original. In the next steps you will use the Trace tool to convert a bitmap image of a cloudy sky into vector artwork that matches the style of this illustration more closely.

1] View the Layers panel by pressing Ctrl+6 (Windows) or Command+6 (Macintosh). Add a layer and name it *Land & Sky*. Move this layer below the Foreground layer.

You worked with layers in Lesson 4, where you learned that layers can help keep different types of artwork separated while you are working on them. That is exactly what you are doing here. The current Persp.Objects layer contains all the artwork you've been working with so far. The land and sky elements will be on a separate layer, located under the other layers.

2] Hide the Persp.Objects layer. Make Land & Sky the active layer by clicking it.
Now you will be able to work on the Land & Sky layer without obstruction. Notice that the active layer is the one with the pen tip icon on the right; just because a layer is highlighted does not mean it is the active layer. You need the Land & Sky layer to be activated so that the objects you create will be located on the right layer.

3] Make sure the Perspective Grid is visible. Draw a rectangle from the horizon line at the left edge of the page down to the bottom-right corner of the page.

This will be the ground, from the bottom of the page all the way up to the horizon line.

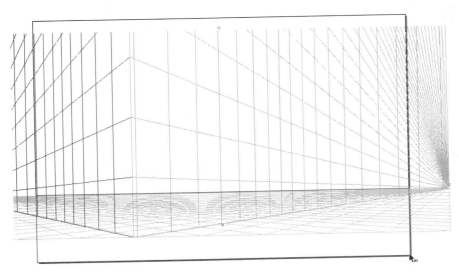

4] Display the Styles panel and assign the Land Fill style to this rectangle. Press the Tab key to deselect all objects, then select the normal style.

This graphic style had already been created, just like the mug styles were created. You need to switch back to the normal style so that future objects don't use the Land Fill Style.

221

5] Scroll your document window so you see a large area of pasteboard to the left of the page. Import the CloudySky.tif file located in the Media folder within the Lesson05 folder and place it on the pasteboard.

This image could be used as the background all by itself, but it would not fit the style of the artwork very well. You are going to use FreeHand's Trace tool to create a vector version of this bitmap image.

6] Double-click the Trace tool in the Toolbox. In the Trace tool settings dialog box, set the options as shown here:

The settings for the Trace tool are very important. If you are working with artwork for the Internet, you will want to use RGB colors. Different tolerance settings can produce vastly different images. If you have time, experiment with different settings to see how they affect the outcome of the trace.

7] Click OK to accept the settings. Drag a marquee around the image with the Trace tool wand.

Everything inside the marquee area will be traced by the Trace tool.

tip *You can also click with the Trace tool wand to activate a selection area. If you click again in that area with the wand, the area will be traced. To deselect an area from the Trace tool wand, press the Tab key.*

8] Without deselecting after the trace, group the traced artwork. Move it down slightly so you can see the original image underneath.

You can see that the colors are significantly different between the original piece and the traced art. You will correct the color in the next step.

223

9] Select Xtras › Color › Color Control. Click the CMYK tab and then drag the Y and K settings all the way to the left. Press Enter.

The Color Control dialog box is a powerful tool in FreeHand. You can edit CMYK or RGB colors directly, or you can work with HLS values.

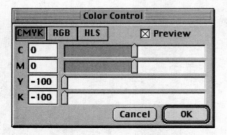

10] Alt+click (Windows) or Option+click (Macintosh) to select the darkest shape at the top of the traced artwork; then delete it.

Sometimes autotrace results need to be adjusted a little to improve their appearance. In this case, simply deleting the extra dark shape at the top is all that is needed.

11] Select the imported image and delete it; then move the traced artwork into place on the page.

You don't need the imported image any more, since it has been traced. Now the land and sky are providing the backdrop you need for your scene.

12] Turn off perspective grid. Display the Layer panel again and make all layers visible. Be sure the Persp. Objects layer is the active layer. Save your work.

The major elements for your scene are now in place. Next you will trim off the excess artwork that is extending beyond the edge of the screen.

TRIMMING EXCESS ARTWORK

In many cases you will have excess artwork extending from the edges of the page. FreeHand offers several different ways to solve that problem. In Lesson 4, you used the Intersect command to trim artwork for the road. However, if there are many objects (as in this scene) the Intersect command is not a good choice, since it would need to be applied separately to each object. You could also use Paste Inside to hide the excess artwork in a rectangle that is sized to match the page. This has the added benefit of preserving all the artwork so that it can be accessed at a later date. In this case, though, that is not necessary. Your best option in situations like this is to create a closed path that completely covers the excess artwork, then use that path to trim the excess artwork with the Punch command. The next steps will take you through the process of punching excess artwork so that it ends cleanly at the edge of your page.

1] Select the parking lot and sidewalk elements; then choose View › Perspective Grid › Release with Perspective.

Objects that have been attached to the Perspective Grid can be released from the grid and returned to normal grouped objects.

tip *Up until you release the object with perspective, you have the option of removing the perspective completely. You could distort the art to nearly unrecognizable form and still return the artwork to its original state. However, once you release the object with perspective, it is locked in. That is one reason why it's important to work with copies of objects rather than originals.*

226

2] Draw a rectangle from the left edge of the page down and to the right so that it completely covers the part of the sidewalk that extends beyond the page. Draw a similar rectangle from the right edge that covers the excess of the parking lot, and a third rectangle on the bottom edge that overlaps the other two rectangles and also covers the parking lot excess.

You created a series of overlapping rectangles that will be combined into a single shape with the Union command so that together they will form a single mask that can punch out the excess artwork.

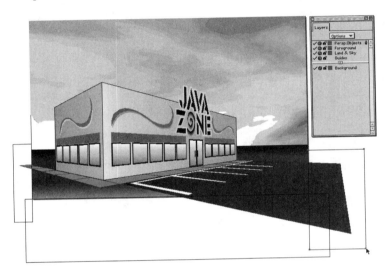

3] Create a single mask element by selecting the three rectangles and then clicking the Union button on the Xtra operations toolbar or choosing Modify › Combine › Union.

Now you are ready to punch out the excess artwork.

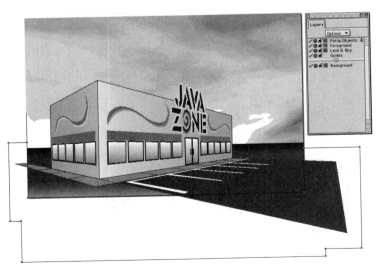

227

**4] Select the mask element, the parking lot, and the sidewalk and then click the
Punch button on the Xtra operations toolbar or choose Modify › Combine › Punch.**

This is the same principle you applied when you created the handle for the coffee
mug, except now you are punching more than one object at a time.

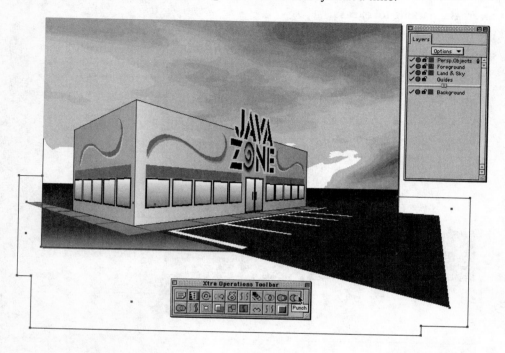

5] Save your work.

Now the artwork has been trimmed, and the scene is complete. There are just a few
more things to add before you finish the project.

ADDING TEXT AND OTHER ELEMENTS

Sometimes artwork doesn't say the whole story, and you need to add text to finish the piece. Rather than import the artwork into a page layout program to add a single block of text, you can add it directly in FreeHand. As you will see in the next steps, FreeHand offers all of the text controls offered in most page layout programs. You will explore even more of the options in Lesson 7 and Lesson 8.

1] Open your MyRibbon document and copy the ribbon.

This will be an element in the final piece.

2] Return to MyMain and paste the ribbon. Position it in the sky on the right side of the page.

The exact location is not critical; use your best judgment for balanced placement.

3] Select the Text tool and type *"Best thing since fried ice cream."* (with the quotation marks); then press Return and type *—Metro News* on the second line. Make the text 48-point News Gothic T Bold.

This is the location for a quote typical of that which you might see from a reviewer for a restaurant, movie, or other entertainment service.

4] Insert a soft return (line break) just before the word fried by pressing Shift+Return or choosing Text › Special Characters › End of Line. Add an en space to the start of the second line by choosing Text › Special Characters › En Space. Give the Metro News line right paragraph alignment by clicking the Align Right button on the text toolbar.

You have access to special typography controls in FreeHand. Many of these can be accessed in the Text > Special Characters submenu. Here you are adding an en space to line up the second line of text, providing a more balanced look to the quote.

5] Select the Metro News line by highlighting it with the Text tool and then change its type size to 24 points. Position it in the sky so that it is visually balanced.

Any time you need to change individual characters in a text block, you need to select them with the Text tool. If you are applying changes to the entire text block, you can select the block with the Pointer tool instead.

6] Save your work.

If you like, you can add finishing touches to your scene, such as copying one of the trees from Lesson 4 and pasting it in various places in the scene. Or if you prefer, create your own artwork by using autotrace on an imported picture of a tree.

231

USING THE LIVE ENVELOPE FEATURE

Many designers and artists encounter situations where they want to distort artwork in such a way that it stretches to fit a particular shape, such as the mug you created at the beginning of this lesson. Other times, a more random distortion is desired, such as when you want artwork to seem like it follows a banner or some other uneven surface. In the past, third party vendors have provided Xtras or plug-ins that provide this envelope functionality. However, these third party solutions required the artwork to be displayed in a dialog box, and it was applied when you dismissed the dialog.

FreeHand 9 has an envelope feature that allows you to work with the artwork directly on the page. In addition, you can save and print your document with the artwork still in an envelope. You can go back to an envelope at any time and edit it, as long as the artwork has not been released. So why would you ever release artwork in an envelope? Just like artwork that is applied to the Perspective Grid, you cannot subselect artwork in an envelope to edit it directly. (In fact, perspectified artwork is actually in an envelope. The difference with perspectified artwork is that the envelope is attached to the Perspective Grid.)

You can work with the envelope just like a regular path, adding and deleting points, manipulating control handles, changing point types, and more. You can even turn on a Mapping feature which allows you to see more easily how your changes will affect the artwork. You will explore the features of the live envelope in the next steps.

The CD that came with this book contains a Quicktime movie which demonstrates how to use Envelopes. Go to Lesson05\Bonus\EnvDemo.mov.

1] Open MyLogo and copy the Java Zone logo you created.
This is the same logo that you added to the top of the store front.

2] Open MyMug and paste the Java Zone logo in your document.

The logo is a little too large for the mug. You will fix that in the next step.

3] Position the right edge of the logo at the right edge of the mug. Resize the logo so that it fits with plenty of space between the handle and the start of the logo.

Now the logo fits much better on the mug. To make the distortion look better, you are going to change the fill of the black Java Zone text so that it has a highlight on the end.

4] Alt+click (Windows) or Option+click (Macintosh) the _J_; then press the accent key (`) once or choose Edit › Select › Superselect.

The black Java Zone text was converted to paths and turned into a composite path. When you Alt+click or Option+click the _J_, that path was subselected. You were selecting inside a group and picking a part of a composite path. When you pressed the accent key (`), which is located above the Tab key on most U.S. keyboards, you superselected the path, or went up one level. Now you have the entire composite path selected.

233

**5] Display the Fill Inspector and change the fill type to Gradient. Set the angle to 0°
and make the top color black and the bottom color 35% black; then drag a black
swatch about halfway down the color ramp. Press Tab to deselect all artwork.**

Now the logo will fit better with the rest of the mug when it is distorted.

6] Display the envelope toolbar by choosing Window › Toolbars › Envelope.

The envelope toolbar contains all the commands you'll need to work with envelopes.

**7] Select the logo on your page; then choose one of the preset envelopes from the
pop-up menu in the envelope toolbar. Press the Create button when you have made
your choice.**

FreeHand offers a number of different preset types. Select several to see the
differences.

8] Turn on the mapping feature by clicking the Show Map button on the envelope toolbar.

The map is a feedback feature that lets you see how the movement of points and control handles on the envelope affects the object you're manipulating.

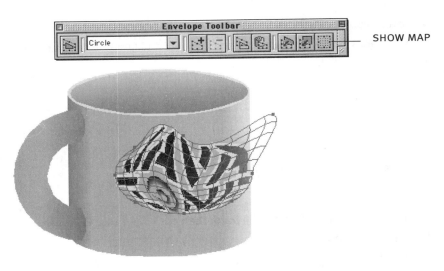

SHOW MAP

235

9] Click the Remove button in the envelope toolbar to return the logo to an unaltered state.

As long as you haven't released an envelope, it can be returned to its original state by selecting Remove.

10] Choose View > Custom > MugEnv. Select the shape and copy it.

You can save and store your own envelope shapes in your document or in the Preset menu on the envelope toolbar.

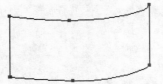

11] Return to the main page and select the logo; then click the Paste Clipboard button on the envelope toolbar.

When you copied the object, it was added to the clipboard. By selecting the logo and choosing Paste Clipboard, you are applying that path shape to the logo as an envelope.

12] Select the top three points on the envelope and stretch the envelope straight up until the letters appear to be a normal height.

Objects may need some adjustment after an envelope has been applied to them. In this case, you simply need to drag straight up on the top three points.

13] Position the logo so that it looks natural on the mug. Cut the logo and select the body of the mug; then choose Edit › Paste Inside. Select the finished mug and group it.

Congratulations! The mug is ready to be used for promotional purposes.

14] Save your work.

Now you have successfully used live envelopes in FreeHand. As you can see, they are extremely powerful. All kinds of artwork can be altered in extreme ways—even live text. You can even edit the text (in the Text Editor) and have it update inside the envelope.

In addition, you have seen how easy it is to work with perspective artwork when you have FreeHand's Perspective Grid at your disposal. Along with the path operations you learned in this lesson and the drawing tool features from previous lessons, you are equipped to create all kinds of artwork. In the next lesson, you will learn how to use blends to create realistic shading to simulate highlights and shadows on complex shapes.

ON YOUR OWN

Look on the CD for Lesson05\Bonus\Thingie.fh9 to find another sample illustration that used the Perspective Grid to create a three-dimensional scene. The Bonus folder also contains Quicktime movies that demonstrate how to set up the Perspective Grid and use the Perspective tool at Lesson05\Bonus\PerspDemo1.mov and Lesson05\Bonus\PerspDemo2.mov, respectively. A third Quicktime movie demonstrates the Envelope feature at Lesson05\Bonus\EnvDemo.mov.

WHAT YOU HAVE LEARNED:

In this lesson you have:

- Used path operations such as Punch, Union, and Inset Path [pages 186–192]
- Assigned graphic styles to objects [pages 188–193]
- Used FreeHand to perform math calculations in panel fields [page 190]
- Attached text and blends to paths [pages 196–203]
- Imported artwork from other FreeHand files [pages 203–205]
- Set up the Perspective Grid options [pages 205–207]
- Manipulated the Perspective Grid on your page [pages 208–210]
- Applied artwork to the Perspective Grid [pages 211–219]
- Automatically traced imported images [pages 219–225]
- Used the envelope feature to distort artwork [pages 232–238]

for shading

blending shapes

LESSON 6

In this lesson, you will complete a robot illustration for a postcard by applying skills you learned in previous lessons to add the fills and shading needed to finish the robot. You will create blends, use Paste Inside, apply Gradient and Lens fills, and import an image to create an illustration that looks three-dimensional. At the end of this lesson, you will learn how to customize FreeHand's toolbars and keyboard shortcuts.

If you would like to review the final result of this lesson, open FlexBotz.fh9 in the Complete folder within the Lesson06 folder.

This robot illustration demonstrates how you can blend shapes and apply fills to add distinctive shading affects to your artwork, making the finished piece look three-dimensional.

Designed by Stewart McKissick

WHAT YOU WILL LEARN

In this lesson you will:

- Create blends for shading

- Paste blends inside paths

- Move copies of artwork into different documents

- Apply Gradient fills

- Apply a Lens fill

- Create a custom page size

- Import an image

- Customize your working environment

APPROXIMATE TIME

This lesson takes about 1 hour and 15 minutes to complete.

LESSON FILES

Media Files:

Lesson06\Media\Planet.tif

Starting Files:

Lesson06\Start\Outline.ft9

Lesson06\Start\Parts.ft9

Lesson06\Start\FlexBtz2.ft9

Completed Project:

Lesson06\Complete\FlexBotz.fh9

Lesson06\Complete\Postcard.fh9

Bonus Files:

Lesson06\Bonus\PillowProcess.fh9

GETTING STARTED

The paths required in this robot illustration have already been created for you and saved in two template files.

1] Open the document named Outline.ft9 in the Start folder within the Lesson06 folder.

Since Outline.ft9 is a template, FreeHand opens an untitled copy of the file, which contains the robot figure.

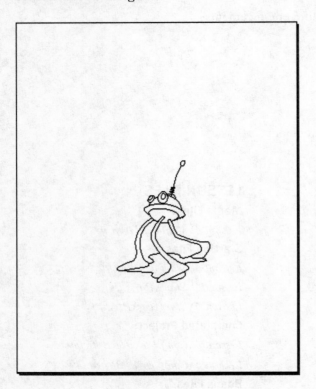

tip *Remember that opening a template opens an untitled copy of the template, instead of the template itself. This prevents you from accidentally altering the template. Any document can be saved as a template by selecting FreeHand Template as the file format instead of the default setting, FreeHand Document, in the Save As dialog box.*

2] Save this document as *FlexBotz* in your MyWork folder.

3] Open the template named Parts.ft9 in the Start folder within the Lesson06 folder.

This template contains body part shapes that will be used to create shading for your robot.

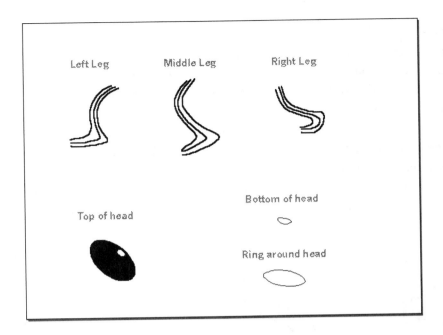

4] Save this document as *MyParts* in your MyWork folder.

CREATING BLENDS

You will be blending the body part shapes to create three-dimensional shading for the robot's legs and body.

1] Zoom in on the Left Leg element and display the Color List panel.

The colors you need were also saved in the template, so they already exist in your document.

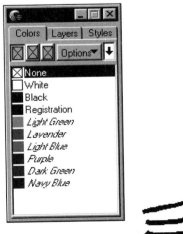

243

tip This document includes a predefined custom view for each part you will be working on. These views are available from the View > Custom menu and from the Magnification menu at the bottom left of the document window. Instead of manually zooming or scrolling to the different parts in this document, you can select the appropriate named view.

2] Using the Pointer tool, select the middle path of the Left Leg element and change the stroke color to Lavender.

Remember that you can change the stroke color by clicking the Current Stroke Color button at the top of the Color List and then clicking the desired color name in the Color List.

CURRENT STROKE COLOR BUTTON

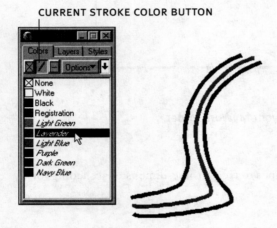

3] Select the two outer paths of the Left Leg element with the Pointer tool and change the stroke color to Purple.

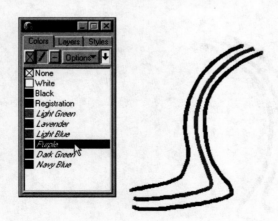

4] Select all three of the Left Leg paths and choose Modify › Combine › Blend.

This creates a blend of the three selected paths. There may be some gaps between the steps in this blend; you will eliminate these in the next step.

5] Change the number of steps in the blend to 15 in the Object Inspector.

Changing the number of steps between paths to 15 smooths out the blend and eliminates any gaps.

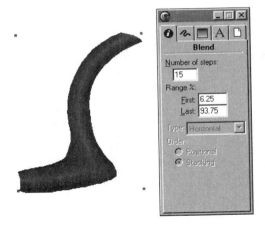

6] Change your view so you can see the Middle Leg paths.

You will now repeat the same procedure for the Middle Leg element.

7] Using the Pointer tool, select the middle path of the Middle Leg element and change the stroke color to Lavender. Select the two outer paths with the Pointer tool and change the stroke color to Purple. Select all three of the Middle Leg paths and choose Modify › Combine › Blend. Then change the number of steps in the blend to 15 in the Object Inspector.

8] Adjust the view to see the Right Leg paths.

9] Select the middle path of the Right Leg element and change the stroke color to Lavender. Select the two outer paths and change the stroke color to Purple. Create a blend of the three Right Leg paths. Then change the number of steps in the blend to 15.

246

10] **Zoom out to see the entire page. Then save your work.**

The three leg blends are ready to be used in the robot illustration.

PASTING BLENDS INSIDE PATHS TO CREATE THREE-DIMENSIONAL SHADING

Although you could fill the legs of your robot with graduated fills, the colors would not follow the contours of the legs. Instead, you blended shapes together to create three-dimensional shading that does follow the contours of the legs. In this task, you will add these blends to the robot by combining them with the paths for each leg using the Paste Inside feature.

1] **Select all three blended leg shapes.**

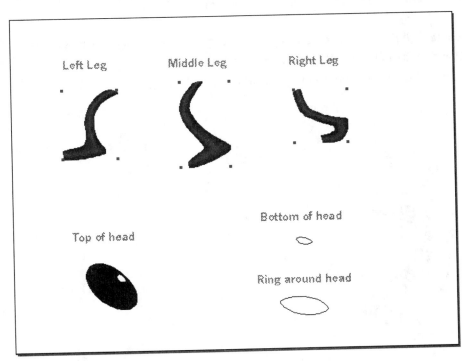

2] Choose Edit › Copy.

You will be pasting the blends into the robot document.

3] Choose Window › FlexBotz to switch to that document and bring it to the front. Then choose Edit › Paste to add the three blends to this document.

Remember that all of the open documents are listed at the bottom of the Window menu so you can easily switch from one to another.

You will reposition the blends in the following steps.

4] Deselect all items. Then select the Middle Leg blend and move this blend into position directly in front of the robot's middle leg.

The blend should completely cover the path for that leg.

Now you will cut the blend and paste it inside the leg path.

5] Cut the blend. Then paste it inside the leg path with Paste Inside. Change the stroke width to 0.5 point.

The lightest part of the blend should be roughly in the middle of the foot, and the blend should completely fill the leg path. If either is not the case, drag the Paste Inside control handle to reposition the blend.

6] Repeat steps 4 and 5 for the left leg and then the right leg.

Now all three legs are complete.

7] Save your work.

249

BLENDING SHAPES FOR SHADING

CREATING SHADING FOR THE TOP OF A SPHERE

The head of this robot is a sphere with a ring around the middle. To add realistic shading, you will create a separate blend for both the top and bottom portions of the sphere.

1] Return to the MyParts document by selecting it from the Window menu. Zoom in on the top of the head elements.

These two ellipses will be used to create shading for the top portion of the robot's head.

2] Using the Pointer tool, select the small oval. Change the fill to Light Blue and make sure that the stroke is set to None.

This will become the highlighted area of the top of the head.

3] Select the large oval and change the fill to Navy Blue. Make sure that the stroke is set to None.

This will be used to create the darker areas of the top of the head.

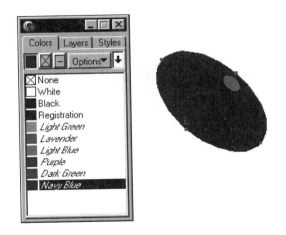

Now you will blend these two shapes together.

tip   *When creating a blend of two closed shapes, make sure that the stroke for each shape is set to None. Otherwise, each of the intermediate shapes will have a stroke, which will disrupt the smooth change of color desired.*

4] Create a blend of the two ellipses. Then change the number of steps in the blend to 30 in the Object Inspector to create a smoother color transition.

This blend is ready to be added to the robot illustration.

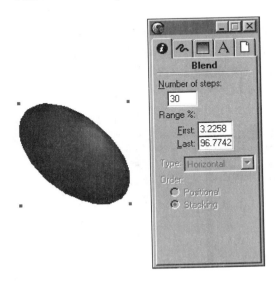

tip   *If you have difficulty selecting both ellipses, be sure you select the smaller shape first; then hold Shift and click the larger one.*

5] Save your work.

Now you will add this blend to the robot.

6] Copy the blend. Then switch to the FlexBotz document and paste the blend.

Before you move this blend into position, you will change the fill and stroke for the path itself. If you need to, move the blend out of your way temporarily.

7] Select the path that defines the top of the head. Change the fill to Navy Blue and set the stroke to None.

Changing the fill to match the darkest color of the blend is a precaution. Occasionally, when you paste a shape inside a path that has no stroke, a bit of the fill color for the path is visible on the screen around the pasted object.

8] Move the blended ellipses into position on the top of the head, as shown here.

9] Cut the blend and use Paste Inside to paste it inside the path for the top of the head.

The highlight should appear on the upper-right part of the head. Drag the Paste Inside control handle to reposition the blend if necessary.

The top of the head was originally behind the eyes in this illustration. Pasting the blend inside this path does not change its current position on the page, which is why the top of the head remains behind the eyes.

10] Save your work.

CREATING SHADING FOR THE BOTTOM OF A SPHERE

Now you will create the bottom head element.

1] Return to the MyParts document and change the view to see the bottom of the head element. Select this shape using the Pointer tool and then change the fill to Light Blue and the stroke to None.

You will use this shape to create the highlighted area for the bottom of the head.

2] Save your work.

Now you will paste this shape in the robot document.

3] Copy the light blue head shape. Then switch to the FlexBotz document and choose Paste.

You will use this shape as the highlight for the lower part of the robot's spherical head. You will move this shape into position in the next step.

254

4] Change to the Fast Keyline mode using the menu at the bottom of the document window.

A shape located on the background layer is now visible on the bottom of the head to help you position the highlight shape correctly.

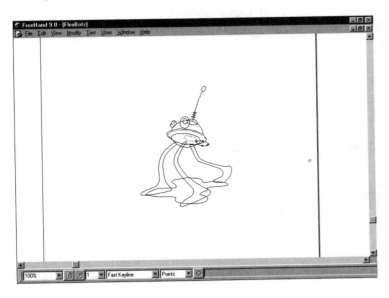

5] Move the highlight element into position on top of the gray background element.

Remember that you move an element by pointing to the middle and dragging with the Pointer tool.

tip *You may find it helpful when repositioning shapes to click and hold the selection until the cursor changes to a four-direction arrow. Then when you drag, you will see the actual shape moving instead of a rectangular bounding box.*

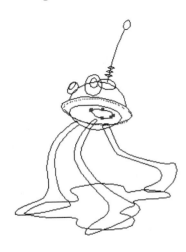

255

6] Change back to the Preview mode and select the path that defines the bottom portion of the head. Change the fill to Navy Blue and set the stroke to None.

This defines the characteristics of the darker areas for the lower head element.

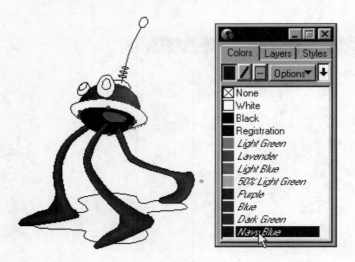

7] Create a blend of the highlight element and the bottom head path. Then make sure the number of steps in the Object Inspector is set at 16.

These shapes created the shading effect for the bottom of the head. However, because the blend is a new element on the page, it is automatically placed in front of the other elements, covering the tops of the legs.

8] Select the middle and right legs and choose Modify › Arrange › Bring to Front. Then save your work.

The legs and two head sphere elements are complete.

CREATING SHADING FOR A CYLINDRICAL RING

Next you will add the appearance of a ring going around the head.

1] Return to the MyParts document and change your view to see the path for the ring around the head.

2] Using the Fill Inspector, apply a gradient that begins and ends with Dark Green. Drag the Light Green swatch from the Color List and drop it just above the middle of the color ramp in the Fill Inspector, as shown here. Change the angle of the gradient to 344 degrees and set the stroke to None.

You will use this shape to add dimension to the ring surrounding the head.

3] Copy the ellipse. Then switch to the FlexBotz document and choose Paste.

4] Zoom in on the head using the Zoom tool. Then change the view mode to Fast Keyline.

You can now see the background elements, including a gray elliptical shape near the ring ellipse to help you position the pasted ellipse accurately.

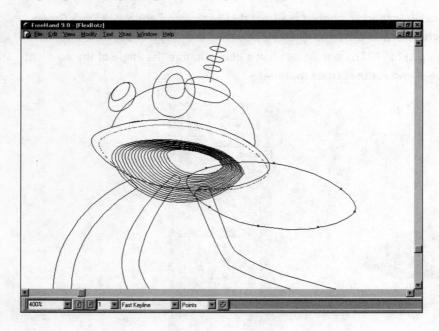

5] Using the Pointer tool, position the ring ellipse on top of the background ellipse.

The ring ellipse filled with gradient color should extend a bit below the bottom (back) edge of the ring.

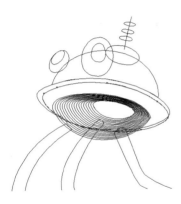

6] Return to the Preview mode. Select the white ellipse behind the green ring shape.

The path is currently filled with white and has a black stroke.

7] Apply a gradient fill that begins and ends with Light Green. Using the Color Mixer, create the color 17c2m26y0k. Add this color to the middle of the gradient on the color ramp as shown here. Then change the angle to 339 degrees and set the stroke to None.

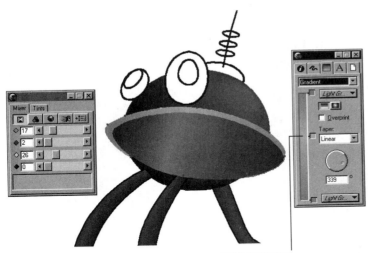

POSITION THE NEW COLOR SWATCH HERE

You will now complete the robot's ring by combining the two ellipses.

259

8] Cut the dark green ellipse and paste it inside the light green ellipse.

The head and ring are now complete.

9] Save your work.

You are finished with your MyParts document, so it does not need to remain open.

10] Switch to the MyParts document and close it.

You will continue your work on the FlexBotz document.

ADDING DIMENSION WITH RADIAL FILLS

The robot's eyes will be shaded using radial fills, which will make them look three-dimensional.

1] Using the Pointer tool, select the larger path for both of the eyes.

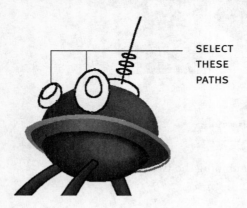

SELECT
THESE
PATHS

The outer shapes use the same fill, so you can apply the fill to both paths at the same time.

2] Using the Fill Inspector, change the type of fill to Gradient. Then click the Radial Fill button. Set White as the starting color (at the bottom of the panel) and set the ending color to Light Blue. Add another White swatch in the middle of the color ramp by dragging the White swatch at the bottom and dropping it approximately one-third of the way up the color ramp.

Using white for two of the three swatches along the color ramp in this gradient will make the white parts of the eyes appear larger than if white was used only once.

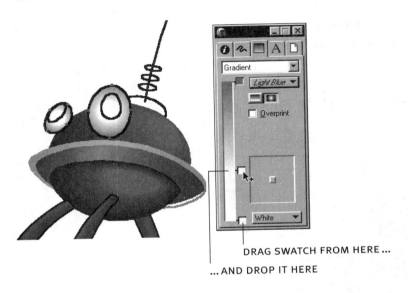

DRAG SWATCH FROM HERE...

...AND DROP IT HERE

3] Move the centerpoint of the radial gradient up and to the right as shown here and change the stroke width to 0.5 point.

The outer paths of the eyes are complete.

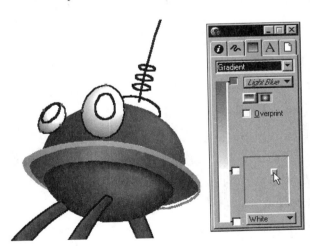

261

Since the desired shading for the eyes could be achieved using a radial gradient, you did not need to create clipping paths by pasting blends inside the paths. Radial and graduated fills are less complex than blends and clipping paths and will usually print faster. Create blends and clipping paths when a radial or graduated fill cannot achieve the desired shading, such as when you need to create a highlight shape that is not circular.

4] Select the smaller path for each eye. Change the stroke to None and then apply a radial gradient fill. Select White as the starting color and Blue as the ending color of the gradient. Drag and drop the Blue color swatch on the middle of the color ramp. Using the blue for two of the three swatches in this gradient makes the transition between white and blue take place over a shorter distance and fills the remaining portion of the paths with solid blue.

5] Move the centerpoint of the radial gradient up slightly and to the right as shown here.

You are almost finished with the eyes.

6] Deselect all elements. Then select just the smaller path of the eye on your left. In the Fill Inspector, move the middle Blue swatch down slightly on the color ramp and move the centerpoint slightly up and to the right.

This subtle change makes the highlight in the eye that is farther away appear smaller, which adds a realistic touch to the illustration. Adjusting the position of the centerpoint makes the eyes appear to be looking in different directions.

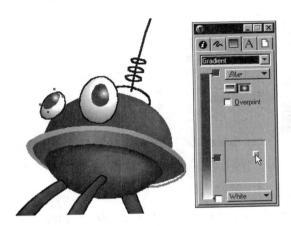

The eyes are now complete.

7] Deselect all elements and save your work.

COMPLETING THE FIGURE

You will complete the antenna by applying basic and Gradient fills.

1] Zoom out, if necessary, so you can see the entire antenna.

The antenna consists of six shapes.

263

2] **Select the long path extending the length of the antenna. Change the stroke color to Purple.**

The width of this line should already be set to 1 point.

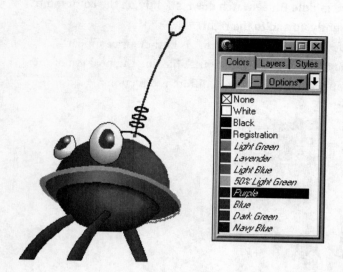

3] **Select the three small oval shapes. Change the fill color to Lavender and the stroke to None.**

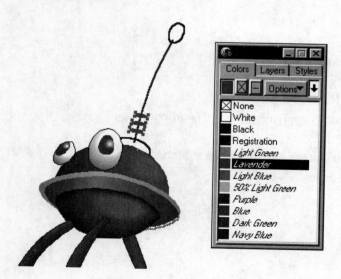

4] **Select the ellipse at the top of the antenna and change the stroke to None. Apply a Radial Gradient fill, with Dark Green as the starting color and 50% Light Green as the ending color. Move the centerpoint up and to the right as shown here.**

5] **Select the element at the base of the antenna and change the stroke to None. Apply a Linear Gradient fill, with Purple as the starting color and Lavender as the ending color. Then change the angle of the gradient to 250 degrees.**

The antenna is now complete.

6] **Save your work.**

CREATING A REALISTIC SHADOW

The shadow will be filled with a lens fill.

1] Zoom out so you can see the entire robot.

2] Select the shadow shape and change the stroke to None. Using the Fill Inspector, apply a Lens fill. Change the type of Lens fill from Transparency to Darken and set the percentage to 35.

For a Darken Lens fill, a value of 0 percent would not darken the background element at all, and a value of 100 percent would make the element completely black. You will see the full effect of this fill later when you add an image behind the shadow.

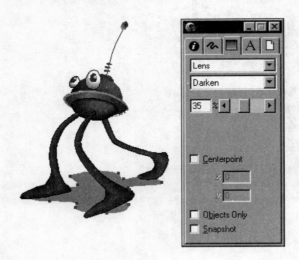

3] Save your work.

CREATING THE FINISHED DOCUMENT

Your robot illustration is so nice that you want to send it to your friends as a postcard. You need to create a new document and specify a custom page size for your postcard. You will then add the completed robot to this new document. For a finishing touch, you will import a TIFF file created in Photoshop as a background image for your robot.

1] Select all of the elements on the page and group them together.

This will make it easier to move and manipulate the robot as one object.

2] Copy this group. Then create a new document and choose Paste.

267

3] Save this document as Postcard in your MyWork folder.

4] Using the Document Inspector, change the page size to 4 inches by 5 inches.
Remember to change the unit of measurement to inches in the menu at the bottom of the document window. Then choose Custom from the list of page sizes in the Document Inspector to enter new dimensions for the page.

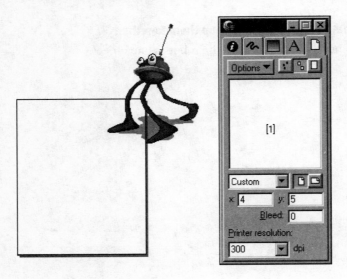

5] Move the robot so it is visually centered on the page. Then choose View › Fit to Page.

You will adjust the position of the robot one final time once the background image is in place.

6] Choose File › Import. Then select the Planet.tif graphic located in the Media folder within the Lesson06 folder. Click near the top of the page to position the image on the page.

The imported image now covers the robot artwork.

7] With the imported graphic still selected, choose Modify › Arrange › Send to Back.

Now the robot appears in front of the background image. Notice how the Darken Lens fill in the shadow actually darkens the texture of the image behind it.

The next step will position the graphic and robot so they are centered on the page.

8] Select both the imported background graphic and the robot. Display the Align panel by choosing Window > Panels > Align. Click the center of the preview grid to change both the vertical and horizontal alignment settings to Align Center. Turn on Align to Page and click Apply (Windows) or Align (Macintosh).

The robot and background image are now centered on the page.

9] Save your work.

Congratulations—your robot postcard is now complete!

CUSTOMIZING FREEHAND'S TOOLBARS AND SHORTCUTS

FreeHand allows you to customize its toolbars by adding, deleting, or repositioning items. You can also define your own keyboard shortcuts or use the keyboard shortcuts from other applications.

1] Choose File › Customize › Shortcuts. Open the Keyboard Shortcuts Setting menu to see a list of available shortcut sets.

FreeHand lets you choose the keyboard shortcut sets from other popular programs to make it easier for you to switch from one program to another as you work.

(Additional preset shortcuts from other programs are available on the Macintosh. See Appendix C, "Moving to FreeHand," for more information.)

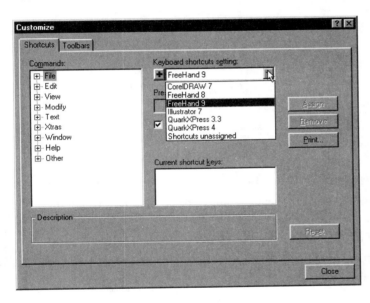

FreeHand also lets you assign keyboard shortcuts to any command. You first select the command from the list on the left, and then you click the Press New Shortcut Key box and type the shortcut you want to assign to that command. Go to Conflict on Assign is turned on by default, so FreeHand will not allow you to assign the same shortcut to different commands.

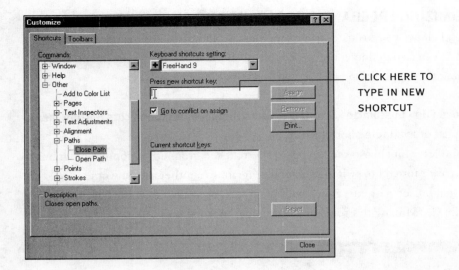

CLICK HERE TO
TYPE IN NEW
SHORTCUT

tip *If you make any inadvertent changes in this dialog box, click the Reset button in the lower-right corner before you close it.*

Now look at how you can customize the toolbars.

2] Close the Customize Shortcuts dialog box and choose File › Customize › Toolbars.
This dialog box enables you to add or delete commands on the toolbars. On the left is a list of FreeHand commands. You can click the + sign (Windows) or triangle (Macintosh) to the left of a command name to view the commands in that command group. On the right are several buttons that represent different specific commands. The button display changes according to the command selected on the left.

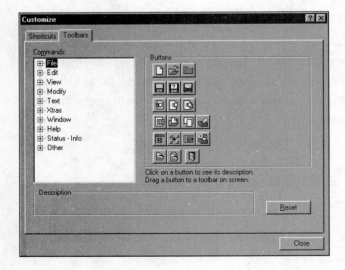

To see how easy it is to customize your toolbars, you will add the Blend command to the main toolbar, so that feature is available at the click of a button.

3] In the Commands list, click the + sign (Windows) or triangle (Macintosh) next to Modify to expand that group and see the commands on the Modify menu. Scroll down the list to Combine and click its + sign (Windows) or triangle (Macintosh) to view the various Combine commands. Click Blend to select this command.

A dotted line (Windows) or heavy line (Macintosh) now appears around the Blend button on the right of the dialog box.

BLEND BUTTON

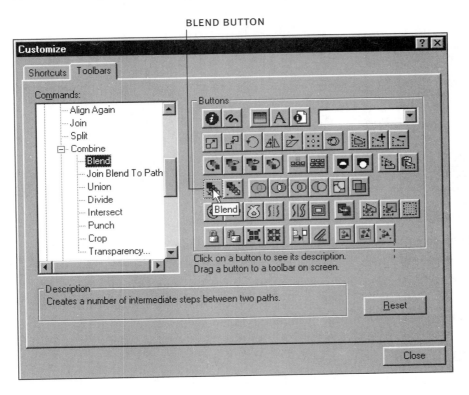

4] Drag the Blend button icon from the right side of the dialog box and drop it where you would like it positioned on the main toolbar.

If you drop a button on top of an existing button, your new button will appear directly to the right of that button. In this example, the Blend button was dropped on top of the Split button so it appears to the right of Split and before Lock.

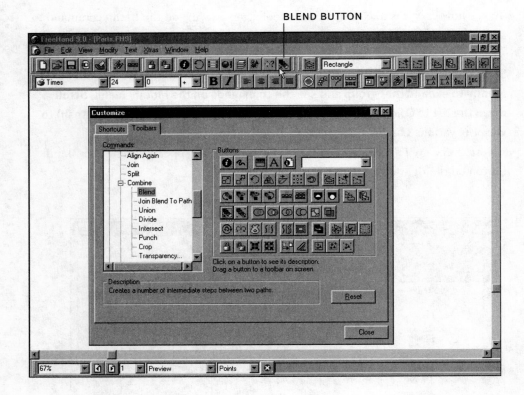

5] If you do not want to apply the change you just made, click Reset. Otherwise, click Close.

Customizable shortcuts and toolbars enable you to fine-tune your working environment, helping you take advantage of the power FreeHand provides in the manner that best suits your own working style and needs.

ON YOUR OWN

Practice the techniques you used in this lesson by adding shading effects to another robot. Open FlexBotz2.ft9, a template you will find in the Start folder within the Lesson06 folder. This document contains the outline shapes for another robot. As with the robot you just completed, you will need to add fills, strokes, and shading to give this new robot three-dimensional qualities. Experiment with blends, Paste Inside, and Gradient and Lens fills as you create a new illustration.

WHAT YOU HAVE LEARNED

In this lesson you have:

- Created blends to add three-dimensional shading effects [pages 243–247]
- Practiced creating clipping paths with the Paste Inside feature [pages 247–249]
- Practiced copying and pasting artwork between documents [pages 250–253]
- Created shading effects using Linear and Radial Gradient fills [pages 254–265]
- Created a realistic shadow using a Darken Lens fill [page 266]
- Practiced creating a custom page size [pages 267–268]
- Imported a Photoshop TIFF document as a background image [pages 269–270]
- Customized FreeHand's keyboard shortcuts and toolbars [pages 271–274]

in FreeHand

page layout

In this lesson, you will create a one-page ad designed to go in a magazine. In the process, you'll learn to use FreeHand's text editing tools by working with imported text, multicolumn text blocks, in-line graphics, imported image files with runaround, and more.

All of the elements in this ad are vector objects created in FreeHand. The pillow is the same one that you had the opportunity to create in the bonus round of Lesson 6. Text was imported into FreeHand and formatted using the text editing tools available within the program. You will learn how to format text in a variety of ways in this lesson.

Designed by Tony Roame of Illustrated Concepts.

FreeHand excels at working with one-page, graphics-intensive documents. It has all of the text editing features you would expect in a typical page layout program, and even some features most page layout programs lack. In addition, you have the advantage of working with fewer imported objects, because all of your vector artwork can stay right in FreeHand.

If you'd like to review the final result of this lesson, open LPad.ft9 in the Complete folder within the Lesson07 folder.

WHAT YOU WILL LEARN

In this lesson you will:

- Import text from an external source
- Toggle text blocks between fixed width and auto-expand
- Control the size and position of text blocks
- Create multicolumn text blocks
- Import vector objects from an external file
- Create text runaround for imported objects
- Export a document as a PDF file

APPROXIMATE TIME

This lesson takes approximately 45 minutes to complete.

LESSON FILES

Media Files:

Lesson07\Media\LabelsText.rtf
Lesson07\Media\BodyCopy.rtf
Lesson07\Media\3LLSlogo.eps
Lesson07\Media\Slogan.eps
Lesson07\Media\LP3D.eps
Lesson07\Media\LCard.eps
Lesson07\Media\FactBox.eps

Starting Files:

Lesson07\Start\LPstart.ft9

Completed Project:

Lesson07\Complete\LPad.ft9

ASSEMBLING THE TOP SECTION

FreeHand can be used very effectively as a page layout solution. You are going to learn how to take elements from various FreeHand documents and from documents created by other applications and bring all that information together in one place to create an effective ad.

You will start by opening a document already in progress, and you will bring in the rest of the elements and format them as necessary.

1] Open the document LPstart.ft9 in the Lesson07\Start folder.

A document opens on your screen that contains the headline text. You can also see guides on the bottom and sides of the page. These guides indicate the margin required on the page, so you will need to make sure that all elements stay inside the guides.

Now you are ready to start importing the rest of the elements that will be used in this ad.

PAGE GUIDES

2] Choose File › Import and select LP3D.eps located in the Media folder within the Lesson07 folder. Click below the word *Smart* to place the pillow in your document.

Alternatively, if you completed the bonus round in Lesson 6, you could select the pillow artwork you created yourself.

3] With the pillow still selected, open the Align panel (Window › Panels › Align). From the second pop-up menu, choose Align Center. Check the box marked Align to Page and click Apply (Windows) or Align (Macintosh). Now use the up and down arrow keys to visually center the pillow vertically between the words *Smart* and *Learning*.

The pillow is the focal point for this ad, so it needs to be centered on the page.

279

4] Choose File › Import again, and this time select the file LPcard.eps. Click the page in FreeHand to place it and then import the file LabelsRaw.rtf. (Both files are located in the Lesson07\Media folder.)

Now you have the elements you need to import for the top half of the ad, and you're ready to start arranging them.

5] Select the learning card and send it to the back (Windows Ctrl+B, Macintosh Command+B). Double-click the card to display the transform handles; then move the mouse outside the transform handles and drag so that the card is rotated clockwise approximately 20 degrees.

You can see the angle of rotation you just made by looking at the Rotate section of the Transform panel after you release your mouse.

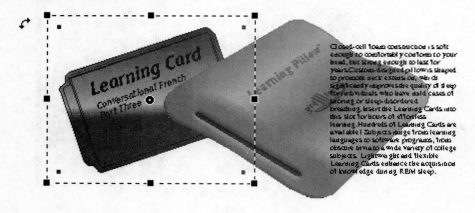

To see the angle of rotation while you are dragging with the transform handles, turn on the Info toolbar and watch the number after the word Angle. Once you double click to activate the transform handles, you will see the Angle number changing based on your mouse position. Move your mouse to the right of the object until the Angle number is 0, then click and drag up until the Angle number is correct. This technique also works when using the Rotate tool instead of the transform handles.

6] Duplicate the card by choosing Edit › Duplicate (Windows Ctrl+D, Macintosh Command+D). Move the duplicate to the left and up slightly; then send it to the back. With the transform handles still active, move your mouse outside of the handles and drag to rotate the duplicate card approximately 10 degrees counterclockwise.

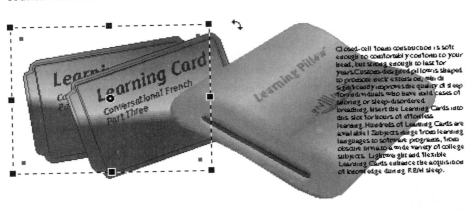

Now you have a second card in position behind the first. You will repeat this step one more time to create a third card.

7] Duplicate the learning card you just created, move it up and to the left, and send it to the back. If the transform handles are not already active, double-click to display them; then rotate this third duplicate card counterclockwise 10 degrees.

Now the three cards are created and in place. If you need to adjust the positions of the cards relative to each other, do so at this time.

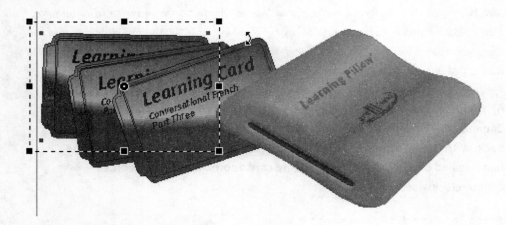

8] Select the three cards with the Pointer tool by holding the Shift key as you click each card. Position the cards behind the pillow so that the bottom lines of text on the first card are partially hidden by the pillow.

In this step, you are getting the cards in the right position relative to the pillow. When you are finished, your page should look like the following illustration.

9] Save your work.

SEPARATING THE TEXT LABELS

Sometimes you will receive text in a single file that belongs in separate locations on the page. In this case, the labels were all written in a single text file. After importing that file, you need to break it into individual text blocks so the labels are easy to position in various locations around the illustration.

1] Choose File › Preferences and click Text. Uncheck the box marked Text Tool reverts to pointer; then close the Preferences dialog box.

Unchecking this preference will enable you to perform the next steps more quickly. This preference activates the Pointer tool every time your cursor moves outside the active text block. In many instances, this is extremely useful, but if you'll be manipulating a significant amount of text, it's much better to have this option unchecked. Now the Text tool will still be active when you move it outside the active text block, and clicking will create a new text block, rather than just deactivating the current text block.

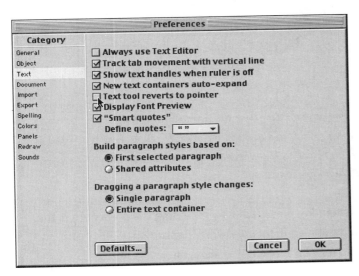

2] Select the bottom paragraph with the Text tool and cut the text. With the Text tool still active, click and drag a rectangle in the space above the learning cards. Paste the text by choosing File › Paste.

You have just separated the label from the body of the text you imported. You will follow this sequence to separate the rest of the labels.

CLICK AND DRAG WITH THE TEXT TOOL

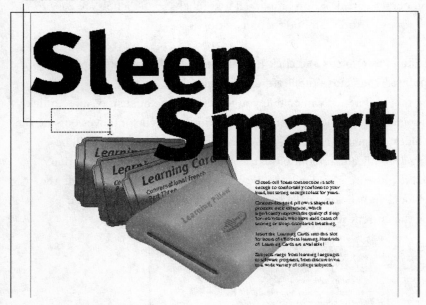

tip *By dragging a selection with the Text tool, you are creating a fixed-width text block. That is, you are confining the text you placed to a specific area. If you had simply clicked with the Text tool and then pasted the text, FreeHand would have created an auto-expanding text block, and all the text would be on one long line.*

3] Separate each of the remaining paragraphs by repeating the procedure in the previous step. Place them as shown in the following illustration.

The five text blocks should now be separated as shown here.

PLACE THE TEST
PARAGRAPHS
LIKE THIS.

A SOLID CIRCLE IN THE
LINK BOX INDICATES
TEXT OVERFLOW

tip   *When you are working with fixed-width text blocks, sometimes not all the text will fit within the visible area. Text overflow is indicated by a solid circle in the Text Block's Link box, which is visible when the text block is selected. You can see an example of this in the illustration below. The best way to fix this problem is to double-click the Pointer tool on the bottom center handle of the text block. This makes the text block auto-expanding going down, while maintaining a fixed width side to side.*

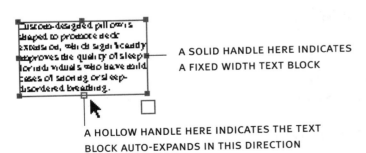

A SOLID HANDLE HERE INDICATES
A FIXED WIDTH TEXT BLOCK

A HOLLOW HANDLE HERE INDICATES THE TEXT
BLOCK AUTO-EXPANDS IN THIS DIRECTION

285

You can easily tell whether a text block is auto-expanding by looking at the bottom or side handle. If the handle is hollow, the text block is auto-expanding in that direction; if it is solid, then the text block is fixed in that direction.

4] Make sure each of the labels displays all of the text by double-clicking the Pointer tool on the bottom center handle of each text block. Then make sure each of the text blocks is a short distance from the illustration (see the following figure). Select the Line tool and draw a one-point black line from each label to the appropriate area on the illustration.

Move the text blocks and lines as necessary to achieve an aesthetically pleasing and balanced look. You can resize the text blocks by dragging either of the bottom corner handles. Dragging other handles on the side and bottom will change the range kerning and the leading of the text. If this happens, choose Undo.

Now the top half of the ad is complete. Next you'll work with the body copy by importing text and formatting it with the tools available in FreeHand.

CREATING MULTI-COLUMN TEXT BLOCKS

In this part of the lesson, you'll learn how to make one text block behave like two. FreeHand makes this process both fun and easy.

1] Import the file BodyCopy.rtf located in the Media folder within the Lesson07 folder.
This file comes in as one large text block. It will be much more appealing and easy to read when it has been divided into two columns and formatted.

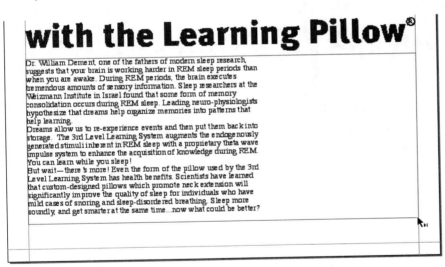

with the Learning Pillow®

Dr. William Dement, one of the fathers of modern sleep research, suggests that your brain is working harder in REM sleep periods than when you are awake. During REM periods, the brain executes tremendous amounts of sensory information. Sleep researchers at the Weizmann Institute in Israel found that some form of memory consolidation occurs during REM sleep. Leading neuro-physiologists hypothesize that dreams help organize memories into patterns that help learning.

Dreams allow us to re-experience events and then put them back into storage. The 3rd Level Learning System augments the endogenously generated stimuli inherent in REM sleep with a proprietary theta wave impulse system to enhance the acquisition of knowledge during REM. You can learn while you sleep!

But wait—there's more! Even the form of the pillow used by the 3rd Level Learning System has health benefits. Scientists have learned that custom-designed pillows which promote neck extension will significantly improve the quality of sleep for individuals who have mild cases of snoring and sleep-disordered breathing. Sleep more soundly, and get smarter at the same time...now what could be better?

2] **Select the Pointer tool and drag the text block so that the left edge is touching the left guide. Then drag the bottom-right corner of the text block until it touches the right guide.**

Now your text block is the proper width. Next you'll format it into two columns.

with the Learning Pillow®

Dr. William Dement, one of the fathers of modern sleep research, suggests that your brain is working harder in REM sleep periods than when you are awake. During REM periods, the brain executes tremendous amounts of sensory information. Sleep researchers at the Weizmann Institute in Israel found that some form of memory consolidation occurs during REM sleep. Leading neuro-physiologists hypothesize that dreams help organize memories into patterns that help learning.

Dreams allow us to re-experience events and then put them back into storage. The 3rd Level Learning System augments the endogenously generated stimuli inherent in REM sleep with a proprietary theta wave impulse system to enhance the acquisition of knowledge during REM. You can learn while you sleep!

But wait—there's more! Even the form of the pillow used by the 3rd Level Learning System has health benefits. Scientists have learned that custom-designed pillows which promote neck extension will significantly improve the quality of sleep for individuals who have mild cases of snoring and sleep-disordered breathing. Sleep more soundly, and get smarter at the same time...now what could be better?

3] **Select the Text Inspector by choosing Window › Inspectors › Text. Click the fourth button in the Text Inspector, which is the Column Inspector. In the Columns field, enter *2* and press Enter.**

Changing a text block into multiple columns is as simple as changing one field. You could just as easily create a three-, four-, or five-column text block. You can leave the Height and Spacing fields the way they are for now.

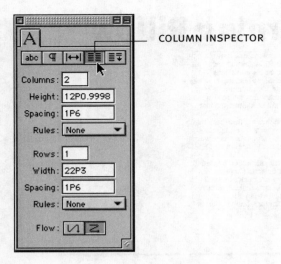

COLUMN INSPECTOR

You want the text to break in a specific location. You are going to guarantee that break in the next step.

4] Select the Text tool and click to the left of the word *Dreams* near the bottom of the first column. Choose Text > Special Characters > End of Column.

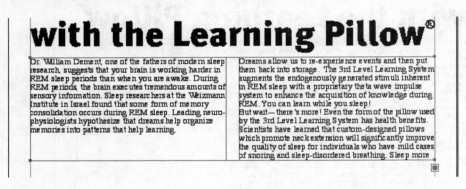

Notice that the text block's link box now has a solid circle filling it. That means that some of the text in the story is not being displayed. You will fix this in the next step.

5] With the Pointer tool, drag one of the bottom handles of the text block down about an inch.

Now there should be plenty of room for the text to appear. The text block's Link box should be empty. If it is not, drag one of the corner handles of the text block down a little further.

6] **Select the Text tool and click anywhere in the text block and choose Edit › Select › All (Windows Ctrl+A, Macintosh Command+A). On the text toolbar, select the Utopia font, the size 9.4, and the style Plain. Then set the leading symbol to = and enter the value *13.5*.**

These are the correct settings for the second column. Now you'll select the text in the first column and change its font settings to make it unique.

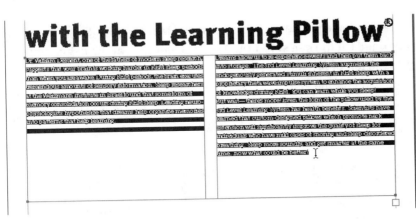

If this font is not available on your system, use a similar serif font that is available. You may need to adjust the size to match the layout. For instance, you could use Times at 10.5 type size instead.

7] **Select the text in the first column with the Text tool. Change the leading to 22, the type size to 11.8, and the font to MetaPlus Bold Italic.**

Now the type is a little more interesting, but the introduction of some in-line graphics would make it stand out even more. This would provide more entry points for the reader.

If this font is not available on your system, use a similar sans-serif bold font that is available. You may need to adjust the size to match the layout. For instance, you could use Trebuchet MS at 11.5 type size instead. The Trebuchet MS font can be downloaded from the Microsoft Web site.

In the next section, you will insert vector graphics into a text block.

USING IN-LINE GRAPHICS

It can be very useful at times to place vector graphics right inside a text block. If you make an adjustment to the text that causes line breaks to shift, for instance, in-line graphics will be repositioned with the rest of the text. Another benefit is that the text automatically moves to make space for the graphic. In the next steps, you will learn a simple but very useful technique for adding in-line graphics.

1] Import the file FactBox.eps located in the Lesson07 Media folder. Select the imported Fact box and cut it. Then select the Text tool and click at the beginning of the body (just to the left of *Dr.*) and paste.

You have just added an in-line graphic to your text block. Vector objects in FreeHand can be pasted inside text blocks, where they will be treated just like ordinary text characters. You will see how that works in the next step.

2] Click with the Text tool after the graphic and press the spacebar to add room between the graphic and the text. Now drag across the graphic with the Text tool to highlight it. Go to the Character Inspector section of the Text Inspector and change the Baseline Shift field to -0p3.

Here you can see that by highlighting the graphic with the Text tool, you can control the positioning of the graphic just as you can any character of text. In this case, you are adjusting the baseline shift to move the graphic down 3 points so that it fits better with the line of text. If you are using a different font, you may need to adjust the leading and baseline values to match the illustration.

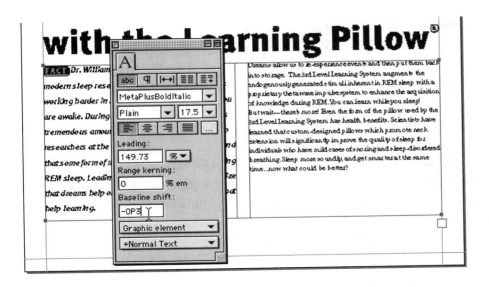

3] Highlight the graphic with the Text tool again, copy it, and paste it at the beginning of each sentence in the first column.

Simply click with the Text tool and choose Edit › Paste at each location where you want to add the in-line graphic. When you are finished, the first column should contain four in-line graphics, as shown in the following illustration.

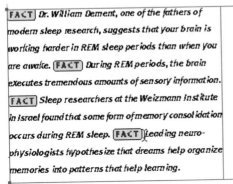

Now you are ready to add the Third-Level Learning System logo.

291

MAKING TEXT FLOW AROUND GRAPHIC ELEMENTS

Keeping text in rectangular boxes is easy, but your design will be more interesting if you break up the monotony by making your text flow around graphic elements on your page. **Run Around** is a common term for text that wraps around graphics. In the next section, you will make the body copy in the second column flow around the logo, rather than simply overlapping it.

1] Import the file 3LLSlogo.TIF. Position it so the right edge of the logo touches the right guide on the page and move it vertically so that the top of the logo is almost touching the baseline of the last full line of text (slightly more than an inch from the bottom of the page).

You need to leave room for the slogan and a disclaimer at the bottom of the page, so the logo shouldn't really go much lower. You don't want the logo to run too close to the body copy, so now you need to assign runaround to this logo so that the text will automatically flow around it.

2] Select the Pen tool or the Bezigon tool and draw a path around the logo, staying about one pica (⅛ of an inch) from the edge of the artwork. Make sure the path is closed.

This path will define the runaround for the logo.

Dreams allow us to re-experience events and then put them back into storage. The 3rd Level Learning System augments the endogenously generated stimuli inherent in REM sleep with a proprietary theta wave impulse system to enhance the acquisition of knowledge during REM. You can learn while you sleep!

But wait—there's more! Even the form of the pillow used by the 3rd Level Learning System has health benefits. Scientists have learned that custom-designed pillows which promote neck extension will significantly improve the quality of sleep for individuals who have mild cases of snoring and sleep-disordered breathing. Sleep more soundly, and get smarter at the same time…now what could be better?

3] With the path selected, choose Text › Run Around Selection. In the Run Around dialog box, click the right icon; then press Enter or click OK.

When you dismiss the Run Around dialog box, the runaround is applied to the path. You may need to adjust the path a bit so that the text lines break where you want them to.

Dreams allow us to re-experience events and then put them back into storage. The 3rd Level Learning System augments the endogenously generated stimuli inherent in REM sleep with a proprietary theta wave impulse system to enhance the acquisition of knowledge during REM. You can learn while you sleep!

But wait—there's more! Even the form of the pillow used by the 3rd Level Learning System has health benefits. Scientists have learned that custom-designed pillows which promote neck extension will significantly improve the quality of sleep for individuals who have mild cases of snoring and sleep-disordered breathing. Sleep more soundly, and get smarter at the same time…now what could be better?

You don't want this path to appear in the printed piece. You also want to make sure that the path stays with the logo in case you have to make any size or position adjustments later.

4] **With the path still selected, go to the Stroke Inspector and set the path to None. Select the Pointer tool, hold down the Shift key, and click the logo. Choose Modify › Group (Windows Ctrl-G, Macintosh Command-G).**

Now the runaround path and the logo are grouped together, and the path itself is invisible.

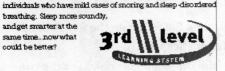

tip *If you need to edit the runaround path later, switch to the Keyline view at the bottom of the document window, and you'll be able to see the line again.*

note *You will need to use Alt+click (Windows) or Option+click (Macintosh) to select the line to edit it, since it is part of a group now.*

The ad is nearly finished. All you have to do now is import the slogan and the disclaimer text.

5] **Import the file Legal.rtf, change it to 6-point Helvetica type, and stretch the text block so that it reaches from the left margin all the way to the right margin. Then move the text block down until the bottom of the block touches the bottom guide.**

Now the disclaimer looks just like the fine print you've come to expect in many modern ad campaigns.

6] **Import the file Slogan.eps and position it just above the disclaimer text block. With the slogan still selected, open the Align panel and adjust the settings to center the slogan on the page.**

Make sure you check the Align to Page box.

Use the up and down arrow keys to visually center the slogan between the disclaimer and the body copy.

Now your ad is complete! Are you ready to learn some more?

SAVING THE DOCUMENT AS A PDF FILE

Adobe's portable document format (PDF) has been gaining momentum over the last few years as a cross-platform solution for delivering documents that preserve the design integrity of the original document, regardless of its origin or destination. In addition, many printers and service bureaus are now accepting PDF files for output to film. FreeHand does an excellent job of integrating support for PDF, both by importing PDF documents into FreeHand and by exporting FreeHand documents in the PDF format.

These next steps will take you through the process of exporting a FreeHand document as a PDF file.

1] Choose File › Export. In the Save as File type (Windows) or Format (Macintosh) pop-up menu, choose PDF. Make sure your file is going to land where you want it to go and check that it is named correctly.

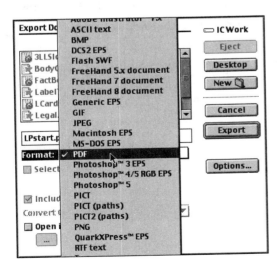

2] Click the Setup (Windows) or Options (Macintosh) button, located below the Export button. Select the desired options for your document, including the page range, compression, color conversion, and compatibility settings. Click OK or press Enter when you're done.

Note especially the option to embed fonts in your PDF document. Although it adds slightly to the file size, embedding fonts is the best way to ensure that your document appears the way you designed it. If you don't embed the fonts, people who do not have those fonts may see a document that looks significantly different than your original. Make sure also to select the version of Acrobat compatible with your version of Acrobat Reader.

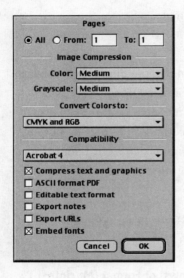

3] If you want to open the file immediately in Adobe Acrobat Reader, click the Open in an External Application check box. Then click Next button and locate the Acrobat Reader you want to use. When you're done, click Save (Windows) or Export (Macintosh) or press Enter.

A dialog box will display the progress of your PDF file as it is being saved. Be sure to check the PDF file to be certain that everything turned out the way you intended.

WHAT YOU HAVE LEARNED

In this lesson you have:

- Imported graphics from other FreeHand documents [pages 278–280]
- Used the transform handles to rotate objects [pages 280–281]
- Separated one text block into multiple text blocks [pages 283–286]
- Formatted a single text block into two columns [pages 286–288]
- Selected fonts, sizes, leading, and other text properties [page 289]
- Placed graphics in line with text [pages 290–291]
- Used text runaround with a placed object [pages 292–295]
- Exported a FreeHand file as a PDF document [pages 295–296]

documents

multiple-page

LESSON 8

In addition to creating a wide variety of graphics and illustrations, you can use FreeHand to design and construct multiple-page documents by adding pages to documents and flowing text from one page to the next. As you learned in Lesson 2, FreeHand allows you to create several different-sized pages within the same document.

In this lesson, you will construct a three-page catalog insert for a real estate company. If you would like to review the final result of this lesson, open RREfinal.fh9 in the Complete folder within the Lesson05 folder.

This three-page catalog was created entirely in FreeHand using the program's page layout tools, which combine the text-handling features you find in page layout programs with the graphics management features you expect from a professional-level drawing program.

Designed by Tony Roame of Illustrated Concepts.

WHAT YOU WILL LEARN

- Add new page sizes to the Document Inspector
- Add and edit ruler guides
- Create path guides
- Create custom process colors
- Blend Gradient fills
- Import text into a layout
- Flow text from one page to another
- Format text using styles
- Use Xtra tools and path operations
- Wrap text around graphics
- Use and edit custom text effects
- Copy colors from imported images for use elsewhere in the document
- Print your document
- Prepare files for a commercial printer

APPROXIMATE TIME

This lesson takes approximately 2 hours to complete.

LESSON FILES

Media Files:

Lesson08\Media\House1.TIF

Lesson08\Media\House2.TIF

Lesson08\Media\House3.TIF

Lesson08\Media\House4.TIF

Starting Files:

None

Completed Project:

Lessons08\Media\RREfinal.fh9

SPECIFYING A CUSTOM PAGE SIZE

The catalog insert you'll be creating requires a custom page size, plus a specific amount of bleed area around the page. In addition, you'll enter the printer resolution of the output device that will be used to print this document. This allows FreeHand to optimize the resolution of Gradient fills and blends for the best printed results.

1] Close any open FreeHand document windows and then choose File › New to create a new document.

A page appears within a new document window. You'll change the page size and document settings to match the layout. Since this catalog is part of an ongoing project, you're going to add this custom page size to the pop-up menu in the Document Inspector. This will make it easier to select the correct page size for future pages in this document.

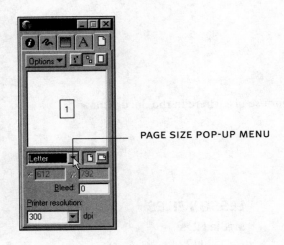

PAGE SIZE POP-UP MENU

2] Choose Windows › Inspectors › Document to display the Document Inspector. From the Page Size pop-up menu, select Edit Pages. In the Edit Pages dialog box, click the New button. In the first field, type *5 x 7 catalog*; then type *7i* as the value for x and *5i* as the value for y. Click the Close button when you are done. Back in the Document Inspector, select 5 x 7 Catalog from the pop-up menu and then select Landscape Orientation.

Creating a custom page setting will let you more easily select the correct page size when you need to add pages to this document later.

Currently, the measurement units for your document are points, so the values in these fields are displayed in points. To enter a value with a different unit of measure than the unit displayed, simply add the unit of measure to the number you enter.

For instance, when you want to enter 7 inches in a field that displays values in points, FreeHand understands that *7i* indicates 7 inches instead of 7 points.

When you click the Close button, the values you specify will be converted to the current measurement unit. Thus, your 7-inch by 5-inch page will appear as a 504-point by 360-point page in the Document Inspector.

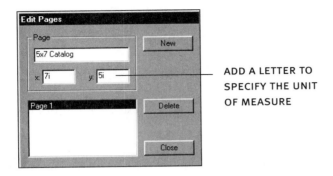

ADD A LETTER TO
SPECIFY THE UNIT
OF MEASURE

3] Choose View › Fit to Page. Type *9* as the bleed size in the Document Inspector and press Enter.

The bleed size defines how much beyond the edge of the page FreeHand will print when this document is output. Bleed size is important when preparing artwork for printing on a press. The measurement of 9 points is equal to the standard one-eighth–inch bleed you specified for the letterhead in Lesson 2.

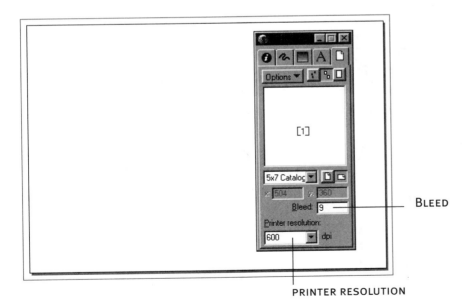

BLEED

PRINTER RESOLUTION

301

4] In the Document Inspector, set the printer resolution to 600.

Setting the printer resolution to match the characteristics of the printer or an output device that this project will be printed on enables FreeHand to optimize color transitions—Gradient fills and blends in the document—so you get the best possible results. Set this value to the resolution of your final output device. For example, as you are creating a document, you may print it on a 600-dot-per-inch (dpi) printer, and then you may send it to a service bureau for final output at 1,270 dpi. Since the final output is what you are concerned with, you would type *1270* as the printer resolution in FreeHand for that document.

5] Choose View > Magnification > 100%.

Working at actual size makes it easier to precisely adjust the size and position of the elements.

6] Close the Document Inspector and save the document as *MyCatalog* in your MyWork folder.

Instead of adding the two additional pages at this time, you will first set up one page with all the elements and guides you want to appear on every page. Then you will duplicate that page, which duplicates the elements as well, so you don't have to copy, paste, and reposition items manually.

CREATING GUIDES FOR A CONSISTENT LAYOUT

To position elements in your page consistently, you will set up several nonprinting guides on the page.

1] Show the rulers by choosing View > Page Rulers > Show and activate the Info bar by choosing Window > Toolbars > Info.

The rulers must be visible for you to add ruler guides to the page. The Info bar will help you position them accurately.

tip *The Info bar works just like the Toolbox and other toolbars. If it is docked at the top of the screen and you prefer to have it displayed as a floating panel, simply drag it toward the center of the screen.*

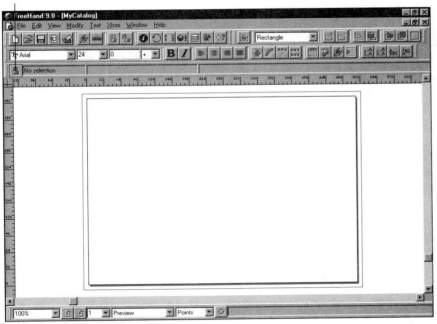

2] Change the unit of measure for this document to picas by using the Units menu at the bottom of the document window.

Picas and points are units of measurement widely used in the graphic arts field. You already have been using points to specify type sizes and strokes. There are 12 points per pica and 6 picas per inch. Each inch, therefore, is equivalent to 72 points. Using this system, you can avoid having to deal with the fractional or decimal values required when working with inches.

3] Drag a ruler guide out from the center of the vertical ruler on the left side of the document window. Watch the Info bar at the top of the window and release this guide when the x value is 31 picas.

This nonprinting guide is 31 picas out from the left edge of the page.

tip   *Make sure to drag the ruler guide out from the center of the ruler. If you drag from the top left corner of the rulers, where the vertical and horizontal rulers intersect, you'll reposition the zero point on the page. If the zero point is repositioned, all of the values for the horizontal (x) and vertical (y) positions will be measured from that new point. If this ever happens by mistake, double-click the point where the rulers intersect to reset the zero point to the lower-left corner of the page. All measurements in these lessons assume that the zero point is in this default position: the lower-left corner of the page.*

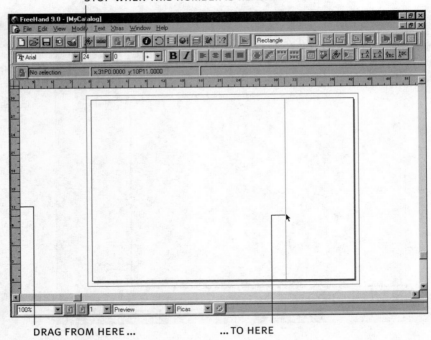

DRAG FROM HERE ...   ... TO HERE

4] Drag a ruler guide out from the horizontal ruler down to 25 picas.

You can pull ruler guides from the vertical or horizontal ruler as needed.

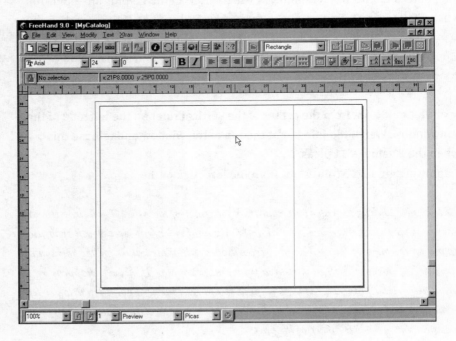

In addition to the ruler guides, elements on the page can be converted into guides. In the next step, you will create a rectangle to indicate the position of a future text block and then convert that rectangle into a guide.

5] Create a rectangle anywhere on the page using the Rectangle tool; then choose Window › Inspector › Object Inspector to display the Object Inspector. For the x dimension in the Inspector, type *3p0*. Press the Tab key to select the y value and type *3p0*. Press Tab again to select the w (width) value and type *26p0*. Then press Tab and type *19p0* as the h (height) value. Press Enter.

This rectangle is now the precise size and in the correct location required for this layout.

tip *Entering specific values in the Inspectors helps you position elements with precision.*

6] Click the Layers button on the main toolbar to display the Layers panel, or choose Window › Panels › Layers. With the rectangle selected on the page, click the name of the Guides layer to convert the selection into a guide.

If you move elements to the Guides layer, they automatically become nonprinting guides, just like the ruler guide you created earlier. You have used foreground and background layers in previous lessons. The Guides layer is special—even though it appears above the divider line in the Layers panel, elements on the Guides layer do not print. You can move this layer above or below other layers, depending on how you want the guides to appear. You can also hide and lock the Guides layer the same way you can with other layers.

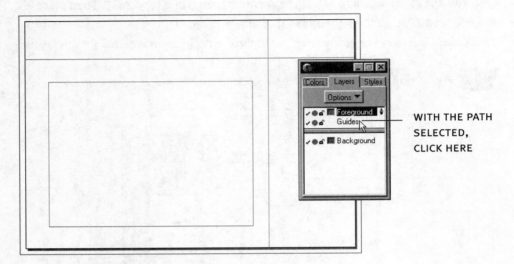

WITH THE PATH
SELECTED,
CLICK HERE

7] Create another rectangle. Position it so that the x value is *13p9* and the y value is *11p0*, and set the width to *20p0* and the height to *12p3*. Then convert this rectangle into a guide as well.

All the guides you need to position elements in this document are now in place.

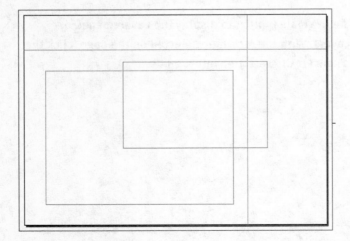

8] Hide the page rulers and the Info bar and save the document.

Now you are ready to begin assembling elements on the page.

USING THE EDIT GUIDES COMMAND

Another way to set up and manipulate guides is to use FreeHand's Edit Guides controls. In the Guides dialog box, you can create new guides in precise positions, adjust the positions of existing guides, evenly distribute guides across a page, and release guides. The next steps will help you explore these controls.

1] Create a new document. Choose View › Guides › Edit.

A new document window appears in front of your current document, where you can experiment with ruler guides. The Guides dialog box displays a list of the guides on the designated page. No guides have been created for this new document, so the list is blank.

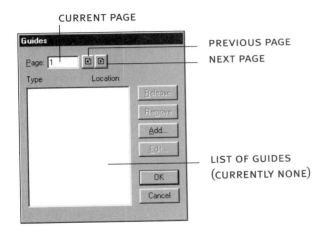

2] Click Add. Click Vertical and type *6* in the Count field, *.5i* in the First Position field, and *8i* in the Last Position field.

The First and Last Position values allow you to enter a distance in from the edge of the page where you want the first and last guides to be placed. As in all FreeHand entry fields, if you want to enter an inch value in a field that currently displays points or picas, simply add the unit after the value, such as *.5i*.

307

These settings will create six vertical ruler guides that are evenly spaced across the page, starting and ending 0.5 inch in from the left and right edges of the page.

3] Click Add to return to the Guides dialog box.

All of your new guides now appear in the Guides list, which displays the type and location of each guide.

4] Click OK in the Guides dialog box to apply these changes and view your document.

FreeHand has added the six guides to the page, positioned precisely as you indicated in the dialog boxes.

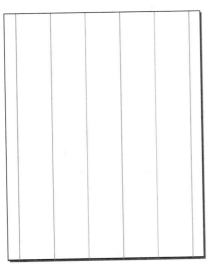

5] Return to the Guides dialog box and experiment with the other options: deleting, editing, and releasing guides.

The Edit button allows you to position each guide at a specific location on the page.

The Release button actually releases a guide from the Guides layer and changes it into a printing path on the active layer in your document. Ruler guides created by dragging out from the rulers become lines when released.

Delete will do exactly as you would expect, removing the selected guide completely from the document.

If you add a path to the Guides layer, the Guides dialog box will display the path as one of the guides in the list, and it can be modified in the same ways as any other guide.

6] Close this document and return to the MyCatalog document window.

You do not need to save changes to the Untitled document.

MIXING CUSTOM PROCESS COLORS AND BLENDING GRADIENTS

In Lesson 4, you learned that documents that use many colors (especially those that include photographic artwork) are usually printed with process colors. The real estate insert you are designing fits this description, so you will specify process colors for this document.

In the first step, you'll create a rectangle on the right side of the page. Then you will fill the rectangle with a custom process color gradient, duplicate the rectangle, and blend two gradient rectangles for a special color effect.

1] Draw a rectangle that begins at the upper-right corner of the bleed area (off of the page) and extends to the top edge of the page at the vertical ruler guide.

The bottom edge of the rectangle should be resting on the top edge of the page, and the left side of the rectangle should meet the vertical ruler guide.

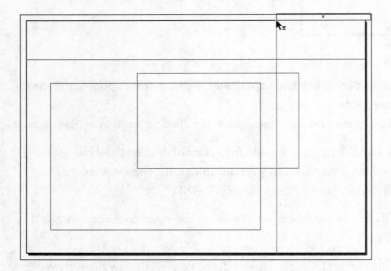

2] Display the Color Mixer by clicking the Color Mixer button on the toolbar, or choose Window › Panels › Color Mixer. Make sure the CMYK button is selected.

When you are designing artwork for print, it's important to use CMYK color. RGB color is great for the Internet and for other on-screen destinations, but it often translates poorly to paper.

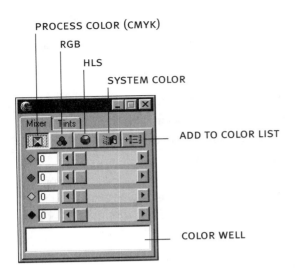

PROCESS COLOR (CMYK)
RGB
HLS
SYSTEM COLOR

ADD TO COLOR LIST

COLOR WELL

3] Move the sliders (or type in the fields) to create a new color that is 100c, 60m, 0y, 0k. When you're done, click the Add to Color List button. In the dialog box that pops up, make sure Process is selected and click the Add button. Now mix a color for 100c, 0M, 85y, 0K and add it to the Color List using the same method. Finally, mix a rich black color that is 100c, 60m, 0y, 100k.

The three new colors have been transferred to the Color List. You will use the blue and green colors right away, and you will learn about the extra black color later in this lesson.

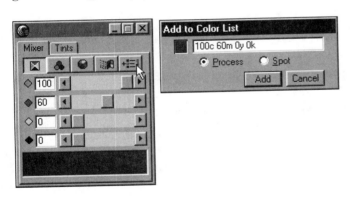

4] Double-click the color well of the Color Mixer to display the Color List; then close the Color Mixer.

Double-clicking the color well of the Color Mixer is a fast way to bring up the Color List. You can also use this technique the other way—double-click any color swatch in the Color List to bring up the Color Mixer.

311

In earlier lessons, you created Gradient fills by assigning them in the Fill Inspector. In the next step, you will learn a new way to create Gradient fills with a drag-and-drop method.

5] Click the blue swatch in the Color List and drag it toward the rectangle you just created. As you drag, hold the Control key (both Windows and Macintosh). Keep this key pressed as you release the swatch over the left side of the rectangle. Then use the Color List to set the stroke of this rectangle to None.

You can assign Gradient fills in one quick step by holding the Control key as you release a color swatch over an object. Notice that as you hold down the Control key, the swatch changes to a diamond shape. This is FreeHand's way of letting you know what will happen when you release the swatch.

...RELEASE HERE, WITH THE CONTROL KEY PRESSED

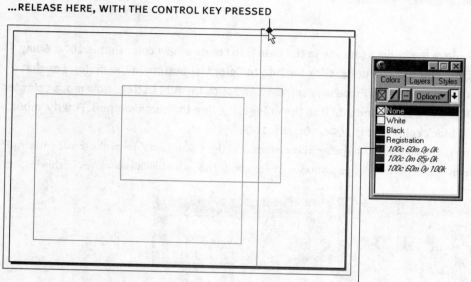

DRAG FROM HERE, AND HOLD THE CONTROL KEY...

tip   *You can also use the other modifier keys to affect the drag-and-drop behavior of color swatches. For instance, Alt (Windows) or Option (Macintosh) will make the swatch become the center color of a Radial fill. The Shift key will force the swatch to affect only the fill of an object, regardless of where the swatch is dropped on that object. Holding the Command key on a Macintosh forces the swatch to affect only the stroke, regardless of where the swatch is dropped.*

This modifier technique is especially useful when the exact angle of the gradient is not important. In this case, however, the angle of the gradient needs to be correct, so you will verify it in the next step.

312

6] Open the Fill Inspector and make sure the angle of the gradient is set to 180 degrees; then close the Fill Inspector.

Now you're ready to duplicate this rectangle to set up the other side of your blend.

7] Select the rectangle and drag it to the bottom of the bleed area. As you drag, hold the Shift key to keep the rectangle aligned correctly, and at the same time hold Alt (Windows) or Option (Macintosh) to duplicate the rectangle.

Make sure both keys are pressed when you release the mouse button. The top edge of the second rectangle should now be touching the bottom edge of the page.

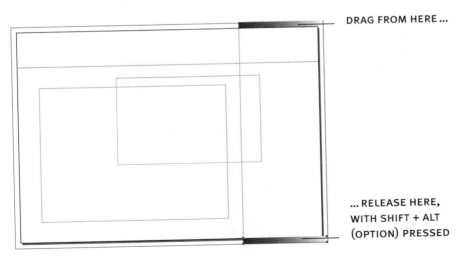

DRAG FROM HERE...

...RELEASE HERE,
WITH SHIFT + ALT
(OPTION) PRESSED

313

8] Without holding any modifier keys, drag the green swatch from the Color List to the left side of the new rectangle.

The new rectangle now has a Gradient fill from green to white. Because you did not hold down a modifier key, FreeHand did not reset the angle of the gradient. It only swapped the blue color value for the green color value, which means you will not have to return to the Fill Inspector.

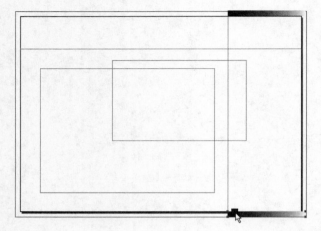

9] Select both rectangles and choose Modify › Combine › Blend.

The band of color that now appears on the right side of the page has color changing in two directions: blue to green from top to bottom, and 100 percent of a color to white from left to right.

FreeHand's ability to blend gradients opens up a whole new world of creative possibilities. Traditionally, a bitmap program such as Adobe Photoshop would be required to achieve this type of effect. By using vectors in FreeHand, you can create artwork that takes up less space, redraws faster, and can be updated more easily.

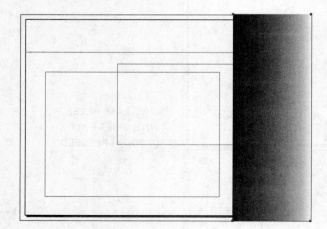

314

Notice how the color bleeds off the edge of the page.

tip *When setting up a bleed, you must do two things. First you need to specify the desired bleed size in the Document Inspector. (Your commercial printer can tell you the size of the bleed you need.) Then you need to make sure all elements you create that should run off the edge of the page also extend out to or beyond the edge of the bleed.*

10] Save your work.

CREATING TEXT AND GRAPHIC ELEMENTS

Now you will add other text and graphic elements that should appear on each page of the catalog.

1] Using the Text tool, click on the top of the page and type *roamer real estate* (all lowercase). Highlight all of the text by dragging across the type with the Text tool and then use the controls in the text toolbar to change the text to 20-point News Gothic T Bold.

You could also select the text with the Pointer tool to change all the text in the text block.

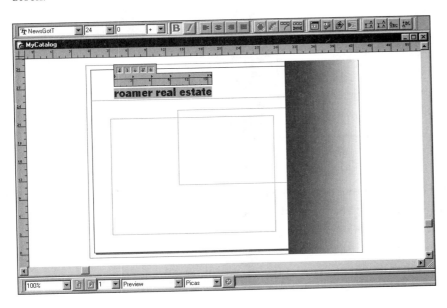

2] Move your mouse away from the text block and click another part of the screen. Then select the text block with the Pointer tool and choose Text › Convert Case › Upper.

315

When you move your mouse away from an active text block, FreeHand automatically switches to the Pointer tool. If you move back over the text block before you click an empty portion of the screen, FreeHand will switch back to the Text tool.

tip *This behavior can be turned on or off in the Preferences dialog box. Choose File > Preferences, click the Text section, then check or uncheck Text Tool Reverts to Pointer.*

FreeHand has case-conversion capabilities, so you can easily convert text to uppercase (as in this example), lowercase, title case, and sentence case.

tip *If you are likely to use the case conversion features in FreeHand regularly, you can add the convert case toolbar icons to the text toolbar. Choose Window > Toolbars > Customize and go to the Text area to find the icons you want.*

3] Position the Pointer tool over the middle handle on the right edge of the text block and click and drag about an inch to the right.

You can visually adjust the range kerning in a text block by dragging the middle handle on either side of the text block. This can be a fast and easy way to experiment with different design and typography options.

DRAG THIS HANDLE

◎ POWER TIP *You can also use the Pointer tool to adjust the size and leading of text within a text block. To change the leading in a multiple-line text block, simply drag the middle bottom handle of the text block. To adjust the size of text within the text block, drag any corner handle and hold Alt (Windows) or Option (Macintosh) when you release the mouse button. The text will expand or reduce the font size and horizontal scale to fit the size of the text block you drag.*

In this design, a specific range kerning is required. You will define the range kerning numerically in the next step.

4] Display the Text Inspector by choosing Window › Inspectors › Text. With the text block selected, change the range kerning to 15 and press Enter.
Now the range kerning is correct for the last two words. You will adjust the word *Roamer* next.

5] Double-click the text block to switch to the Text tool; then double-click the word *Roamer* **to select it. In the Text Inspector, change the type size to 50 and the range kerning to 30; then press Enter.**

To change some of the text within a text block separately, you must use the Text tool to select the desired characters.

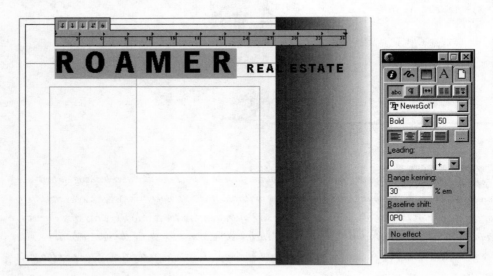

6] Click with the Text tool to the left of the word *Real* **and delete the space between** *Roamer* **and** *Real.*

Now the spacing of the words is more visually balanced.

7] Click the text with the Pointer tool to select the text block. Position the tip of the Pointer tool cursor precisely on the bottom edge of the first character in the text. Hold down the mouse button and drag the cursor toward the ruler guide that runs across the top of the page. Release the mouse when FreeHand snaps your cursor— and the baseline of the text—to the ruler guide.

This demonstrates FreeHand's Snap to Guides feature. When an object you're moving or creating comes within a few pixels of a guide, FreeHand snaps the object to the guide. You can snap the edges of objects to guides; or you can position your cursor at a significant location on the object (as you did here in pointing to the bottom of the text), and FreeHand will snap the object into position when the cursor nears the guide.

The baseline of text is the imaginary line on which all the characters sit. For example, the lowest parts of the character *m* are touching the baseline. Some characters (such as *g* and *p*) have descenders that hang below the baseline.

RELEASE WHEN THE CURSOR SNAPS TO THE GUIDE

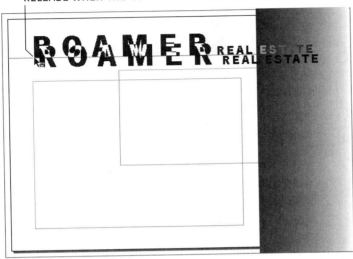

tip *Notice the snap cursor that appears as you move an element when that element is snapped to a guide. Occasionally, the snap feature can interfere when you are trying to position an element near, but not on, a guide. You can deactivate this feature by choosing View > Snap to Guides (a check mark next to this menu item indicates that the feature is turned on).*

8] With the text block selected, use the left and right arrow keys to adjust the position of the text block so that the space between *Real* and *Estate* is evenly divided by the left edge of the color band. Then press the Tab key to deselect all elements; save your work.

Use the arrow keys to tweak the position of elements in small increments.

You can control how far the arrow keys move an object in FreeHand by choosing Modify > Cursor Distance. In the dialog box that pops up, you will also notice that holding the Shift key while pressing the arrow key can cause the object to move a different distance. You can set these cursor distance fields to meet your custom needs.

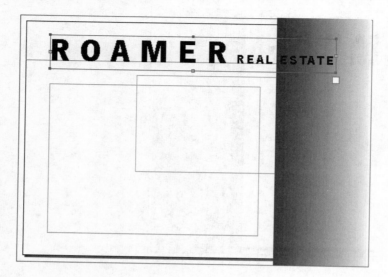

Now you'll add a rectangle below the text and fill it with a multicolored gradient.

9] Draw a wide, short rectangle below the text that extends the length of the text box. Use the Object Inspector to set the value for x to 2p0, y to 24p0, w to 36p0, and h to 0p4.

Using the Object Inspector to set precise values guarantees repeatable results.

10] Fill this rectangle with a gradient that goes from the rich black color (100c 60m 0y 100k) to white. Change the angle of the fill to 180 degrees. Now drag the rich black swatch down the color ramp until it's just above the field where you entered the degrees for the fill angle. Change the top color to blue (100c 60m 0y 0k), and set the stroke to None.

This is where the rich black you created earlier is required. If you were to use an ordinary black with process color printing, you would get an undesirable gray tone in the transition between the black and blue colors (even though everything looks fine on your monitor).

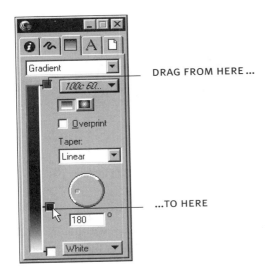

DRAG FROM HERE ...

...TO HERE

Next you will create a duplicate of this element and position it at the bottom of the page.

11] Choose Edit › Clone to create a copy of this rectangle directly on top of the original. Begin to move this copied object with the Pointer tool and hold down the Shift key after you've started to move it. Position the rectangle just above the bottom of the page so that the bottom of the rectangle is at 1p6 (about a quarter of an inch above the bottom).

321

Again, holding down Shift constrains the movement of an object.

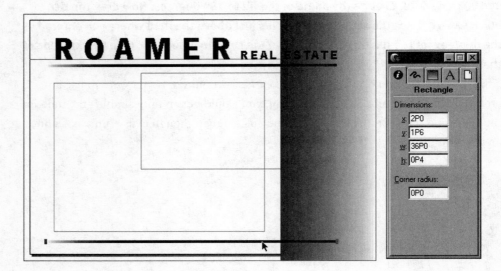

12] Save your work.

There are a few more elements to add before you are ready to duplicate the page.

USING THE XTRA OPERATIONS

The Xtra Operations toolbar offers a variety of useful features. You have already used some of them in other lessons, such as the Intersect path operation in Lesson 4. You will explore two more Xtra operations in the following steps.

1] Hold down the spacebar to activate the grabber hand; then click and drag to the left so you can see some additional pasteboard area on the right side of your page.

You're going to use this area to create a graphic element for your document.

2] Select the Line tool from the Toolbox and draw a vertical line an inch or two from the right edge of the page. The line should start above the bleed area at the top of the page and extend below the bleed area at the bottom of the page. Hold the Shift key as you release the mouse button to force FreeHand to draw a straight line.

This line is the starting point for a special graphic element.

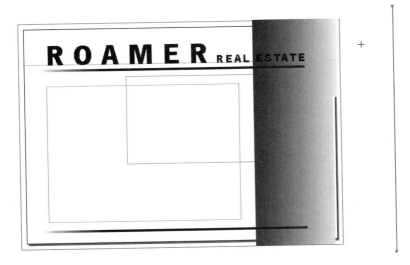

3] Display the Xtra Operations toolbar by choosing Window > Toolbars > Xtra Operations. Click three times on the Add Points button.

The Add Points button places an additional point between each existing point on the path, each time you click. This path now contains 9 points.

ADD POINTS

4] Select the top point of this path and delete it. Starting with the new top point, select every other point, so that alternating points are selected. Position your mouse over one of the highlighted points and then click and drag about 3 picas to the right.

This procedure can be a quick way of achieving a sawtooth effect. In this case, however, you're going to go a little further.

323

5] Use the Pointer tool to drag a selection marquee around the entire path. With all points highlighted, bring up the Object Inspector, click the Curve Point Type button, and check the box for Automatic.

FreeHand converts all the selected points to curve points, and because you checked Automatic, the control handles extend to provide the smoothest possible curves between these points.

CONTROL HANDLES EXTEND WHEN AUTOMATIC IS CHECKED

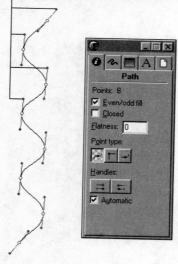

6] Switch to the Stroke Inspector and enter a stroke width of 0p23. Set the Cap option to Round (the middle button).

Now you have a very thick stroke with rounded ends, and you're ready to use another path operation in the Xtra Operations toolbar.

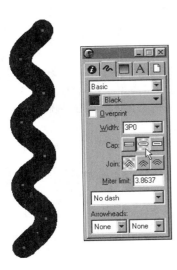

7] Make sure the path is selected; then click the Expand Stroke button in the Xtra Operations toolbar. When the dialog box pops up, click OK or press Enter.
The Expand Stroke operation in FreeHand recognizes the attributes of the line that you have selected and automatically uses those values in the dialog box. Since this is exactly what you want, all you have to do is click OK.

Now this element has been converted from an open path with a black stroke to a closed path with a black fill and no stroke. The shape, however, remains identical.

EXPAND STROKE

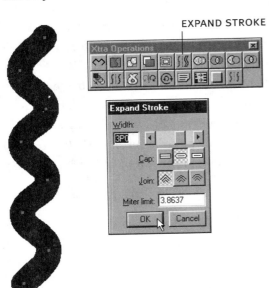

325

In the next step, you're going to use one of FreeHand's specialty tools.

8] Choose Window › Toolbars › Xtra Tools. Double-click the 3D Rotate tool to bring up its settings panel. Set the perspective amount to 33p0, and make sure that Rotate From is set to Mouse click.

This controls the amount of perspective that FreeHand applies to a path, and the point from which 3D rotation occurs. If you click the Expert button, you will have the option of specifying the projection behavior in addition to the rotate behavior. For this exercise, though, the Easy setting is sufficient.

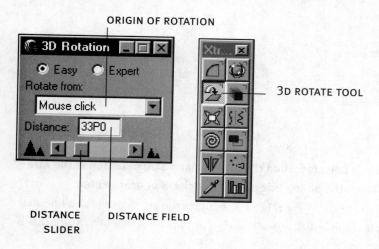

ORIGIN OF ROTATION

3D ROTATE TOOL

DISTANCE SLIDER

DISTANCE FIELD

9] Position the 3D Rotate tool in the center of the path. Notice your vertical position as indicated by the gray line on the vertical ruler at the left edge of the screen. Click and drag up approximately 3 picas, holding the Shift key as you drag. Release the mouse button; then release the Shift key. Now position the 3D Rotate tool over the same spot on the path and click and drag up 3 picas, again holding the Shift key. Then repeat one more time, again dragging up 3 picas from the center of the path.

By repeating this step three times, you achieve a more exaggerated effect, which in this case is exactly what you want. If your path does not look similar to the examples here, select Undo from the File menu a few times and try again. The 3D Rotate tool can have a significantly different effect, depending on where you first click and drag.

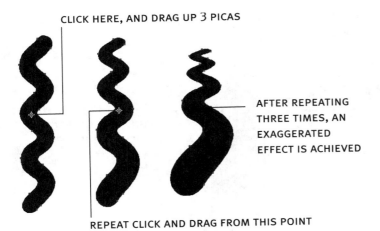

CLICK HERE, AND DRAG UP 3 PICAS

AFTER REPEATING THREE TIMES, AN EXAGGERATED EFFECT IS ACHIEVED

REPEAT CLICK AND DRAG FROM THIS POINT

10] Close the Xtra Tools toolbar; then switch back to the Pointer tool by pressing the zero key on your numeric keypad or keyboard. Select your reshaped path and move it until it is centered over the band of color on the right side of the page.

The path still needs to be adjusted a little. You will make the necessary adjustments with the transform handles.

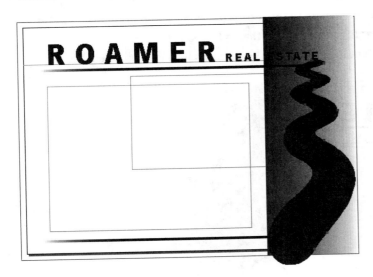

11] Double-click the path to activate the transform handles. Move the cursor over the dotted line at the top of the transform handles. When the skew icon appears, drag to the right until the top of the path touches the outer edge of the bleed area on the right side.

327

Skewing the path brings it more closely into the position you want. Now all you have to do is adjust the height slightly.

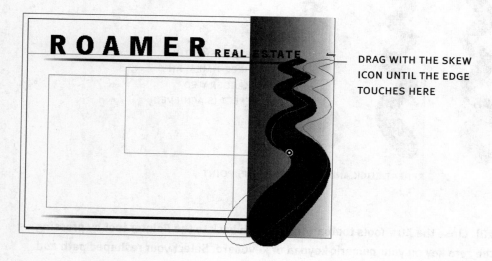

DRAG WITH THE SKEW ICON UNTIL THE EDGE TOUCHES HERE

12] With the transform handles still active, position the mouse over the bottom-center handle and drag up until the bottom of the path touches the bottom of the bleed area. Then move the mouse to the top-center handle and drag down until the top of the object is slightly under the bar that is beneath the text.

Now this graphic element is in place. All that remains is to give it the correct fill.

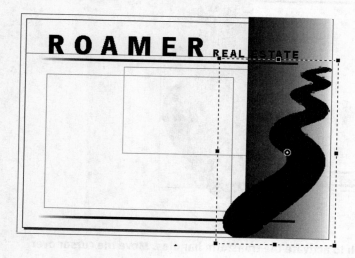

13] Save your work.

In the next steps, you will work with transparency in FreeHand.

USING TRANSPARENCY IN FREEHAND

The Lens fills in FreeHand seem to offer an endless variety of creative possibilities. In the next steps, you will explore three different transparency options provided by the Lens fills.

1] Open the Fill Inspector and set the fill for this object to Lens. Click OK if the spot color warning dialog box pops up; then set the Lens type to Transparency, the color to blue (100c 60m 0y 0k), and the opacity to 15%. Select the Objects Only check box near the bottom of the Fill Inspector.

Now this graphic element is complete. Did you notice the effect of the Objects Only option? The colored fill disappears over blank parts of the page; now only actual objects on the page are affected by the Lens fill.

note *If you are working with spot colors in your document, any portions of spot color that appear under a Lens fill will be converted to process color when you output the file. Also note that EPS files are affected by Lens fills only on your monitor. Lens fills have no effect on printed EPS files. The only exception is that when you use the Magnify Lens fill, EPS files are magnified properly. You are better off using TIFF files for bitmap images. Since FreeHand now recognizes clipping paths in TIFF files, you will be able to use TIFF files the same way as you use EPS files.*

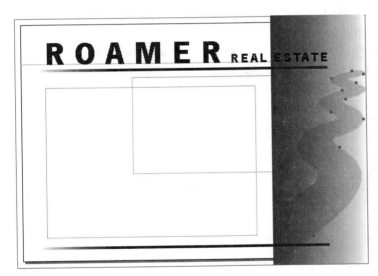

2] Create a rectangle that is 10p0 wide and 6p6 high and position it about 1 pica above the bottom line.

The rectangle is in position vertically, but to get it in position horizontally, you will need to change your view mode.

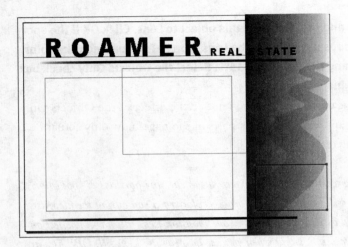

3] Switch to Keyline view using the pop-up menu at the bottom of your screen. Zoom in to 200% for a better view and then use the left and right arrow keys to move the box so that it is centered between the left edge of the color band and the right edge of the page.

It's always a good idea to zoom in when you need to fine-tune elements, and sometimes it's necessary to switch to Keyline view, where fills and strokes don't obscure your view (in this case, your view of the edge of the page).

330

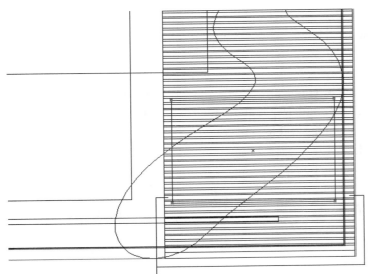

ADJUST SO THE SPACE IS EVEN ON EITHER SIDE OF
THE RECTANGLE, BETWEEN THE EDGE OF THE PAGE
AND THE EDGE OF THE COLOR BAND.

4] Switch back to 100% magnification and to Preview mode. In the Fill Inspector, give this rectangle a Lens fill and set the Lens type to Lighten, with a 50% value. Set the stroke to None.

Here you can see the effect of a different type of Lens fill. The color of objects under this fill are always 50% lighter—no other color shifting takes place.

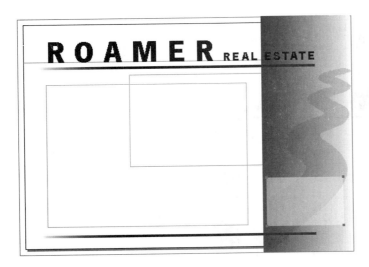

To draw the next object, you need to see the guides without obstruction. The best way to make guides appear above the other elements on your page is to adjust their position in the Layers panel.

5] Open the Layers panel by choosing Window › Panels › Layers; then position your mouse over the Guides layer and drag it above the Foreground layer.

When you need to make guides visible over other artwork, simply drag the Guides layer above the other layers.

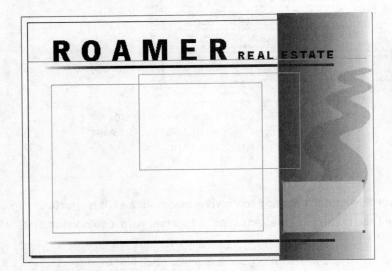

6] Draw a rectangle over the upper path guide on the page.

This will become a drop shadow for your photos.

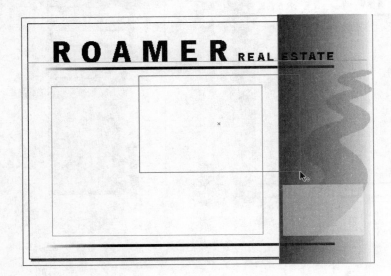

7] Display the Transform panel by double-clicking one of the transform tools in the toolbox, or choose Modify › Transform › Move. Make sure the far-left icon is selected in the Transform panel; set the move distance to -0p4 in both the x and y fields and then press Enter or click Move (Windows) or Apply (Macintosh).

The Move section of the Transform panel is a great way to move objects specific, repeatable distances.

8] In the Fill Inspector, give this rectangle a Lens fill and set the Lens type to Darken. Set the darken percentage to 30% and set the stroke to None.

Now all of the constant, unchanging graphics for this layout are in place.

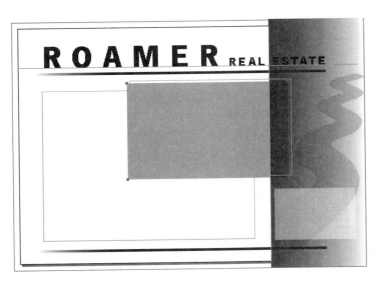

333

USING LAYERS TO SEPARATE TYPES OF ARTWORK

As you learned in Lesson 4, layers can be used to make the stacking order of artwork more manageable. You can also use layers to separate constant foreground elements from changeable foreground elements. Assigning unique color swatches to the layers helps you distinguish which elements are on certain layers.

1] Deselect all elements. Display the Layers panel and double-click the Foreground layer to highlight it. Rename the Foreground layer *Constant*. **Add a new layer by choosing New from the Options pop-up menu and name the new layer** *Changing*. **Make sure the Constant layer is below the Guides layer, and the Changing layer is above the Guides layer.**

It's important to name layers so you can readily determine the purpose of each layer and easily identify the stacking order. The Guides layer is positioned in the stacking order so that you can see the guides over the constant elements, but the guides will not obscure the changing elements you will be working with for the rest of the project.

2] Display the Color Mixer and the Color List by double-clicking the Changing layer's color swatch. If the Layers panel is docked with the Color List, switch back to the Layers panel by clicking its tab in the panel.

As you can see, the double-clicking method you learned earlier in this lesson also works when you double-click a swatch in the Layers panel.

3] Create a bright red color in the Color Mixer and drag a color swatch from the color well in the Color Mixer over the color swatch for the Changing layer. Close the Color Mixer when you are done.

Assigning a unique color to this layer will help you distinguish which layer a selected object is located on, since the color of points and handles of selected objects will be the same as the color of the layer

4] Lock the Constant layer and close the Layers panel. Save your work.

Locking the Constant layer prevents you from accidentally moving or altering the constant objects. Now you are ready to add a text block and use one of FreeHand's text effects.

USING TEXT EFFECTS

Text effects in FreeHand provide a unique way to assign graphics to individual characters of text. Each of the text effects has characteristics, such as color and position, that you can control. You are going to explore one of these effects in the next steps.

1] Choose File > Import, and select RREcopy1.rtf from the Media folder within the Lesson08 folder. Position the cursor in the upper-left corner of the white box at the bottom of the color band.

The text you imported has already been formatted. All you need to do is assign a text effect to the first line of text.

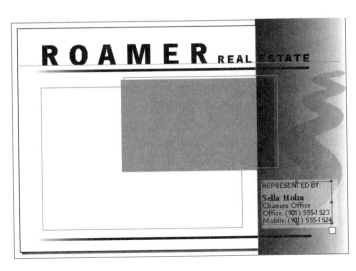

2] Select the first line of text by dragging across it with the Text tool. Display the Text Inspector by choosing Window › Inspectors › Text. Click the Effects pop-up menu (which currently says No Effect) and select Underline.

The Underline effect is applied to the text you highlighted on the first line.

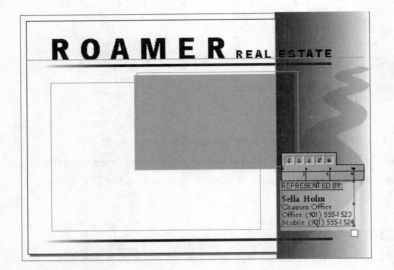

3] Click the Effects pop-up menu again and this time select Edit. In the dialog box that is displayed, set the position to –4, leave the width at 1, and set the color to green (100c 0m 85y 0k). Press Enter or click OK when you are done.

The Underline effect is now lower and colored correctly. Other text effects, such as highlight and shadow, have similar editing options.

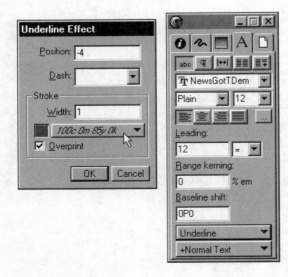

In the next step you are going to align the text block inside the white box.

4] Display the Layers panel and unlock the Constant layer. Select the text block and Shift-click the white box. Display the Align panel (Window › Panels › Align) and center the text block in the white box. Lock the Constant layer again when the objects are aligned; then close the Layers panel.

Zoom in if you have trouble selecting both elements. The fastest way to center two objects with the Align panel is to click in the center of the grid in the Align panel and then press Enter or click Apply (Windows) or Align (Macintosh).

Notice that when you selected the text and the white box, it was easy to tell they were on different layers because their handles were different colors.

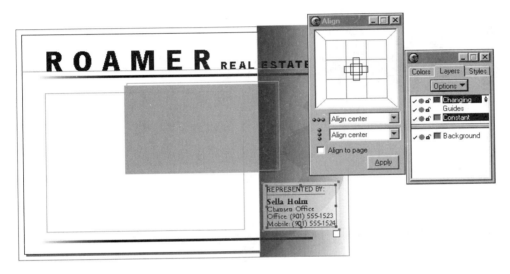

Now you are ready to duplicate the page.

DUPLICATING PAGES IN A DOCUMENT

The basic design you just created will serve as a master for all the pages of the catalog. You will now create two additional pages that look just like the one you have been working on.

1] Zoom out to 50% by choosing 50% from the Magnification pop-up menu at the bottom of your document window. Hold the spacebar to activate the grabber hand; then drag to the left until you see a large area of the pasteboard to the right of the page.

Reducing the view enables you to see where your pages will be going.

2] Select the Page tool from the toolbar; then drag page 1 to the right. Press Alt (Windows) or Option (Macintosh) as you drag. Release the mouse button first; then release the Alt or Option key.

Using the Page tool is the fastest and easiest way to duplicate and move pages exactly where you want them on the pasteboard. Simply click and drag with the Page tool to move pages, or hold down the Alt or Option key at the same time to duplicate pages.

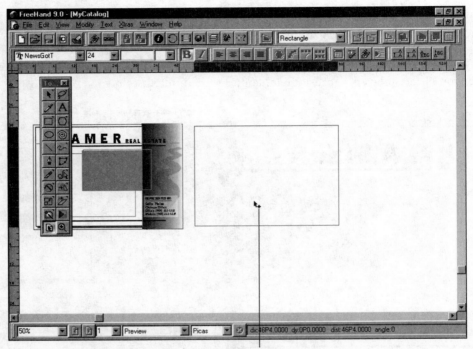

HOLD ALT (OPTION) AS YOU DRAG

3] Click page 2 with the Page tool and drag it to the right in the same manner, holding down Alt (Windows) or Option (Macintosh) as you release the mouse button. Make page 1 fill your document window by selecting Page 1 from the Page Selector menu at the bottom of the document window.

Now all of the pages are in place. You can switch between page views in several ways. You can use the pop-up menu, as you did here, or you can click the Previous Page and Next Page buttons. You can also switch pages from the keyboard by pressing Ctrl and Page Up or Page Down (Windows), or Command and Page Up or Page Down (Macintosh).

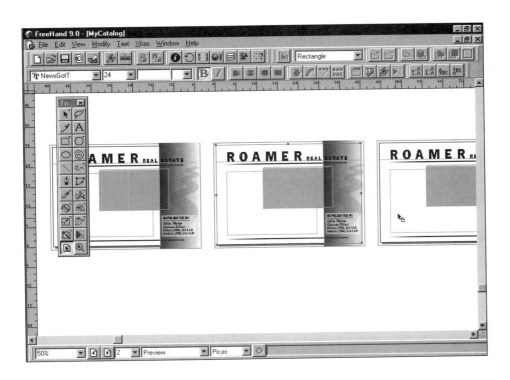

IMPORTING TEXT AND LINKING TEXT BLOCKS

The text for this project has already been entered into a word processor and saved as a Rich Text Format (RTF) file. FreeHand can import RTF files, which retain text formatting characteristics, and ASCII text files, which do not retain any formatting.

In this task, you will import the text into your layout, starting on page 1. Then you will continue the text on the other two pages by linking text blocks together, allowing the text to flow from one text block to another.

The text will flow into text blocks that duplicate the size and position of the large rectangular guide you positioned on the page earlier.

1] Choose File › Import, locate RREcopy2.rtf in the Media folder within the Lesson08 folder, and click Open. Position the import cursor at the upper-left corner of the large rectangular guide, drag down to the bottom-right corner of this rectangle, and then release the mouse.

Formatted text flows into this text block. RTF files contain both text and formatting.

The text will not look like the finished layout yet—some of the text is not formatted properly, and this page contains more text than you need for page 1.

Notice the large solid circle in the Link box, the small square near the bottom corner of the text block. This indicates an overflow: there is more text than will fit within the current text box.

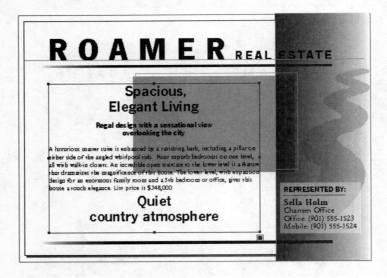

Before you can flow the remaining text onto the other pages, you must first create a text block for the text to flow into on each of those pages.

2] Change to page 2. Use the Text tool to create a text block the same size and position as the large rectangular guide. Then change to page 3 and create a new text block in the same position on this page. Save your work.

Now each page has a text container, so you are ready to link the text blocks together.

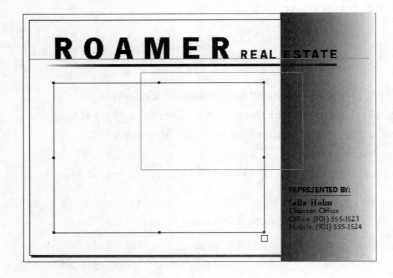

3] Choose View › Fit All. Close any panels that interfere with your view of the pages (except the Toolbox).

This reduces the view so you can see all of the pages within your document. This will help in the next step, where you will link the text block on page 1 to the text blocks on the other two pages.

4] Select the text block on page 1 with the Pointer tool to see the Link box with its filled circle indicating an overflow. Point to the Link box and drag a link line to the inside of the empty text block on page 2.

  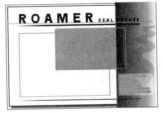

The text will flow into the text block on page 2, and the Link box for this text block will also indicate an overflow.

5] Repeat this process for page 3 by dragging a link line from the Link box on page 2 into the empty text block on page 3.

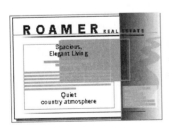 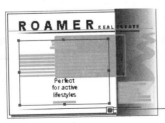 

The text is now linked across all three pages. All of the text fits.

6] Select the text block on page 1 and choose View › Magnification › 100%.

FreeHand centers the selected elements on the screen when you change the magnification, so you now see the text block on page 1.

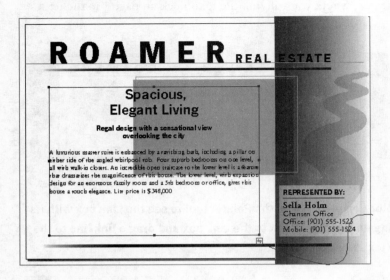

7] Save your work.

DEFINING PARAGRAPH STYLES

In Lesson 4, you used object styles to apply preset fill and stroke attributes to multiple objects. Paragraph styles can provide similar benefits for text.

1] Choose Window › Panels › Styles to display the Styles panel. Use the Text tool to select the title at the beginning of the text ("Spacious, Elegant Living").

This was imported as 24-point News Gothic T Demi. Now create a style based on the selected text.

2] Choose New from the Options menu at the top of the Styles panel.

A new paragraph style named Style-1 appears in the panel. Paragraph styles can record text formatting information, including font, size, alignment, color, and leading, that you can apply to paragraphs elsewhere in the document.

3] Double-click Style-1. Type a new name, *Headline*, and press Enter.

The style automatically picks up the formatting of the selected text, and that text now is linked to the Headline style.

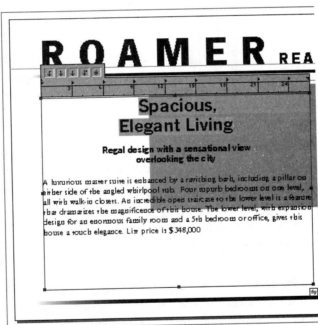

4] Using the Text tool, double-click the word *Regal* in the second paragraph to select that word. Create another new style and name it *Subhead*.

Styles apply to entire paragraphs. Selecting just a portion of a paragraph when creating a style records the characteristics of that text and assigns that new style to the entire paragraph to which the selected text belongs.

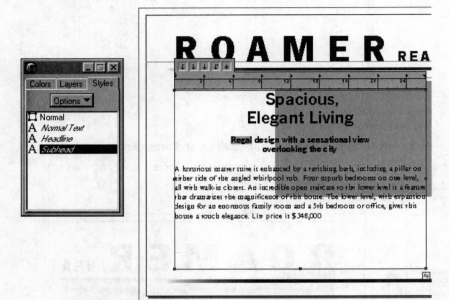

The last remaining new style you need is for the description. However, suppose you select the word *luxurious* in the first line of the description paragraph. This text is 10-point URW Garamond Regular—but the price at the end of this description is in the demi version of the same font. Styles apply to entire paragraphs, so you will create a style for the regular text and then manually apply the demi weight of the font to just those words within the paragraph that require it.

5] Select the description paragraph and display the Text Inspector. Choose the equal sign from the Leading Options menu and specify a leading of 12 points to specify a fixed leading. Then create a new style and name it *Body*.

When you create a new style, the characteristics of the style are set to match those of the first character selected. Assigning this new style to the paragraph eliminated the boldfacing used for some of the words in the paragraph.

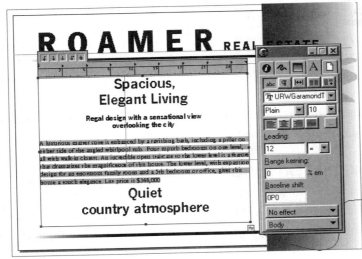

6] Select the last sentence of the description ("List price is $348,000") and change it to bold type.

Local formatting of individual characters within a paragraph must be performed manually, one selection at a time—you cannot select separate portions of the text at the same time. When local formatting has been applied to selected text, the Styles panel displays a plus sign next to the style name, to indicate that this text no longer exactly matches the style characteristics.

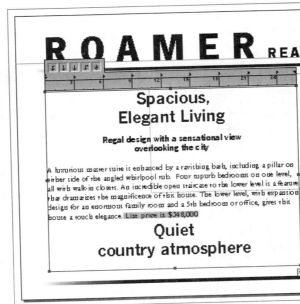

Depending on the level of magnification, you may not be able to readily distinguish bold type from plain type with certain fonts. If you want to be certain that the change was made, zoom in to get a closer, more accurate view.

7] Save your work.

The three styles you need have been defined, so now you can apply them throughout the remaining text.

USING THE TEXT EDITOR

In addition to directly editing the text on the page, you can also open text in FreeHand's Text Editor. This enables you to edit an entire text block and apply formatting and paragraph styles without having to change from page to page.

1] Click the "Spacious, Elegant Living" text block with the Pointer tool and choose Text › Editor to open the Text Editor window. Adjust the size and position of the Text Editor so you can also see the Styles panel.

The Text Editor displays the contents of the selected text block (and all linked text blocks) in a word processor view. This enables you to edit and apply formatting to this entire text block without changing pages.

The Text Editor displays the text in the actual font and type size unless you turn on the 12 Point Black option, which changes the display to 12-point black text. (This option is especially useful when editing white or light-colored text.) However, alignment settings, paragraph spacing, and leading are not visible in the Text Editor; all text is aligned on the left side and single spaced.

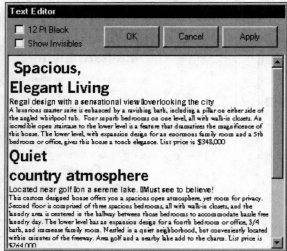

2] Turn on Show Invisibles by clicking its check box at the top of the Text Editor window.

FreeHand now displays all of the nonprinting characters in your text, making it easy to see where spaces, returns, and tabs are entered. Paragraph marks indicate returns. The small dots that appear between words indicate spaces. Tabs are displayed as small right-pointing arrows, although this text block does not contain any tabs.

note   *You can see the invisible (nonprinting) items only within the Text Editor window. Leaving this option on in the Text Editor has no effect on the display of text on the pages or on the printing of your documents.*

3] Scroll down in the Text Editor window and select the starting lines for the second house described in the text, "Quiet country atmosphere." Click Headline once in the Styles panel to apply the Headline formatting.

The font, size, and alignment of the Headline paragraph style are applied to the paragraph containing the selected text. Most importantly, the text is connected to the style name, and now the attributes of the text can be edited without selecting the text directly. You can simply make a change once by editing the style itself, and all text connected to that style will be changed at the same time.

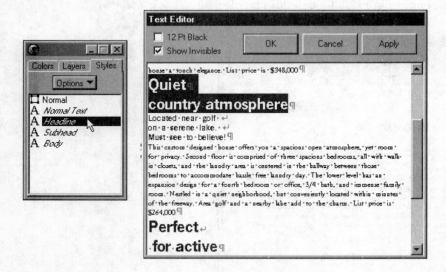

Styles apply to entire paragraphs, even though you may have selected only one word within the paragraph, as the next step demonstrates.

4] Select one word of the next paragraph ("Located...") and apply the Subhead style. Then select a word in the description paragraph and apply the Body style.

As you work through the rest of the text applying styles in the Text Editor, you don't have to worry about changing pages.

5] Apply local formatting by changing the last sentence of the description (the price of the house) to bold type.

The "List price..." sentence should be set to URW Garamond Demi.

6] Select a word in the starting line for the last house ("Perfect for active lifestyles") and apply the Headline style. Repeat steps 4 and 5 to format the remaining text.

The description of the last house also has a "List price..." sentence at the end that should be changed to URW Garamond Demi.

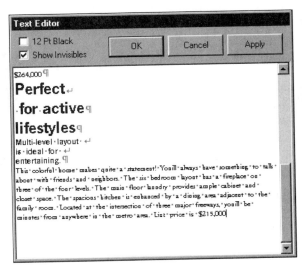

7] Click OK to close the Text Editor window. Switch to page 2 and then to page 3 to see the formatted text on all of the pages.

The text is completely formatted, but it will not fit the pages properly until you add the graphics.

8] Select the Pointer tool and click an empty part of the pasteboard to deselect all elements. Return to page 1.

tip You have used the Tab key to deselect elements as you work. Be careful not to press the Tab key when text blocks are being edited, or FreeHand will enter a Tab character in the text instead of deselecting the element.

◉ POWER TIP Macintosh users can also press Command+Tab to safely deselect text blocks, even when they are being edited.

Before you finish with the text, it is a good idea to check the spelling.

9] Choose Text › Spelling to display the Spelling window. Click Start and review each suspected error.

Suspected errors will be identified for your review. For actual spelling errors, such as the word *supurb*, click the Change or Change All button. In this document, you will be asked about possible duplication errors, such as the word *Office* where it appears twice in the white box at the bottom of the page. In addition, FreeHand's dictionary will not recognize the name *Sella* and will present it as a possible error. When the capitalization or spelling displayed for your review is actually correct (such as the name *RoamerReal* which appears as one word, since you took out the space), click Ignore to skip this occurrence or click Ignore All to skip all occurrences of the suspected error. If a misspelling is found, FreeHand will suggest possible alternatives to choose from. Select the correct spelling and then click Change to correct this instance or click Change All to automatically correct every occurrence of this error in the document.

Remember that, like the spell check features in other applications, the Spelling feature will help you identify obvious errors. It is not, however, a substitute for careful proofreading of your work.

UNRECOGNIZED WORD

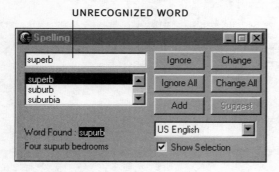

10] When FreeHand indicates that it is finished checking the document, close the Spelling window and save your work.

IMPORTING IMAGES

Next you will import the photographs for this catalog insert.

1] Return to page 1. Choose File › Import, locate House1.tif in the Media folder within the Lesson08 folder, and click Open. Position the import cursor at the upper-left corner of the small rectangular guide and click once to place the graphic on the page.

When importing graphics, always just click to put the image on the page, rather than dragging the import cursor as you do to define a text area when importing text. Clicking once will put the image on the page with its original size and proportions. If you drag the cursor, you will distort the graphic to fit between the points on the page where you start and stop dragging.

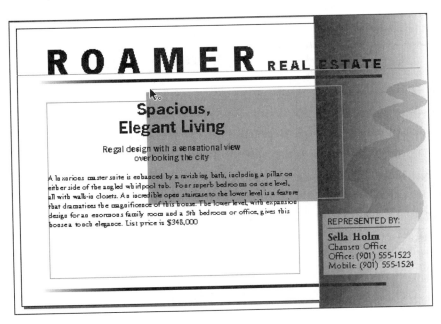

tip *If the CMYK image appears murky and dark on your monitor, you can adjust your color preferences in FreeHand to improve its appearance. Choose File > Preferences and select the Color section. At the bottom of the Color section, choose Color Tables from the Type pop-up menu, and from the Monitor Simulates pop-up menu choose Separations Printer. Your image quality should improve significantly.*

2] Switch to page 2 and repeat step 1 to import the House2.tif image.

3] Repeat step 1 again to position the House3.tif image on page 3.

As you can see, the image on page 3 is marked FPO, which means For Position Only. You will learn how to substitute one placed image for another later in this lesson.

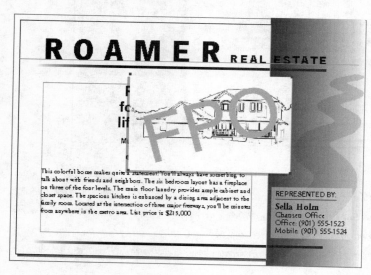

All three images are in the correct position on their respective pages. However, the images overlap the text on all three pages. You will fix this in the next task.

4] Return to page 1 and save your work.

WRAPPING TEXT AROUND GRAPHICS

FreeHand can easily run text around graphics. You will use this capability to fit the images into the layout without overlapping the text.

1] Select the image on page 1 and choose Text › Run Around Selection. Assign text wrapping to the selected image by clicking the button at the top right of the dialog box. Specify a space of 11 points along the left and bottom edges of the image.

Since your document is set to measure in picas, the values in this dialog box are displayed as 0p0, which represents zero picas and zero points. You must type *11pt* to specify 11 points. (Alternatively, you could type *0p11*, which represents zero picas and 11 points.) If you just type *11* with no units, FreeHand will set the standoff, or space between the text and the graphic, to 11 picas (11 picas equals nearly 2 inches).

The left and top standoff values can remain at zero, since text will not be touching the image along those edges in this layout.

CLICK TO REMOVE TEXT WRAPPING FROM A SELECTED OBJECT

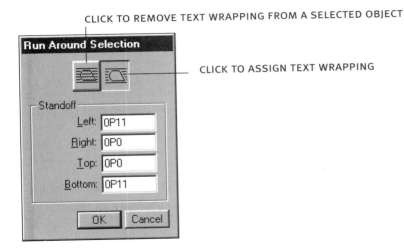

CLICK TO ASSIGN TEXT WRAPPING

2] Click OK in the Run Around Selection dialog box.

The text now flows around the graphic, with a small space between the graphic and the text along the image's right and bottom edges.

If your text stays about an inch away from the right and bottom edges of the graphic, go back to the Run Around Selection dialog box and type *0p11* (that is, 11 points instead of 11 picas).

If the text does not wrap around the image at all, choose Modify > Arrange > Bring to Front—graphics must be in front of text for this feature to work.

The text should wrap around the image, and the entire description should fit on this page. (The description on each page ends with the price of the house.)

No text below this paragraph should appear on page 1. If text does appear below this point, you will need to adjust the size of this text block. (If the text fits properly on this page, skip to step 4.)

3] If the start of the next headline appears at the bottom of page 1, use the Pointer tool to drag the bottom corner handle of the text block up slightly so the next headline no longer fits in this block.

You must drag a *corner* handle to make this adjustment. Dragging the bottom middle handle of the text block adjusts the leading for the text block, but will not change the amount of text that the block contains.

When you make this text block shorter, the text that no longer appears in the block is automatically pushed to the top of the text block on the next page, where it belongs.

Once the text on this page fits as it should, you are ready to go to the next page.

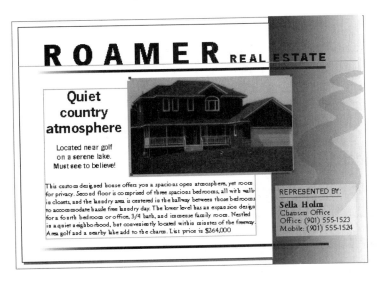

4] Repeat steps 1 through 3 for pages 2 and 3.

The text should now flow around the graphic on each page as desired.

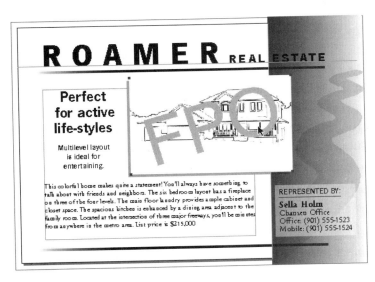

5] Save your work.

355

USING THE LINKS DIALOG BOX

In this task, you will replace the FPO image on page 3.

1] Choose Edit › Links to display the Links window.

The Links window lists the three TIFF images you imported. It shows that they are CMYK TIFF files as well as their sizes and the pages where the graphics are located.

One of the advantages of linked files is that if the original image is modified after it has been imported as a linked image, FreeHand will automatically update the image in your FreeHand document.

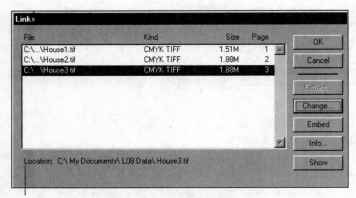

FULL DIRECTORY PATH OF THE SELECTED LINK

The buttons on the right side of this window provide direct control over the images in your document. Info provides more detailed information about the selected graphic. Change enables you to substitute another graphic for the one currently in place. Select the desired graphic and click Embed if you want the selected graphic to be completely contained within the FreeHand document. Embedded graphics are not linked to disk files, so you can achieve high-resolution printing without supplying the original disk files for the embedded images. Using embedded graphics can make it easier to transfer FreeHand files without having to worry about auxiliary images.

Embedded graphics do have their drawbacks, however. Embedding many high-resolution images will dramatically increase the size of your FreeHand document and may slow down FreeHand's performance (though you may be able to counteract that drawback somewhat by switching to the Fast Preview mode).

When an embedded image is selected, the Extract button is available so you can export the image as a linked file on a disk.

2] In the Links dialog box, click the House3.tif link and click the Change button. In the Change dialog box, select House4.tif in the Media folder within the Lesson08 folder. Click Open to select the correct image; then click OK to save your change and dismiss the Links dialog box.

The correct image now appears in place of the FPO image on page 3. Notice that the text wrapping is the same as it was with the FPO image.

There is one last task remaining before you complete your work on this layout.

USING COLORS FROM BITMAP IMAGES

Another exciting tool allows you to copy a color from any element in the document, including colors within a bitmap image. You can then use that color elsewhere within your document.

1] Select the Eyedropper tool from the Toolbox. Then display the Color List.

You will pick up a color from the image on this page and use that color for the subhead. This will tie the text and illustration together nicely.

2] Position the tool over the garage door and select a medium tan color. Drag the color swatch into the Color List.

Your color is added to the list, so you can use it for other elements in your document. It is defined in this list by its CMYK values since the image is a CMYK TIFF file.

3] With the Text tool, select the entire subhead on page 1, "Regal...city." Drag the color swatch for your new color from the Color List and drop it on the selected text. Click an empty part of the pasteboard to see the results.

The subhead text now appears in the color that you picked up from the image.

4] Go to page 2 and add a medium green color from the side of the garage near the window to the Color List. Apply that color to the entire subhead on this page, "Located...believe!" Repeat this process for page 3, applying a color of your choice from the image on page 3 to the entire subhead "Multilevel...entertaining."

The three new colors are displayed in the Color List.

5] Return to page 1 and save your work.

The layout is now complete.

USING FIND AND REPLACE GRAPHICS FOR TEXT

Sometimes clients change their minds at the last minute. They want colors adjusted, text emphasized differently, and other countless time-intensive tasks. Some of the features in the Find and Replace Graphics panel can help you make these changes more easily.

In this layout, the client wants to add more emphasis to the last sentence of each description, where the list price is shown. You are going to provide that emphasis by changing the font to a bolder face, but rather than selecting each sentence manually (which would take some time), you are going to let Find and Replace Graphics come to the rescue.

1] Choose Edit › Find and Replace › Graphics. Click the Find and Replace tab; then select Font in the Attribute pop-up menu. In the Change In menu, select Document. The Font attribute allows you to find and replace text based on typeface, style, and size criteria. In this case, you are going to search for URW Garamond Demi and replace it with URW Garamond ExtraBold.

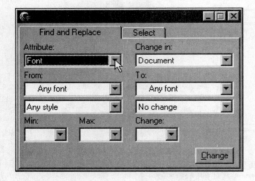

2] In the From pop-up menu, select URW Garamond Demi. In the To menu, select URW Garamond ExtraBold. Type *10* in each of the fields labeled Min, Max, and Change.

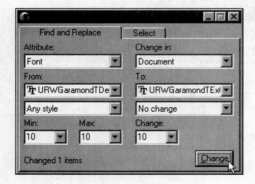

360

Notice that you could have changed the text to a larger point size at the same time, if that had been requested. This section of the Find and Replace Graphics panel can be very useful in situations like these.

3] Click the Change button.

FreeHand now seeks out all 10-point URW Garamond Demi text and replaces it with 10-point URW Garamond ExtraBold. Go to the text on page 1 to see for yourself that the change occurred.

You can imagine how much time you would have saved if this was a 20-page document, and multiple changes needed to be made on each page. Keep this feature in mind when you are working with text in FreeHand.

4] Save your work.

Now you are ready to print your document.

PRINTING YOUR DOCUMENT

Now it is time to print your work. FreeHand is designed to take full advantage of PostScript printers and high-resolution output devices, which are the standard for desktop publishing and the graphic arts community. However, FreeHand can print to other types of printers as well. If you are printing to a non-PostScript printer, the options displayed in the Print dialog box will vary depending upon the type of printer selected.

If your system is configured to print to a PostScript printer or other high-resolution output device, FreeHand offers several special capabilities when it comes time to print. The steps in this task illustrate the options available for PostScript printers.

1] Choose File › Print to display the Print dialog box.

On Macintosh computers running OS 8.0 and later, you will need to select FreeHand from the General pop-up menu in the Print dialog box. If your system is not configured to print to a PostScript output device, the dialog box will be different than the example shown here.

A variety of controls enables you to set the most common printing options within this dialog box. The Print Setting menu provides quick access to preset or custom print setup configurations.

2] Click the Setup button to display the Print Setup dialog box.

Print Setup enables you to customize settings for this print job or specify print settings you can use for future print jobs. The preview window on the left shows how the document will print on the page with the current settings. At the right, three tabbed panels allow control over printing separations, imaging options, and paper size and orientation. At the top left, the name of the current print settings file is displayed.

You can save your print settings in a settings file that then becomes available from a menu in the Print dialog box. You record custom settings by clicking the Save Print Settings button (the Plus sign) at the top left of the Print Setup dialog box.

The Print Setup dialog box has three tabbed sections. The first one you see, Separations, controls how your printer will print the colors in your document—as a composite image, with all the colors printing on the same page, or as separations, with each color printing on a different sheet (this is the setting used by printers to create separate printing plates for each color). A commercial printer can advise you how to use the other settings in this dialog box when you need output for a printing press.

362

> **tip**   *Print settings can also be shared easily with other users. Each of the settings files are saved in a folder called PrintSet installed with FreeHand. Simply copy the specific settings files into the PrintSet folder on another workstation to make them available on that system.*

SAVE PRINT SETTINGS BUTTON

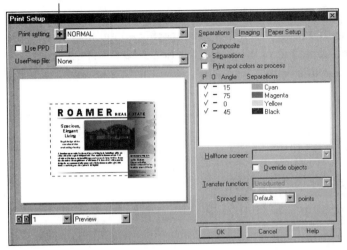

3] Click the Imaging tab at the top of the dialog box and click Crop Marks to turn on that option.

Crop marks indicate the edges of your page. (They will print only if your document's page size is smaller than the paper size, as it is here.)

The Imaging tab also contains an option that allows you to choose whether to print invisible (hidden) layers. There are no hidden layers in this document, so in this case it does not make any difference whether this option is selected or not.

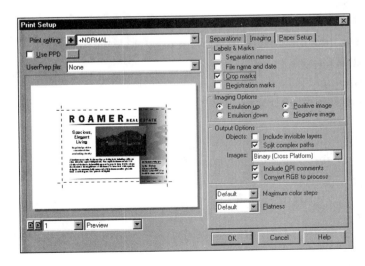

363

4] Click the Paper Setup tab.

Here you can select the paper size and orientation for output. The Automatic Orientation default setting tells FreeHand to automatically determine the optimum orientation based on the size of the pages in your document, the output device, and the paper size.

5] To select from among other paper sizes that your specific printer may offer, click the Use PPD button at the upper left of the dialog box and select the PostScript printer description file for your printer.

These PPDs, or PostScript printer descriptions, contain optimized print settings for specific PostScript printers. You will achieve the best printing results when you use PPD information, and FreeHand will be able to support the full range of features and paper sizes your printer offers.

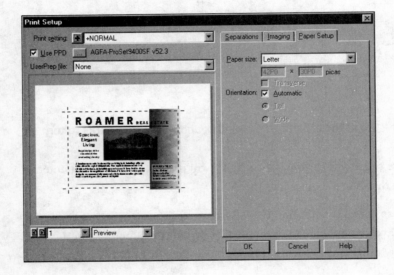

6] Click OK to return to the Print dialog box. If you want to print at this time, click the Print button. If not, click Cancel.

Remember that this is a multiple-page document, so you have the choice of printing the entire document or just specific pages.

7] Save your work.

You have now completed the three-page catalog insert.

COLLECTING FILES FOR OUTPUT

The TIFF images you imported into this document were imported as linked graphics by default, which means that a preview image was imported for you to work with. When you print the document, FreeHand sends the high-resolution information from the individual disk files for each image. That means that the images must remain with the FreeHand document.

When sending your completed documents to a service bureau or commercial printer for high-resolution output, you must also include any linked graphics so they can be output at high resolution as well.

FreeHand offers two features to help you prevent problems when printing or transferring files: Links and Collect for Output. You already explored the Links dialog box earlier in this lesson. When you are ready to send files to a service bureau or commercial printer, check the Links dialog box to make sure that all links to your images are intact, and make sure the images conform to the requirements set by your output provider (for instance, using CMYK rather than RGB images). Then you will be ready to collect your files for output.

1] Choose File › Collect for Output.

This feature is designed to collect all of the elements required to send this document to your service bureau or commercial printer for output. The first thing you will see initially is an alert reminding you that fonts are copyrighted works, and you should check your font license before sending copies of your fonts to your output service.

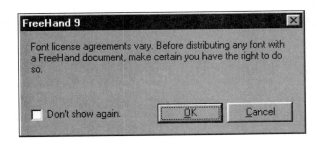

2] Click OK in the font license alert box.

The Document Report window appears. This enables you to specify what information you want collected in a report on this document. Notice that the report can list all the placed images used in your document, along with specific font information, including the font names, PostScript names, font file format, and style. These pieces of information can be very useful information to your service bureau or commercial printer.

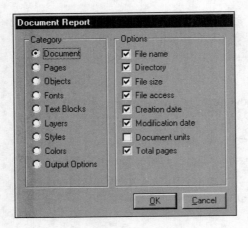

3] Accept the default settings and click OK (Windows) or Report (Macintosh).
A Save dialog box appears, asking for a location for all of the files needed to output this FreeHand document and requesting a name for the report that summarizes the document characteristics. Typically, you would select the disk or cartridge you want to send to the printer.

Collect for Output will save the text file report and copy the FreeHand document, all linked images, the fonts used in the document, and the active printer description files to the selected folder or disk volume. If you are not saving the file to removable media, you will probably want to create a new folder to keep the collected files from spreading out in the directory you select.

Since you will probably not send this document to a service bureau for high-resolution printing, you do not need to actually complete this process at this time.

4] Click Cancel to return to the document window without collecting the files for output.

ON YOUR OWN

Do you have multiple-page projects you can use FreeHand for? Remember that a FreeHand document can contain different-sized pages, so it is perfect for that corporate identity project. FreeHand is also very capable at handling graphic-intensive newsletters and catalogs. The Collect for Output feature means you won't have to worry about missing a font or image when you send the file to your printer or service bureau. FreeHand files can be output directly to an imagesetter, or you can export a PDF (if your printer supports PDF workflow).

WHAT YOU HAVE LEARNED:

In this lesson, you have:

- Added new page sizes to the Document Inspector [pages 300–302]
- Added and edited ruler guides [pages 302–309]
- Created custom process colors [pages 310–311]
- Blended Gradient fills [pages 312–315]
- Used Xtra tools and path operations [pages 322–333]
- Flowed text from one page to another [pages 339–341]
- Formatted text using styles and text effects [pages 335–337, 342–350]
- Wrapped text around graphics [pages 353–355]
- Copied colors from imported images for use elsewhere in a document [pages 357–359]
- Used Find and Replace Graphics to change text based on specific criteria [pages 360–361]
- Printed your document [pages 361–364]
- Prepared files for a commercial printer [pages 365–366]

animation

setting up

LESSON 9

In this lesson, you will create an animation in FreeHand and export it as a SWF file. SWF stands for Shockwave-Flash, and it is pronounced "swiff," just like the GIF file format is pronounced "giff" or "jiff." SWF is the file format used by Macromedia Flash, which is a program designed specifically to bring high-impact vector animation to the Internet. At the end of this lesson you will have the option of working with the exported file in Flash, where you can add sound, interactivity, and more.

In the process of building this animation in FreeHand, you will learn how to blend to create motion, release blends to layers in a variety of ways, and select various output options to obtain the desired results.

Designed by Tony Roame of Illustrated Concepts.

This is one of the final screens in the Race Fans animation. This animation was created entirely in FreeHand, and published from FreeHand as a complete animation. The exported file is ready for viewing on the Internet or on the desktop of your computer. You will learn the techniques for creating such an animation in this lesson.

The basic process behind standard animation is the rapid replacement of one static image with another, each slightly altered from the previous image. It works much the same way as those flip-books you may have played with as a child. FreeHand can create alternating images by animating from one page to the next, from one layer to the next, or some combination of both. In this lesson, you will learn techniques for setting up both kinds of animation.

If you'd like to review the final result of this lesson, open Raceintro.ft9 in the Complete folder within the Lesson09 folder. If you'd like to see the final animated results, open the Racefinal.swf file from the same folder in the Flash 4 Flash player or in a Web browser with the Flash player plug-in.

WHAT YOU WILL LEARN

In this lesson you will:

- Create blends that are designed for motion
- Animate text in a variety of ways
- Release blends to layers
- Use a variety of animation techniques
- Use the Fisheye Lens tool for 3D animation
- Use various export settings
- Export a document as a SWF file

APPROXIMATE TIME

This lesson takes approximately 1 hour and 30 minutes to complete.

LESSON FILES

Media Files:

None

Starting Files:

Lesson09\Start\Racestart.ft9

Completed Project:

Lesson09\Complete\Raceintro.ft9

Lesson09\Complete\Racefinal.swf

Bonus Files:

Lesson09\Bonus\Bonus9.pdf

Lesson09\Bonus\Bonus9Export.swf

Lesson09\Bonus\Bonus9FL4.fla

Lesson09\Bonus\Bonus9Final.swf

BUILDING THE FIRST SEQUENCE

FreeHand can be a very effective tool for quickly building and testing a variety of animation ideas. In the next few steps, you are going to create some simple blends that will build the backdrop used in the rest of the animation.

You will start by opening a document already in progress. You will be editing and creating a few elements to give you a feel for the creative process, but a majority of the objects are already in place so that most of your time will be spent learning new techniques.

The animation is divided into four sequences, each on a new page. You will set up each page for animation, and then, as the last step, you will create the animation.

1] Open the document named Racestart.ft9 in the Lesson9\Start folder.
A document opens on your screen. The page that's visible contains some text and a rectangle.

The rectangle will be part of the main background in your movie. Rather than have it simply appear, you'd like to have it show up in an interesting way. This can be accomplished by creating a blend, releasing the blend steps to individual layers, and then exporting the layers as steps in an animation. You will make that happen in these next steps.

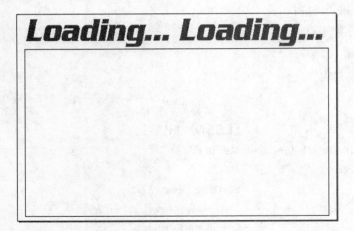

2] Select the rectangle and clone it. Go to the Object Inspector and give the cloned rectangle a height of 10 points (in the "h:" field).
The 10 point height is an arbitrary number. The idea is to have a rectangle that is the same width, but much shorter. By changing a value in the Object Inspector, you avoid the possiblity of inadvertantly changing the width while you adjust the height.

note *When you adjust values in the Object Inspector, the lower left corner of the selection is always the "origin" or the point of change. For instance, the "x:" field refers to the left edge, and "y:" field refers to the bottom edge, so these coordinates taken together point to the lower left corner of the selection. When you change the "w:" or "h:" fields, the bottom and left edges of the selection always stay in their current position, and only the top and right edges are adjusted.*

The new rectangle shares the bottom edge with the original. You will move the alignment to the top in the next step.

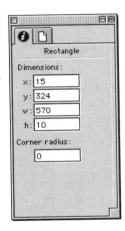

note *This figure shows that some of the Inspector panels have been separated from the Object Inspector. Depending on your workflow, it may be convenient to separate the various Inspector panels, so they can be accessed simultaneously.*

3] Select both rectangles and align them on their top edges in the Align panel. Press Tab to deselect the rectangles.

The new rectangle is already in the correct horizontal position, so it does not need to be adjusted.

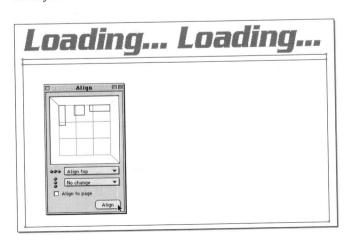

371

tip You can also align objects by adding the toolbar alignment icons to one of the toolbars on your screen, or you can use the keyboard shortcuts. To add toolbar alignment icons for simple one-click alignment action, choose File > Customize > Toolbars and select the "Other" section, then drag the appropriate icons to a convenient toolbar. To look up the keyboard shortcuts for alignment, choose File > Customize > Shortcuts.

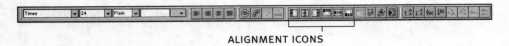

ALIGNMENT ICONS

4] Select the small rectangle and clone it. With the clone selected, change the width in the Object Inspector to 40 points.

These three rectangles will be used to create the blend on the first page.

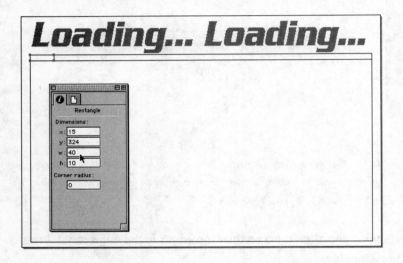

5] Select the smallest rectangle and bring it to the front by choosing Modify › Arrange › Bring to Front (Windows Ctrl+F, Macintosh Command+F). Next click the middle rectangle and bring it to the front. Then click the largest original rectangle and bring it to the front.

As you learned in Lesson 6, the stacking order of objects determines the order in which they will be blended. In general, it's a good practice to bring each of the objects in your blend to the front in the order you want them to appear. That's what you just accomplished in this step.

6] Select all three rectangles and choose Modify › Combine › Blend. Change the number of steps in the Object Inspector to 11.

372

You can see the way the blend will be built by looking at the steps before changing the fill to black. When you animate this blend, the smallest rectangle in the upper-left corner will be displayed first, and then each subsequent step in the blend will be displayed, replacing the one before it. The replacements will happen so quickly that the objects will seem to be in motion.

7] With the blend still selected, go to the Color List and assign a black fill and no stroke.

Once you assign the fill and stroke, it seems like you have just an ordinary black rectangle selected. However, if you look at the Object Inspector, it will tell you that a blend with 11 steps is selected.

Now you're ready to release this blend to layers and create an animation.

8] Select the text at the top (which has already been converted to paths) and choose Xtras > Animate > Release to Layers. In the dialog box that appears, choose Trail from the Animate pop-up menu. Move the slider until the Trail By value is 4; then click OK or press Return.

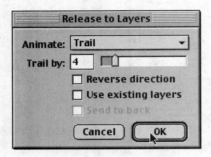

You will see the effect of this type of blend shortly. For now, notice that each of the letters has been broken apart and is located on its own layer.

9] Select the black rectangle blend and choose Xtras > Animate > Release to Layers. In the dialog box that appears, choose Sequence from the Animate pop-up menu and check the box marked Use existing layers.

374

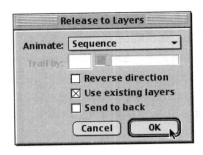

Because you chose Sequence, each step will replace the previous step. Because you checked Use existing layers, the animation of the blend will take place at the same time as the animation of the text. If you did not check Use existing layers, the animation of the rectangles would not start until after the animation of the text was finished.

In the next step, you have the opportunity to see your animation in action.

10] Choose File › Export.
In Windows, in the Save as type pop-up menu, choose Macromedia Flash. Click the Setup button. In the Frames section, click the From radio button and enter 1 in the From and To fields. Change the frame rate to 20 frames per second; then click OK.

On a Macintosh, in the Format pop-up menu, choose Macromedia Flash (SWF). Click the Options button, and in the Frames section, click the From radio button and enter 1 in the From and To fields. Change the frame rate to 20 frames per section; then click OK.

Your options dialog box should look like the following illustration.

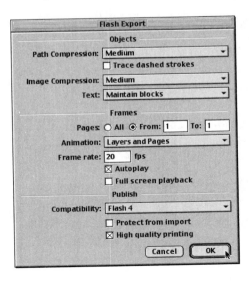

375

11] In the Export Document dialog box, check Open in External Application and then click the button with the ellipsis. In the new dialog box that pops up, navigate to the Flash 4 player located in the FreeHand application folder. Select the Flash 4 player and click Open (Windows) or Choose (Macintosh).

These are the settings you should have in your export dialog box. Notice that the Open in Application box is checked and the Flash 4 Player is selected. The Flash 4 player is located in the FreeHand application folder on your hard drive.

Note that if you don't want to open the exported file in a new application immediately upon expanding it, then clicking the button with the ellipsis is not necessary.

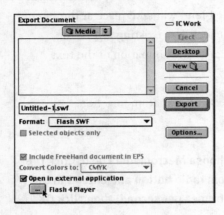

12] Click Save (Windows) or Export (Macintosh).

FreeHand publishes page 1 as an animation in the SWF format, and the Flash 4 player automatically launches and plays the exported file.

tip   If the animation sequence appears in the wrong direction, the stacking order was incorrect when you created the blend. There are two ways to fix that. You can return to the FreeHand document and choose Undo repeatedly until you return to the point where you have three separate rectangles on your page again and then set the correct stacking order and proceed as before. Alternatively, you can undo only until you reach the blend and then release to layers again, but this time check the Reverse Direction option in the Release to Layers dialog box.

13] Close the animation in the Flash 4 player. Make FreeHand the foremost application again. Select Undo from the File menu two times, or until the Layers panel displays only one foreground layer.

Now you should be back to the point where you have a blend on page 1 along with the text at the top, which should be a group again. It's best to wait until the entire document is completed before releasing everything to layers. You are going to work with several more pages before you're ready to take this step.

14] Save your work.

BUILDING THE SECOND SEQUENCE

The second sequence is where the blue screen appears in the window. You are going to use blends, just like in the previous task.

1] Go to page 2 in the document you saved in the previous task.

You can see a black rectangle on the page, and in the middle of the black rectangle is a blue rectangle. You're going to create new blends using each of these rectangles as a starting point.

note *If you were setting up an animation in FreeHand only to export it to Flash and finish editing it there, then step 2 would not be necessary. You would need to create a blend only for new elements that would appear in the animation. Objects that remain in the background, like the black rectangle from page 1, would be handled separately in Flash. However, if you plan to export a finished SWF file from FreeHand, then you need to design it frame by frame using complete images. This means that any element that remains in the background must appear in every layer in your FreeHand document. The best way to make that happen is to clone each constant element and blend it to itself, using the same number of steps as needed for the rest of the objects that appear.*

◎ POWER TIP *It's best to design animations in FreeHand only as a front end for Flash. Although it's possible to export a polished movie directly from FreeHand (as this lesson will demonstrate), you will be better off in most cases if you don't have to try to synchronize the number of background steps with the steps required by the rest of your animation. Let Flash do what it's really good at, and use FreeHand for its strengths, which include its abilities to manipulate vector data, swap colors, and provide access to tools that make the creative process more fluid.*

377

2] **Select the black rectangle and clone it. Select both rectangles (for Windows, click and then Shift+right-click; for Macintosh, click and then Control+Shift+click). Blend the two black rectangles, change the number of blend steps to 23 in the Object Inspector, and send the blend to the back.**

This blend contains the correct number of steps to ensure that the black background element remains constantly visible in the exported movie. You need to send the blend to the back so that you can see the blue rectangle again.

3] **Select the blue rectangle and clone it. In the Object Inspector, make the height of the blue rectangle 255 points. Center the new blue rectangle on the black blend using the Align panel or the toolbar alignment icons.**

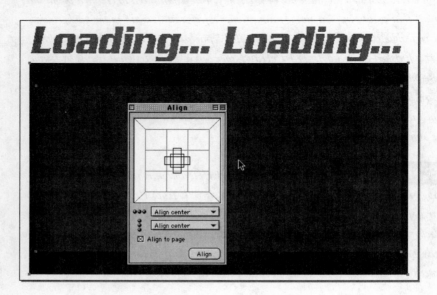

In the next step, you will blend the small blue rectangle with the big blue rectangle. When animated, this will make the blue screen appear to grow out from the middle of the page.

4] Switch to Keyline mode using the pop-up menu at the bottom of the window. Click the line for the small blue rectangle and Shift+click the large blue rectangle. Blend the two rectangles and set the number of blend steps to 23 in the Object Inspector. Switch back to Preview mode.

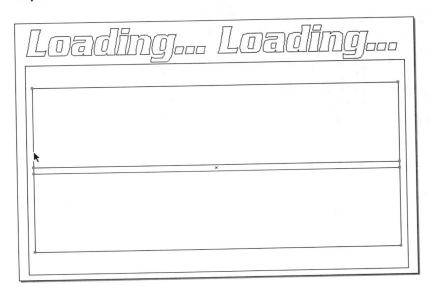

Sometimes it's easiest to switch to Keyline mode when you need to select an object that is otherwise hidden from view.

5] Save your work.
This was the only setup needed for page 2. You will set up animation for page 3 next.

BUILDING THE THIRD, FOURTH, AND FIFTH SEQUENCES
Now you will work on the page where the white checkered strips will make their entrance.

1] Go to page 3 in your saved file.

This page already has the blend created for the black rectangle. It is just like the one you created for the previous page. As before, a blend has also been created for the blue rectangle. The new elements on this page are the white squares in the four corners.

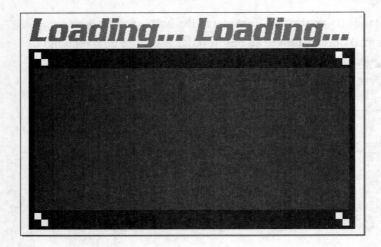

2] Select the set of white squares in the upper-left corner; then Shift+click to select the set of white squares in the upper-right corner. Blend the sets of squares, and in the Object Inspector set the number of steps to 21.

Each set of squares is actually a composite path. FreeHand has the ability to blend composite paths, which can make certain types of blends much easier to create.

3] Select the two sets of squares below the blue box and blend them. In the Object Inspector, set the number of steps to 21.

Now the top and bottom have checkered rows of white squares.

The next page contains artwork that is identical to that which appears on this page. Only the style of animation will be different. The most efficient way to set up the next page is to duplicate this page.

4] Select the Page tool from the Toolbox, click page 4, and press Delete. Then click page 3 with the Page tool and hold down the Alt (Windows) or Option (Macintosh) key as you drag page 3 to the location of page 4; release the mouse button.

Make sure you are holding down the Alt or Option key when you release the mouse button so that the page will be duplicated.

5] Save your work.

6] Go to page 5 in your document.

This page has the same black, blue, and white blends as the previous two pages. However, there is a new block of text at the top, and there are a series of red spheres on the page. These spheres are the new animation on this page. The text will also receive a different style of animation, but you will take care of that later.

7] Select the smallest red sphere, on the left edge of the screen, and bring it to the front. Next click the small red sphere at the bottom and bring it to the front, then bring the small top sphere to the front, and then finally bring the large center sphere to the front.

Now you can be certain that the stacking order is correct and the spheres will be animated in the right sequence.

8] Select all four spheres and blend them. In the Object Inspector, set the number of steps to 5.

The blend will appear as shown in the following illustration.

9] Save your work.

BUILDING THE FINAL SEQUENCE

Now there is only one sequence remaining. In the next sequence, you will create text that appears to rotate three-dimensionally around the sphere.

1] Go to page 6 in your document.

This page contains the text that you will make appear three-dimensional as it rotates around the sphere. The text blocks have already been converted to paths (to avoid potential font conflicts).

2] Select the yellow text and choose Modify › Join to convert it to a composite path. Clone the composite path. Select the clone and the original and blend them; then set the blend steps to 21.

You are converting the text to a composite path so it can be blended, and you are blending the text so that it will appear on every layer, making it constantly visible.

3] Select the white text and choose Modify › Join to convert it to a composite path.

The text in this position will be in the middle of a three-step blend. Next you will create the pieces on either side.

383

4] Clone the white text, then double-click to display the transform handles. Grab the center handle on the left side and drag to the right until all the text is about 5 or 10% of its original width, which is slightly less than the original width of the letter "s".

This will be the text as it is first visible on the right side of the sphere.

5] Drag the scaled text to the right of the sphere so that it is about 12 points from the edge.

Hold the Shift key as you drag and release the mouse to keep the text in line as you reposition it.

Now you are going to move a copy of the scaled text to the other side of the sphere.

6] **With the scaled text still selected, start dragging it to the left side of the sphere. As you drag, hold the Alt (Windows) or Option (Macintosh) key and the Shift key. When the text is the same distance from the sphere on the left side as it is on the right side, release the mouse and then release the keys.**

Now you have the three parts in position. The next step is to fix the stacking order and then blend them.

7] **Select the text on the right and bring it to the front, then click the text in the center and bring it to the front, and then click on the text on the left and bring it to the front. Then Shift+click all three text blocks and blend them. In the Object Inspector, set the number of blend steps to 10.**

This will make the text appear in the order that it will be easiest to read when it is animated. Right now, however, it is just an unintelligible mass of vectors.

385

Next you will set up the Fisheye Lens tool so it is ready to distort the text the way you want it to.

8] From the Window menu, choose Toolbars › Xtra Tools. Double-click the Fisheye Lens tool to change its settings. In the dialog box that appears, drag the slider all the way to the right (100%).

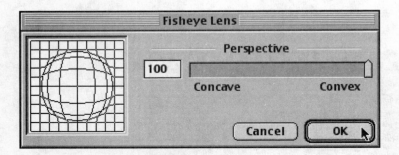

Before you can apply the 3D distortion to the text, the text needs to be released to layers.

9] Select the white text blend and choose Xtras › Animate › Release to Layers. In the dialog box that appears, choose Sequence from the pop-up menu and check Use Existing Layers; then press Return. Leave all the objects selected.

The blend steps are each released to separate layers, which FreeHand will animate when the file is exported as a SWF file. Now you are ready to distort the steps.

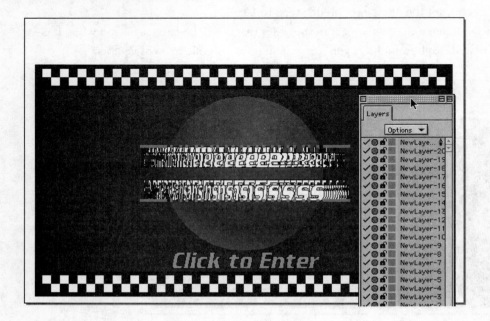

386

10] With all the blend steps still selected, position the Fisheye Lens tool over the center of the red sphere. Hold the Alt (Windows) or Option (Macintosh) key and drag out with the Fisheye Lens tool until the circle you are dragging is completely around the blend.

When you release the Fisheye Lens tool, the distortion is applied individually to each of the blend steps. If you had applied the distortion earlier, the effect would not have been very convincing.

Now you need to create a blend with the red sphere so that the sphere stays visible throughout this portion of the sequence.

11] Select the red sphere and clone it. Select the clone and the original and blend them, setting the blend steps to 21. In the Layers panel, click the name of the foreground layer to make sure the blend moves to the foreground layer.

When you release the first blend to layers, the active layer (indicated by the pen tip symbol) becomes the top layer. When you blend the red sphere, it moves to the active layer. You want to make sure it goes back to the bottom layer so that it animates properly with the rest of the artwork.

12] Save your work.

RELEASING THE BLENDS TO LAYERS

The next steps involve releasing the various blends to layers so they can be animated. For the most part, there will not be any significant visual feedback. You will have to just do things in the right order and keep track of where you are in the process.

1] Select the red sphere blend on page 6. Choose Xtras › Animate › Release to Layers. Choose Sequence from the pop-up menu and check the boxes for Use Existing Layers and Send to Back.

You want each step in the blend to go to the back of each of the existing layers —
that is, behind the white text that is currently on each layer.

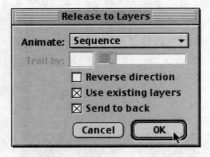

The top red circle will now be in front of the white text objects.

**2] Select the yellow text blend below the red sphere. Release this blend to layers
using the same settings as in the previous step.**

Now the "Click to Enter" text is on every layer.

**3] Select both white checkered blends and choose Xtras › Animate › Release to
Layers. In the dialog box, select Drop from the pop-up menu. Leave the two boxes
checked, but this time also check Reverse direction.**

This is a different animation option. You will see the effect of Drop when you export
the file.

**4] Select the blue rectangle blend and release it to layers, using Sequence from the
pop-up menu. Uncheck Reverse direction, but leave the other two boxes checked. Then
select the black rectangle blend and release it in the same way as the blue rectangle.**

Page 6 is completely animated. Now you will animate the other pages.

**5] Select the blend of red spheres on page 5 and release the blend to layers by
sequence, with the same two boxes checked.**

Notice that this time the highlighted layers stop one short of the top. That means
there weren't enough steps in the blend to fill the existing layers. Since you don't
want the sphere to temporarily disappear from the screen, you will have to manually
clone the top object and move it up a layer.

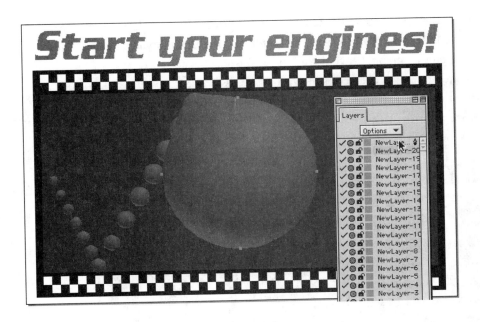

6] **Select the biggest red sphere on page 5 and clone it. Click the name of the next layer up to move the clone to that layer.**

Now the sphere will not disappear from view, since it occupies each layer.

7] **Select the white checkered blends on page 5 and choose Xtras › Animate › Release to Layers. In the dialog box, select Drop from the pop-up menu. Leave the two boxes checked, but this time do not check Reverse direction.**

You will see the effect of Drop when you export the file.

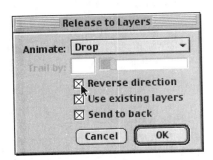

8] **Select the blue rectangle blend and release it to layers, using Sequence from the pop-up menu. Leave the other two boxes checked. Then select the black rectangle blend and release it in the same way as the blue rectangle.**

Next you are going to release the text at the top of the page.

9] Select the text block at the top of page 5. Click the name of layer 5 to move the text up to that layer. Now release the blend, and in the dialog box, choose Build from the pop-up menu. Leave the other two boxes checked.

There aren't enough characters in this text block to last for all 21 steps, so you moved it up a few layers so that it starts later and finishes at the same time as the other steps.

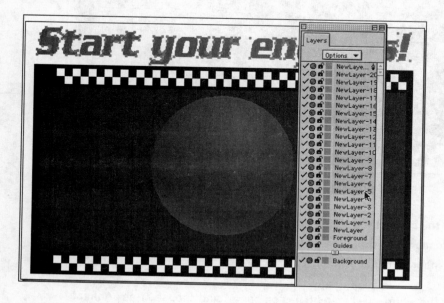

note *Regular text blocks do not need any special treatment before they are released to layers. When you release a text block to layers, the characters are animated one at a time using the pop-up option you have chosen. (The same is true for text that has been converted to paths.)*

10] Select the white checkered blends on page 4 and choose Xtras › Animate › Release to Layers. In the dialog box, select Drop from the pop-up menu. Leave the two boxes checked, and this time also check Reverse direction.

11] Select the blue rectangle blend on page 4 and release it to layers, using Sequence from the pop-up menu. Uncheck Reverse direction, but leave the other two boxes checked. Then select the black rectangle blend and release it in the same way as the blue rectangle.

12] Select the "Loading... Loading..." text at the top of page 4 and choose Xtras › Animate › Release to Layers. In the Animate pop-up menu, choose Trail, and set the Trail by value to 4. Leave the two boxes checked.

This is the same option that you experimented with at the beginning of the lesson.

390

13] Select the "Loading... Loading..." text at the top of the other three pages and release it to layers with the same Trail settings as used in step 12.

If you zoom out far enough, you could release the text on all three pages at one time. If you don't have a large enough screen to make that practical, then you can work with the pages one at a time.

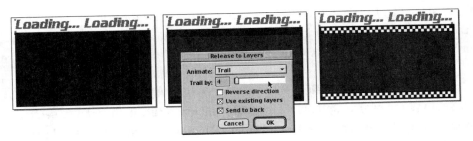

14] Go to page 3 and select the white checkered blends and choose Xtras › Animate › Release to Layers. This time, choose Build in Animation from the pop-up menu. Leave the other two boxes checked.

This is the sequence where the checks first appear on the screen. You want it to build from left to right.

15] Select the blue rectangle blend on page 3 and release it to layers, choosing Sequence from the pop-up menu and leaving the two boxes checked. Then select the black rectangle blend and repeat this step with the same settings.

16] Go to page 2 and release the blue blend; then release the black blend with the same settings as in step 14.

17] Go to page 1 and release the black rectangle blend using the same settings as in step 14.

391

18] Choose File › Save As to preserve the previous version of this file while saving a version with all the blends released.

It is important at this stage to save two versions of the file, because it is very difficult to go back and re-create the blends if something doesn't work right, but you don't want to lose all the work you just did releasing everything, either. If you discover something needs to be fixed in your animation, it is much better to go back to the original blends than to trust that the Undo command can bring you back to an editable state.

note   *When you open released versions of your animations in the future, there may be a noticeable delay before any artwork appears (depending on the speed of your computer). The computer may have to process thousands of pieces of art for each page, depending on what you've created.*

EXPORTING THE ANIMATION

A SWF created by FreeHand can be a finished file ready for professional use, such as on the Internet or in a presentation. However, if you wish to add sound or interactivity, your SWF can be imported into Flash where it can be edited and enhanced.

1] Choose File › Export and select Macromedia Flash (SWF) from the pop-up menu. Click Setup (Windows) or Options (Macintosh) and make sure in the Frames section that Layers and Pages is selected in the Animation pop-up menu, and that all pages are set to export. Set the Frame Rate field to 20.

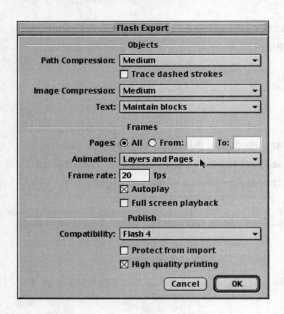

2] Click OK. Make sure the Open in External Application is checked; then click Save (Windows) or Export (Macintosh).

Sit back and enjoy your animation! If you need to fix something, you can either return to the FreeHand file you just exported from and click Undo until you find the problem, or you can go back to the previous version of the file that still has all the blends intact and fix it there.

ON YOUR OWN

Working with a file in Flash has some special benefits, but in many ways Flash interprets objects differently than FreeHand. There are some things that you can do in FreeHand prior to exporting a SWF that will make it easier to edit the file in Flash. A SWF that is set up especially for export to Flash will not look great by itself, but if you have Flash available then you can easily edit the file and quickly create a final SWF that includes sound, interactivity, and is likely to be smaller than the one you created here. Look in the Lesson09\Bonus folder for the instructions and finished files.

WHAT YOU HAVE LEARNED

In this lesson you have:

- Blended objects to create steps for an animation [pages 370–373]
- Created Sequence, Build, Drop, and Trail animation effects [pages 374–381]
- Used the Fisheye Lens tool to create a 3D movement effect [pages 382–387]
- Exported a FreeHand document as a SWF file with different settings [pages 387–393]

storyboards

web site

LESSON 10

In this lesson, you will learn how to use FreeHand to assemble a Web site storyboard, carry out creative concepts, export the results as a PDF or HTML file for client review, and export as a SWF file for editing in Flash. In the process, you'll learn how to use symbols for repeating elements, find an innovative use for one of the Lens fills, use Find and Replace Graphics for efficient editing, and learn how arrange and duplicate individual pages (and groups of pages) to lay out sections of a Web site.

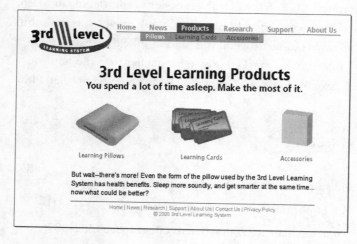

This is one section of a FreeHand document that contains a Web site storyboard. In this lesson, you'll learn how to take advantage of some of the unique tools FreeHand offers for creating Web site storyboards.

What you are not going to do in this lesson is design an entire Web site. That would take hours and hours of work and is beyond the goals of this book. However, you will learn the principles necessary to use FreeHand effectively as a tool for developing Web sites, and you will learn how to send content to a variety of destinations.

If you'd like to review the final result of this lesson, open LPsite2.ft9 in the Complete folder within the Lesson10 folder.

WHAT YOU WILL LEARN

In this lesson you will:

- Create symbols in FreeHand for repeating elements
- Use symbols for repeating elements
- Edit and replace existing symbols
- Edit text styles to update multiple pages simultaneously
- Use Find and Replace Graphics to substitute elements and explore design concepts
- Use the Magnify Lens fill to create master elements
- Duplicate single pages and groups of pages to expedite design
- Export a FreeHand document as a PDF, HTML or SWF document

APPROXIMATE TIME

This lesson takes approximately 45 minutes to complete.

LESSON FILES

Media Files:
None

Starting Files:
Lesson10\Start\LPsite1.ft9

Completed Project:
Lesson10\Complete\LPsite2.ft9

Bonus Files:
Lesson10\Bonus\Bonus10.pdf
Lesson10\Bonus\Bonus10Export.swf
Lesson10\Bonus\Bonus10FL4.fla
Lesson10\Bonus\Bonus10Final.swf

APPROACHING WEB SITE DESIGN

FreeHand can be an excellent tool to help you approach Web site design. The use of graphics styles, Find and Replace Graphics, and symbols, along with the multipage capability allowed by the Page tool, enable you to come up with quick and efficient designs that can easily be moved in a number of directions. You will begin this lesson by exploring symbols and the role they can play in Web site design. But before you start the first task, it's worth taking a moment to think about your general approach.

When designing a Web site, it is of utmost importance that a site map come first. If a site map is not completed, then much of your work may be in vain. Before you really begin designing an interface, you should have two versions of the site map on hand. The first should be a text outline, with written titles for every page that will appear on the site. The second version should be a graphical representation. It should have page icons that represent each page on your site, with lines between the pages to show how they link together.

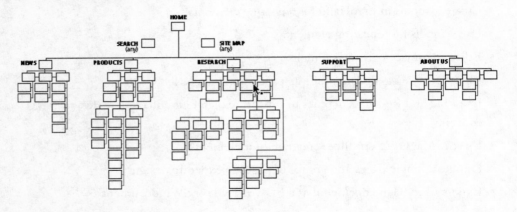

If these maps are not on hand, you're faced with a task similar to building a house without a blueprint—a structure may eventually be assembled, but there will be a lot of mistakes along the way, and it probably won't look or function the way it's supposed to.

The other consideration in Web site design is the user interface—the actual design and navigation that defines the site. This lesson won't cover user-interface design. Volumes have been written on the subject, and it is beyond the scope of this book. Suffice it to say that FreeHand can accommodate any of your design preferences, whether or not they follow the general guidelines for a good user interface. The tools are here at your disposal; you can use them however you please.

396

WORKING WITH SYMBOLS

You will begin this lesson by opening a document that has already been started. You will add and edit symbols and then go on to explore other benefits of using FreeHand in Web site design.

1] Open the document LPsite1.ft9 in the Lesson10\Start folder.

A document opens on your screen, and a site map is visible. If it is not, choose View > Custom > Site map. This is a graphical representation of the pages on the sample site. The Web site you are designing in FreeHand will be based on this layout. It is possible to re-create this site map with actual pages, page for page, all in a single FreeHand document. You will not actually be completing all that work here, but you will learn how you could.

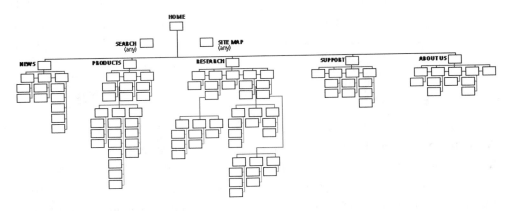

2] Choose View › Fit All to show all the pages that are already part of this FreeHand document.

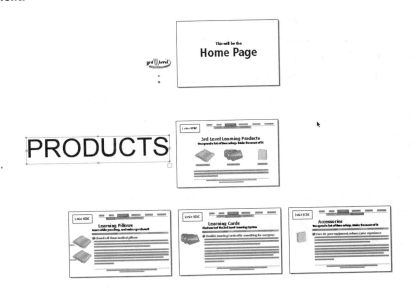

Here you can see the pages that are currently in progress. Many of the design elements are already in place. You are going to use the features of FreeHand to modify and continue developing this Web site, beginning with the Symbols feature.

3] Make sure the Object Inspector is visible; then choose page 2 from the pop-up menu at the bottom of your screen. Click the gray footer text at the bottom of page 2. Notice that the text block is selected like a group, and in the Object Inspector it is called an instance.

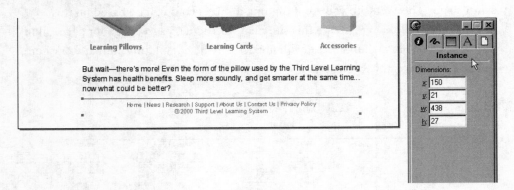

An **instance** is a special type of object in FreeHand. An instance points to a **symbol** in the Symbols library. The symbols stored in this library contain the actual content for the instance. An instance is actually just a pointer that refers to the stored symbol. Instances can be modified with the transform handles, but their actual content (the symbol) can't be modified directly.

There are several advantages to using symbols in a FreeHand document. First, judicious use of symbols can dramatically reduce file size. This is especially true if you have many repeating elements, or if you have very large elements repeated in one or more locations. In addition, it's nearly impossible to accidentally change a symbol. You can be confident that if a symbol is correct in one place, it is correct in all places. Also, the Symbols library records the last time a symbol was modified. This can be great tool for verifying whether or not a particular piece of artwork is current.

tip *Symbols work well in conjunction with the Graphic Hose. Turn elements into symbols before you place them in Graphic Hose sets. Then when you spray Graphic Hose elements on your page, you will actually be using symbols—which means your artwork will take up less file space and will be easier to edit later, should that be necessary.*

4] Open the Symbols library by choosing Window › Panels › Symbols.

The Symbols panel, or library, as it's called, has a preview window at the top that displays the contents of the highlighted symbol. If you resize the library, you can see additional fields for Count and Date Modified. At the bottom of the panel, you'll see icons for adding symbols and folders, and a trash can for deleting symbols or folders. If you've used Macromedia Flash before, these should be familiar to you.

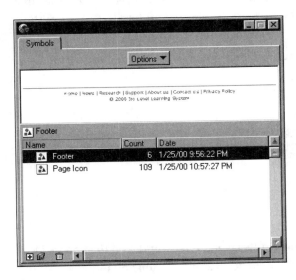

Next you're going to add a symbol to the library and place instances of that symbol in your document.

5] Choose Page 1 from the pop-up menu at the bottom of your screen and scroll to the left until you see the Third-Level Learning System logo. Make sure the Symbol library is visible; then drag the logo into the blank space below the names of the other two symbols. Double-click the default name and rename this symbol *3rd Level logo*.

The artwork you selected is automatically converted to an instance of the symbol and can no longer be modified directly. You will learn how to modify symbols later in this lesson.

When you drag artwork onto the Symbol library, FreeHand assigns a default name of Graphic-01. Be sure to rename your symbols right away so that they're easy to distinguish from each other. Renaming also reduces the risk of inadvertently replacing one symbol with another when copying instances between FreeHand documents.

399

 You can use naming conventions to quickly update multiple documents with a new symbol definition. To do this, change the symbol in one document and then drag and drop the modified symbol onto other existing documents. When the new symbol lands on an existing page, this new symbol automatically redefines all symbols that share its name.

6] Make page 2 visible in the document window; then position your mouse over the 3rd Level logo name (or its picture in the preview window) and drag the logo to the upper-left corner of the page.

A new instance of the logo appears at the position where you release the mouse.

7] Select the instance of the logo and Shift+click the rectangle and the upper-left corner; then use the Align panel to align the logo along the top and left edges of the rectangle. Then delete the rectangle.

To save time, you can click the upper-left grid of the Align panel to select the correct alignment option and then click Align or press Return.

Next you'll distribute instances to the other pages.

8] Choose View › Fit All; then press Alt (Windows) or Option (Macintosh) and drag a copy of the logo (instance) from page 2 onto each of the three lower pages. Align the logos the same way you did on page 2 and then delete the existing rectangles.

Notice that when you press Alt or Option when dragging an instance, FreeHand just places another instance. This can easily be verified by checking the Count column in the Symbol library. When you're done with this step, the Symbol library will show a count of 5 for the 3rd Level logo.

Next you'll use some of FreeHand's powerful document-wide text search features.

9] Choose Edit › Find and Replace › Text. In the Find field, type *Third Level*. Press tab and then, in the Change to field, type *3rd Level*. Click the Find First button and then press Change All when this option becomes available.

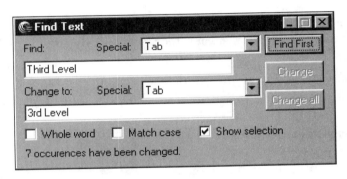

FreeHand alerts you that the document search is complete. The number of occurrences changed is listed at the bottom of the Find Text panel.

Sometimes you will need to change a specific line of text on multiple pages. It may not be practical to search each page individually, and even if you did, there's always a chance you'll miss something. By using Find and Replace Text, you can be sure that every occurrence is changed, even if it is locked, part of a hidden selection, on an invisible layer, or otherwise easy to miss. A notable exception is that Find and Replace Text will not change text that is inside an envelope or part of a symbol. You can see this for yourself by checking the footer symbol at the bottom of any of these pages.

In the next steps, you will learn how to modify existing symbols.

10] Click an instance of the footer that is located at the bottom of one of the pages. Choose Modify › Symbol › Release Instance. Then choose Modify › Ungroup.

When you first release the instance, it might seem like nothing happens, because the selection handles don't change. That's because every time you release an instance, it is released as a group. This ensures that the artwork that was part of the symbol stays together when the instance is released.

11] Select the Text tool and change *Third* to *3rd*.

Now that the change is made, you need to make the new artwork redefine the current footer symbol.

12] Select the text block and the gray line that make up the footer and drag them until your arrow covers the title of the footer symbol in the Symbol library; then release the mouse button.

The text in the footer label is highlighted as your mouse drags over it, indicating that it is active.

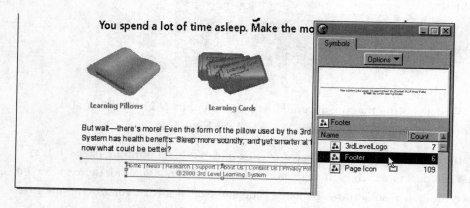

13] When the dialog box appears, press Replace.

When you release the mouse button, a dialog box appears with several choices. The default selection creates a new symbol and does not modify the existing instances of the footer in any way. The Replace option uses the artwork that you are dragging to redefine the contents of this symbol, making all existing instances of the symbol assume the new definition. Convert is an option that allows you to redefine this symbol without changing the definition of any current instances. If you click Convert, all existing instances will become ordinary grouped objects.

402

In this case, you wanted the artwork you were dragging to redefine the current artwork, so you chose Replace.

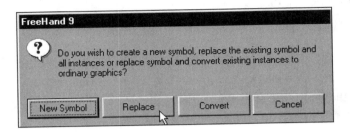

14] Save your work.

MORE POWERFUL EDITING FEATURES

When you're creating a design for something as complicated as a Web site, you can go through a long exploration stage, where you try different colors, styles, fonts, and even graphic elements. Making these changes over and over on page after page can be a tedious chore, to say the least. FreeHand has features that can make these changes happen more quickly, and with considerably less effort. In the next steps, you will experience the benefits of these features.

1] Choose Page 3 from the pop-up menu at the bottom of your document. Open the Styles panel by choosing Window › Panels › Styles.

You can see that many different styles have already been created for this document. There are styles for text and graphics. You are going to explore design variations by altering the colors of some text styles.

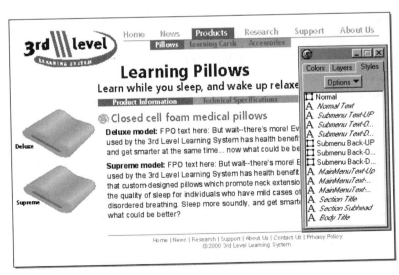

403

2] To discover which styles are used in a text block, watch the Styles panel as you use the Arrow tool to click the Learning Pillows text, the line immediately below that, and then the body title (the line that starts with "Closed cell foam").

As you select each paragraph, the style that is applied to the paragraph is highlighted in the Styles panel.

3] Press the Tab key to deselect all objects. Hold the Alt (Windows) or Option (Macintosh) key and click the Body Title style name. In the dialog box that pops up, select the red color from the Color pop-up menu; then click OK.

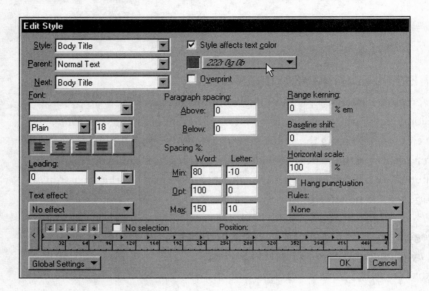

The Edit Styles dialog box contains many other options, but for now you are just experimenting with color.

4] Alt+click (Windows) or Option+click (Macintosh) the Section Subhead style and use the same technique as in step 3 to change the color of this style to green. Click OK when you're done.

You have just changed the way several pages look on your Web site, and you haven't selected a single object. That is the power of using styles in FreeHand. You can use the same technique to edit graphic objects, except in that case, you're controlling fill and stroke attributes rather than text. To verify that several pages have changed, you can click the Next Page icon at the bottom of your screen, or reduce the view magnification so you can see several pages at one time. Notice that the subhead on every page is now green, and the body title on every page is now red.

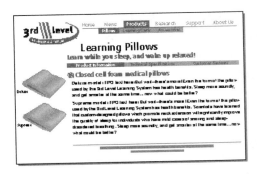
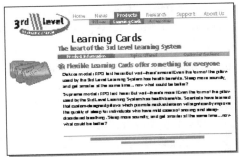

5] Close the Styles panel; then choose Edit › Find and Replace › Graphics. Make sure the Find and Replace tab is active. In the Change in pop-up menu, choose Document. Then select Path Shape from the Attribute menu. In the page select the spiral symbol to the left of the body title and copy it. Then click the Paste in button in the From box in the Find and Replace panel.

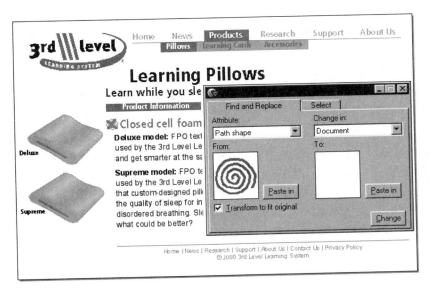

Find and Replace Graphics is an extremely powerful panel that can offer a tremendous boost to your productivity. You can use it to change your entire document, or you can limit its scope to the page you're working on or even just the objects you have selected. In this case, you are going to explore the power of path shape, telling FreeHand to seek out one type of object and replace it with another, regardless of where it exists in your document.

405

6] Choose Page 1 from the Page pop-up menu and scroll to the left until you see the red shapes on the pasteboard. Select the star and copy it; then go back to the Find and Replace Graphics panel and click the Paste in button in the To section. When you have added the star, click the Change button.

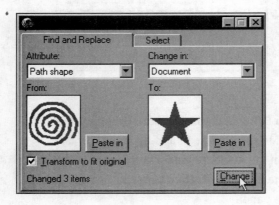

When you click Change, FreeHand seeks out the spiral shape anywhere it exists in the document and replaces it with the star shape. When FreeHand has finished, it lists the number of items that were changed in the bottom-left corner of the panel. To view the changes, select each of the last three pages from the pop-up menu.

Even if you only had to swap out three items, this was a timesaver, because each of the items has been aligned and sized perfectly with just one click. Now imagine if you had dozens of pages, and an element like this needed to be swapped out several times on each of those pages. This feature could save you hours of work all by itself!

tip   *Take the time to explore the other options in the Attribute pop-up menu. Notice that you can have FreeHand automatically seek out and change colors and font characteristics (including font, style, and size), remove invisible objects, simplify paths, rotate or scale multiple objects around their individual centers, and change blend steps.*

In the next steps, you'll learn about another useful feature that saves time and reduces the possibility of error.

7] Choose Page 3 from the pop-up menu at the bottom of the page; then reduce the magnification to about 50%. Select the Page tool; then press Alt (Windows) or Option (Macintosh) and drag a new page immediately below the current page 3. Hold down the Shift key at the same time to keep the pages aligned.

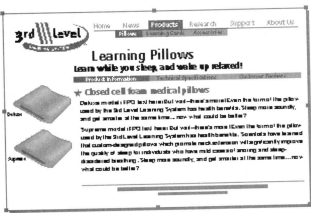

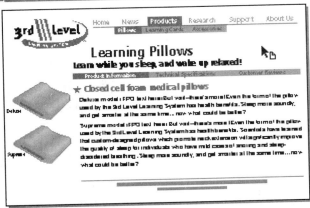

Make sure you're holding the Shift key along with the Alt (Windows) or Option (Macintosh) key when you release the mouse button.

A new page identical to page 3 has been created. This will be the page that holds the technical specifications, as indicated by the submenu above the body title. On this page, the header, logo, section title, and section subhead will all stay the same as they are on page 3—only the submenu, body title, and body copy will change. Any other pages at this level, such as the Customer Reviews page, would also share the same information. As you know, on any given Web site there may be many pages that all have the same information in the same location. Now imagine that a change needs to be made in that location, such as in the header. If you had to work manually, you would have to make the same change over and over on multiple pages, and that could be a very tedious task.

As you will see, FreeHand provides an easier solution.

8] On page 6 (located below page 3), use the Arrow or Lasso tool to select all the items from the top of the page down to the section subhead; then delete them.

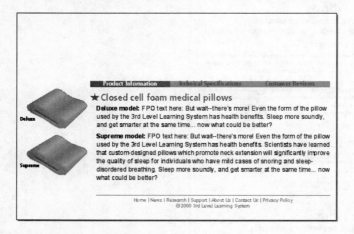

These are the items you are going to reflect from page 3. They will not actually exist on this page, but they will be visible here. You'll see how this works in the next few steps.

9] Scroll up to page 3 so you can see the top of the page. Select the Rectangle tool and draw a rectangle from the upper-left corner of the page 2 to the right side of the page; make sure the rectangle completely covers the subhead.

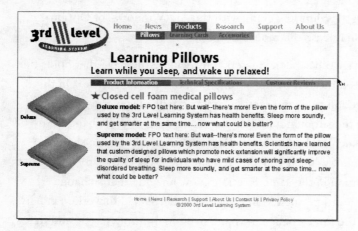

Don't worry about the fill and stroke right now. You will change that in the next step. Just make sure that that rectangle goes from the top corner on the left all the way to the right side and completely covers the top section of the page.

10] Go to the Stroke Inspector and set the stroke to None; then go to the Fill Inspector and change the fill type to Lens. In the second pop-up menu, choose Magnify as the lens type, change the magnification setting to 1, and select the check box for Centerpoint.

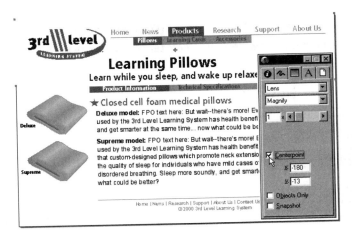

The Magnify Lens fill normally enlarges the artwork underneath it. When you change the magnification setting to 1, the rectangle basically turns into a giant mirror reflecting the original artwork. You checked the Centerpoint option, which means that you can move this rectangle and always refer back to this location, regardless of where the rectangle itself is moved.

11] Reduce the view so you can see the top of both pages 3 and 6 at the same time. Select the rectangle with the Lens fill from page 3 and drag it down to page 6, so that the top of the rectangle is at the top of page 6. Hold the Shift key as you drag to keep the elements aligned.

409

Notice the small diamond icon that appears in the header of page 3 when the rectangle is selected on page 6. This diamond shape indicates the centerpoint for the Magnify Lens fill. As long as you don't move the centerpoint, the Lens fill in this rectangle will always point to this location.

12] Position the Page tool over page 6 and then press Alt (Windows) or Option (Macintosh) and drag down to create a new page immediately below page 6.

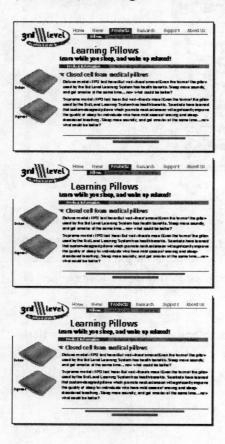

The newest page is identical to page 6. It has a rectangle with a Lens fill at the top, and you will notice that even the duplicated rectangle remembers the original snapshot location—it displays the same header as page 3. In the next step, you will see how this powerful editing tool works when you make a change in the header of page 3 and watch that change reflected in the pages below it.

410

13] Use the Arrow tool to select the word *Research* at the top of page 3 and move it over the word *Support*. Press the Tab key to deselect the word; then click the place where the word *Support* is and drag *Support* to the location where *Research* had been. If possible, work at 50% magnification so you can watch the updates as they occur in the Magnify Lens.

As you can see, you had to make the change on only one page, but the content on all three pages was corrected. Again, even if you had to change only three pages, this feature would be a timesaver. If you had to change dozens of pages, this feature can seem like a lifesaver.

14] **Save your changes.**

With symbols, Find and Replace Text, text styles, graphic styles, Find and Replace Graphics, and the Magnify Lens, you have extremely powerful and compelling reasons to use FreeHand for composing Web site storyboards. But as you'll see in the next sections, it gets even better.

DUPLICATING GROUPS OF PAGES

Earlier you learned that it's essential to have a site map before you begin designing a Web site. At the beginning of this lesson, you saw a sample mock-up for this Web site. Up to this point, you have just been working with one section of this Web site—the Products section. But like most Web sites, this site uses similar templates for each page. The fastest way to create the additional sections you need is to copy the whole group of pages to a new location and then simply make whatever modifications are necessary.

1] **Choose View › Magnification › 6%. Press Tab to deselect all artwork; then hold down the spacebar to activate the grabber hand. With the spacebar down, click and drag until the pages in this document are in the upper-left corner of your screen.**

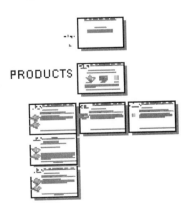

By reducing the view to 6%, you can easily see all of the pages in the document as well as plenty of empty pasteboard where you can place pages. Note that the grabber hand does not change the actual location of the pages on the pasteboard; it only scrolls the view so that a different portion of the document is visible.

2] Select the Page tool and drag a selection around all the visible pages except the top page.

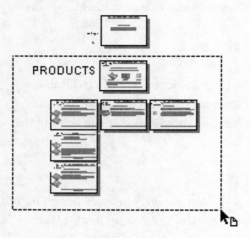

When you release the mouse button, the pages inside your selection are highlighted. You're going to copy all these pages to a new location on the pasteboard.

3] Move the Page tool over the center of one of these pages and press Alt (Windows) or Option (Macintosh) and drag to the right, holding down the Shift key as you drag. Release the mouse button when you have dragged the new pages far enough from the existing pages to fit a page between the two sections.

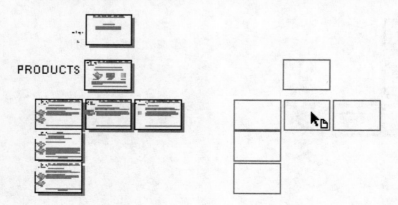

When you release the mouse button, there are six pages identical to the original pages in the new location.

If you were going to finish editing this Web site, this might be the start of the Research section. You could go to the top page of this section and make Research the highlighted option and then change the headline, subhead, and supporting text and artwork. Using the techniques you learned in earlier parts of this lesson, you could make changes to the rest of this section quickly and easily. Although you won't be doing all that work at this time, the important thing to remember is that you can use the flexible, open format in a FreeHand document to organize pages on the pasteboard in a visual arrangement that makes sense, and you can duplicate groups of pages to save time on production.

ASSIGNING ACTIVE LINKS WITH THE URL EDITOR

FreeHand allows you to assign active URL links to text and objects. These can be relative links, such as links between pages in the FreeHand document, or they can be absolute links, such as direct links to a Web site address. These links can be maintained when you export pages out of FreeHand as HTML documents and when you export a document as a PDF file.

In the next steps, you will learn how to assign URL links to text and objects in FreeHand.

1] Select Page 2 from the pop-up menu at the bottom of your screen. Choose Window › Xtras › URL Editor.

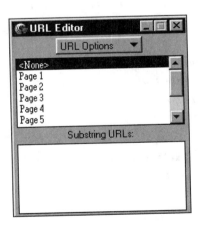

The URL Editor is displayed, and it already lists the pages that are in your document. These are all relative links—that is, they work within the structure of this document, but they aren't part of any named Web site.

2] Move your mouse over the text for page 4 in the URL Editor; then click and drag the mouse to the pillow graphic.

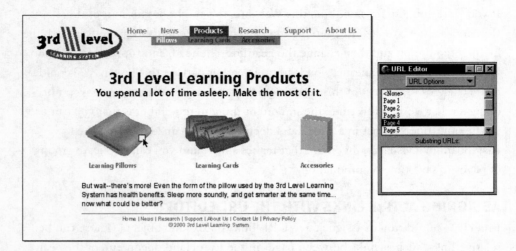

As you start dragging with the mouse, a swatch appears that looks just like a swatch from the Color List. This swatch actually contains the URL link, and when you release this swatch over an object, the URL link will be assigned to that object. This is one way to attach URLs to objects in FreeHand. You will discover another method in the next step.

note *You may have wondered why you are using the Page 4 link for the pillow graphic. This is because the Pillow page has been renumbered as page 4. Page numbers in FreeHand are assigned automatically based on the page's position on the pasteboard (numbers are assigned from left to right, from top to bottom). If a page is moved in front of or behind other pages, each of the affected pages will be renumbered. For this reason, you should use caution when assigning relative page links in FreeHand. While it can be a fast and effective way to preview links, these links can easily be broken. You're better off not assigning links until right before you export—or use absolute links where possible.*

3] Use the Arrow tool to select the Learning Pillows text immediately below the pillow graphic. Then go to the URL Editor and click page 4.

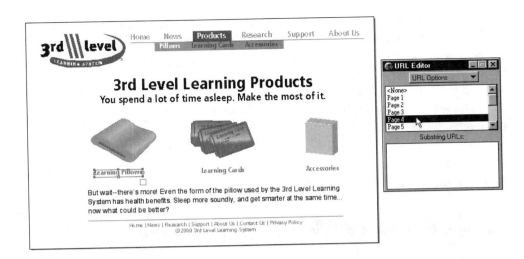

With this method, you selected the text first and then clicked the link in the URL Editor. Both methods work well, and the one you should use depends on the situation and your individual working style.

4] Select Page 4 from the pop-up menu at the bottom of your screen.

As described in the preceding note, pages are renumbered automatically in FreeHand according to their position on the pasteboard. The Learning Pillows page, which had been page 3 earlier, was renumbered as page 4 when you created the new section of pages in your document.

5] Select the word *Products* at the top of page 4 and Shift+click the green rectangle behind it. Group the two objects; then assign page 2 as the active link in the URL Editor.

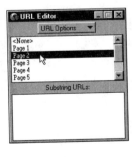

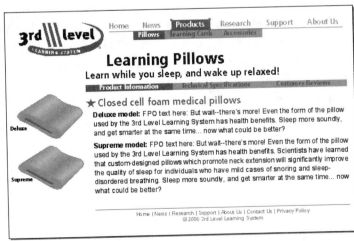

It is important to group text blocks if you want them to be treated as bitmap graphics when you publish documents from FreeHand as HTML pages. Grouping text blocks has no significant effect on the PDF or SWF export options, so you don't need to worry about negative repercussions elsewhere.

You can assign additional relative links in this document if you want to, but it is not necessary for this lesson.

6] Go to the URL Editor and choose New from the URL Options pop-up menu. Type *http://www.3rdlevel.com*. Click OK when you're done.

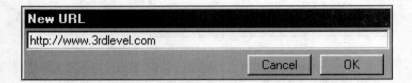

This is how you add your own absolute links to the URL Editor.

7] Assign the absolute link for the 3rd Level Web site to the logo in the upper-left corner of the page and also to the Home text at the top of the page.
You will see how absolute links function differently when you publish the document as HTML pages.

8] Save your changes.

EXPORTING TO VARIOUS FORMATS FROM FREEHAND

FreeHand allows you to take content from one location and move it in a number of different directions. For instance, you could print the file right now to a proofing device or high-end imagesetter. You could also export individual objects or entire pages to EPS files or some other image format. Since you're working on a Web site design, you are most likely going to want to export these pages as a SWF file, a PDF file, or a series of HTML files. The next steps will take you through the options you will encounter with these two last choices.

1] Choose File › Publish as HTML.

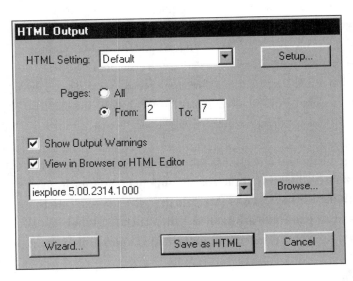

The main HTML Output dialog box appears. Here, you can set a page range, display output warnings, and select a browser or HTML editor for viewing the exported pages. You can also use the Setup and the Wizard (Windows) or Assistant (Macintosh) buttons.

2] Click the Wizard (Windows) or Assistant (Macintosh) button in the HTML Output dialog box. Read the text on the first screen; click Next (Windows) or the right arrow (Macintosh) when you're done. Read the text on each of the following screens, but do not change any of the options. When you reach the end, click the Finish button.
The screens in the HTML Wizard or Assistant explain the various options that FreeHand offers when publishing pages as HTML files. The default options are fine for the purposes of this lesson, so they do not need to be changed.

3] Back in the main HTML Output dialog box, click the From radio button and set the page range to From 2 To 7; then click the Save as HTML button.
When you click the Save as HTML button, FreeHand spends the next several moments going through your document and translating the pages and graphics to the necessary formats. When it completes this process, your browser will launch and display the first published HTML page.

4] Click the links you created in FreeHand (for instance, click the pillow graphic).

Notice that when you click a link, it takes you to the appropriate page. Also notice that text links are automatically underlined, but graphic links are not altered. When you click the 3rd Level logo on page 4, the browser attempts to find the address on the Internet (it won't find one). Do you see the difference between relative and absolute links? Relative links are based on the location of the page (within a directory or folder on your hard drive or on the Internet), but with absolute links, the browser will try to find the indicated address on the Internet, regardless of where the current page is located.

5] Return to your FreeHand document and choose File › Export. Choose PDF from the Save as type pop-up menu (Windows) or the Format pop-up menu (Macintosh) and then click the Setup (Windows) or Options (Macintosh) button. Make sure the options for Export URLs and Embed Fonts are selected; then click OK. When you are done, click Save (Windows) or Export (Macintosh) in the main Export dialog box.

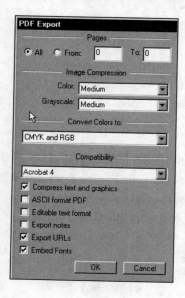

By setting these options, you ensure that the PDF file will maintain the links you created, and the document will appear the way you intended it to. You can distribute the PDF file you exported with confidence, knowing your clients will see the document exactly the way you intended, whether or not they're using the same platform or have the same fonts as you.

note *At the time this book was printed, only absolute links function in PDF files that are exported out of FreeHand. Check the Technotes area of Macromedia's Web site for updates and more information.*

ON YOUR OWN

The optional section of this chapter explores what happens beyond FreeHand in the world of Macromedia Flash. You will export portions of the FreeHand document in the Flash SWF format and then import and edit the SWF files in Flash. Look in the Lesson10\Bonus folder for the instructions and finished files.

WHAT YOU HAVE LEARNED:

In this lesson, you have:

- Created, modified, and used symbols [pages 397–403]
- Used Find and Replace Graphics to substitute elements [pages 405–407]
- Used the Magnify Lens fill to reflect artwork in additional locations [pages 406–410]
- Worked with groups of pages on the pasteboard [pages 411–413]
- Assigned active Web links with the URL Editor [pages 413–415]
- Exported FreeHand documents in a variety of formats [pages 416–418]

windows shortcuts

FreeHand offers lots of shortcuts that, once you learn them, will make your work easier. Many are described in the lessons in this book. This appendix is a quick reference to the default shortcuts in FreeHand for Windows computers.

KEYBOARD SHORTCUTS

FreeHand supports menu command shortcuts throughout the user interface. This section lists the default keyboard shortcuts for issuing commands. FreeHand 9's shortcuts can be customized by choosing File > Customize > Shortcuts. You can then select one of the predefined shortcut sets included with FreeHand, so you can use keyboard shortcuts you may already be familiar with from applications such as Adobe Illustrator, PageMaker, CorelDRAW, or QuarkXPress. You can also assign new keyboard shortcuts to frequently used commands to suit your own individual needs. The Customize Shortcuts dialog box provides a Print button that enables you to print a complete set of the current keyboard shortcuts.

note *O is the alpha character. 0 (zero) is the number.*

FILE MENU

Command	Shortcut
New	Ctrl+N
Open	Ctrl+O
Close	Ctrl+F4
Save	Ctrl+S
Save As	Ctrl+Shift+S
Import	Ctrl+R
Export	Ctrl+Shift+R
Print	Ctrl+P
Preferences	Ctrl+Shift+D
Exit	Alt+F4

EDIT MENU

Command	Shortcut
Undo	Ctrl+Z, Alt+Backspace
Redo	Ctrl+Y, Ctrl+Alt+ Backspace
Cut	Ctrl+X, Shift+Delete
Copy	Ctrl+C, Ctrl+Insert
Paste	Ctrl+V, Shift+Insert
Cut Contents	Ctrl+Shift+X
Paste Inside	Ctrl+Shift+V
Copy Attributes	Ctrl+Alt+Shift+C
Paste Attributes	Ctrl+Alt+Shift+V
Duplicate	Ctrl+D
Clone	Ctrl+Shift+C
Select All	Ctrl+A
Select All in Document	Ctrl+Shift+A
Find and Replace Text	Ctrl+Shift+F
Find and Replace Graphics	Ctrl+Alt+E

VIEW MENU

Command	Shortcut
Fit Selection	Ctrl+0 (zero)
Fit to Page	Ctrl+Shift+W
Fit All	Ctrl+Alt+0 (zero)
Magnification › 50%	Ctrl+5
Magnification › 100%	Ctrl+1
Magnification › 200%	Ctrl+2
Magnification › 400%	Ctrl+4
Magnification › 800%	Ctrl+8
Previous Custom View	Ctrl+Alt+Shift+1
Preview or Keyline	Ctrl+K
Fast Mode View	Ctrl+Shift+K
Flash Anti-alias	Ctrl+Alt+Shift+G
Panels	Ctrl+Shift+H, F12
Toolbars	Ctrl+Alt+T
Page Rulers	Ctrl+Alt+M
Text Rulers	Ctrl+Alt+Shift+T
Snap to Point	Ctrl+Shift+Z
Snap to Guides	Ctrl+Alt+G

MODIFY MENU

Command	Shortcut
Object	Ctrl+I
Stroke	Ctrl+Alt+L
Fill	Ctrl+Alt+F
Text	Ctrl+T
Document	Ctrl+Alt+D
Transform: Scale	Ctrl+F10
Transform: Move	Ctrl+M
Transform: Rotate	Ctrl+F2
Transform: Reflect	Ctrl+F9
Transform: Skew	Ctrl+F11
Transform Again	Ctrl+Shift+G
Bring to Front	Ctrl+F
Move Forward	Ctrl+Alt+Shift+F
Move Backward	Ctrl+Alt+Shift+K
Send to Back	Ctrl+B
Align	Ctrl+Alt+A
Align Again	Ctrl+Alt+Shift+A
Join	Ctrl+J
Split	Ctrl+Shift+J
Blend	Ctrl+Shift+B
Join Blend to Path	Ctrl+Alt+Shift+B
Rasterize	Ctrl+Alt+Shift+Z
Lock	Ctrl+L
Unlock	Ctrl+Shift+L
Group	Ctrl+G
Ungroup	Ctrl+U

TEXT MENU

Command	Shortcut
Size › Smaller	Ctrl+Alt+1, Ctrl+Shift+Down
Size › Larger	Ctrl+Alt+2, Ctrl+Shift+Up
Type Style › Plain	F5 or Ctrl+Alt+Shift+P
Type Style › Bold	F6 or Ctrl+Alt+B
Type Style › Italic	F7 or Ctrl+Alt+I
Type Style › Bold Italic	F8 or Ctrl+Alt+Shift+O
Effect › Highlight	Ctrl+Alt+Shift+H
Effect › Strikethrough	Ctrl+Alt+Shift+S
Effect › Underline	Ctrl+Alt+U
Align Left	Ctrl+Alt+Shift+L
Align Right	Ctrl+Alt+Shift+R
Align Center	Ctrl+Alt+Shift+M
Align Justified	Ctrl+Alt+Shift+J
Special Characters › Nonbreaking Space	Ctrl+Shift+H
Special Characters › Em Space	Ctrl+Shift+M
Special Characters › En Space	Ctrl+Shift+N
Special Characters › Thin Space	Ctrl+Shift+T
Editor	Ctrl+Shift+E
Spelling	Ctrl+Alt+S
Run Around Selection	Ctrl+Alt+W
Flow Inside Path	Ctrl+Shift+U
Attach to Path	Ctrl+Shift+Y
Convert to Paths	Ctrl+Shift+P
Symbols Convert	Ctrl+F8
Xtras Repeat	Ctrl+Alt+Shift+X

WINDOW MENU

Command	Shortcut
New Window	Ctrl+Alt+N
Toolbars › Main	Ctrl+Alt+T
Toolbars › Toolbox	Ctrl+7
Object Inspector	Ctrl+I
Stroke Inspector	Ctrl+Alt+L
Fill Inspector	Ctrl+Alt+F
Text Inspector	Ctrl+T
Document Inspector	Ctrl+Alt+D
Layers Panel	Ctrl+6
Styles Panel	Ctrl+3
Color List Panel	Ctrl+9
Color Mixer Panel	Ctrl+Shift+9
Tints Panel	Ctrl+Shift+3
Halftones Panel	Ctrl+H
Align Panel	Ctrl+Alt+A
Transform Panel	Ctrl+M
Xtras › Operations	Ctrl+Alt+O
Xtra › Xtra Tools	Ctrl+Alt+X
Cascade	Shift+F5
Tile	Shift+F4

DRAWING AND EDITING

Command	Shortcut
Clone	Ctrl+Shift+C
Cut Contents	Ctrl+Shift+X
Thinner Stroke	Ctrl+Shift+1
Deselect All	Tab
Grabber Hand	Spacebar
Group	Ctrl+G
Thicker Stroke	Ctrl+Shift+2
Paste Inside	Ctrl+Shift+V
Preview or Keyline	Ctrl+K

DRAWING AND EDITING (cont'd)

Command	Shortcut
Select All in Document	Ctrl+Shift+A
Select All on Page	Ctrl+A
Snap to Guides	Ctrl+Alt+G
Snap to Point	Ctrl+Shift+Z
Variable Stroke/ Calligraphic Pen Size Down	1 or Left Arrow
Variable Stroke/ Calligraphic Pen Size Up	2 or Right Arrow
Ungroup	Ctrl+U

GENERAL

Command	Shortcut
Close Document	Ctrl+F4
Close All Open Multiviews	Ctrl+Shift+F4
Help Arrow	Shift+F1
Export	Ctrl+Shift+R
Import	Ctrl+R
New Window	Ctrl+Alt+N
Next Page	Ctrl+Page Down
Previous Page	Ctrl+Page Up
Zoom In Magnification	Ctrl+Spacebar+click
Zoom Out Magnification	Ctrl+Alt+Spacebar+ click

PANELS AND TOOLS

To display this	Use
Align	Ctrl+Alt+A
Arrowhead Editor	Alt+Select Arrowhead
Bezigon tool	8
Blend	Ctrl+Shift+B
Color List	Ctrl+9
Color Mixer	Ctrl+Shift+9
Columns Inspector	Ctrl+Alt+R
Copyfit Inspector	Ctrl+Alt+C
Document Inspector	Ctrl+Alt+D
Ellipse tool	3
Fill Inspector	Ctrl+Alt+F
Freehand tool	5
Grabber Hand tool	Spacebar
Halftones panel	Ctrl+H
Hide/show all open panels	Ctrl+Alt+H
Knife tool	7
Layers panel	Ctrl+6

PANELS AND TOOLS (cont'd)

To display this	Use
Line tool	4
Main toolbar (and all other toolbars)	Ctrl+Alt+T
Object Inspector	Ctrl+I
Paragraph Inspector	Ctrl+Alt+P
Pen tool	6
Pointer tool	0
Polygon tool	2
Rectangle tool	1
Page rulers	Ctrl+Alt+M
Spacing/Horizontal Scale Inspector	Ctrl+Alt+K
Stroke Inspector	Ctrl+Alt+L
Styles panel	Ctrl+3
Text tool	. (period) or A
Text toolbar	Ctrl+Alt+T
Toolbox	Ctrl+7
Transform	Ctrl+M
Xtra operations toolbar	Ctrl+Alt+O
Xtra tools toolbar	Ctrl+Alt+X

CONSTRAINING TOOLS

Tool	Shortcut	Action
Pointer	Shift+Pointer tool	Constrain the movement of a selected object to 45-degree increments of the Constrain angle.
Lasso	Ctrl+Lasso tool	Constrain the lasso path to a straight line.
Text	Shift+Text tool	Constrain the text container to a square.
	Alt+Shift+Text tool	Display the Text Editor and create a square text block.
Rectangle	Shift+Rectangle tool	Constrain a rectangle to a square.
	Alt+Rectangle tool	Draw a rectangle from its center.
	Alt+Shift+Rectangle tool	Draw a square along the Constrain angle from its center.
Polygon	Shift+Polygon tool	Draw and constrain based on the Constrain angle.
Ellipse	Shift+Ellipse tool	Constrain an ellipse to a circle.
	Alt+Ellipse tool	Draw an ellipse from its center.
	Alt+Shift+Ellipse tool	Draw a circle along the Constrain angle from its center.
Line	Shift+Line tool	Draw a line along the Constrain angle.
	Alt+Line tool	Draw a line from its center.
	Alt+Shift+Line tool	Draw a line along the Constrain angle from its center.
Crop	Shift+Crop tool	Constrain the crop area to a square.
Text	Alt+Shift+Text tool	Constrain the text block to a square area, drawn from its center.
Freehand	Alt+Freehand tool	Draw a straight line.
	Alt+Shift+Freehand tool	Draw a straight line along the Constrain angle.
	Ctrl+Freehand tool	Erase a path while drawing.
Pen	Shift+Pen tool	Extract a point handle along the Constrain angle.
Knife	Alt+Knife tool	Cut a straight line.
	Alt+Shift+Knife tool	Cut a straight line along the Constrain angle.
Trace	Shift+Trace tool	Constrain the trace selection to a square area.
	Alt+Shift+Trace tool	Constrain the trace selection to a square area, drawn from its center.
Page	Shift+Page tool	Constrain the page to horizontal or vertical movement.
	Shift+Page tool	Drag a corner of the page, resizing it proportionally.
Arc	Shift+Arc tool	Constrain the angle of the arc along the Constrain angle.
Bezigon	Shift+Bezigon tool	Constrain point placement along the Constrain angle.
Rotate	Shift+Rotate tool	Rotate in 45-degree increments from 0 degrees.
Reflect	Shift+Reflect tool	Reflect in 45-degree increments from 0 degrees.
Scale	Shift+Scale tool	Scale proportionally from mouse-down.
Skew	Shift+Skew tool	Skew in 45-degree increments from 0 degrees.
Smudge	Alt+Smudge tool	Smudge from the center of an object.

Note: The Constrain angle defaults to 0 degrees. Choose Modify › Constrain to set a different angle.

TEXT

Category	Activity	Shortcut
Auto-expansion	Switch on and off	Double-click a side or bottom handle
Baseline	Shift down by one point	Ctrl+Alt+Down Arrow
	Shift up by one point	Ctrl+Alt+Up Arrow
Containers	Adjust word spacing for the entire container	Alt+drag a side handle
	Reduce the size to fit text	Double-click the link box
Cursor placement: Char	Previous character	Left Arrow
	Next character	Right Arrow
Cursor placement: Word	Previous word	Ctrl+Left Arrow
	Next word	Ctrl+Right Arrow
Cursor placement: Line	Previous line	Up Arrow
	Next line	Down Arrow
	Beginning of line	Home
	End of line	End
Cursor placement: Sentence	Beginning of sentence	Ctrl+7
	End of sentence	Ctrl+1
Cursor placement: Paragraph	Beginning of previous paragraph	Ctrl+Up Arrow
	Beginning of next paragraph	Ctrl+Down Arrow
Cursor placement: Story	Beginning of story	Ctrl+Shift+Home
	End of story	Ctrl+Shift+End
Delete	Delete the previous word	Ctrl+Shift+Backspace
	Delete the next word	Ctrl+Shift+Delete
Horizontal scale	Increase horizontal scale by 5%	Ctrl+6
	Decrease horizontal scale by 5%	Ctrl+3
Kerning	Adjust range kerning for the entire container	Drag a side handle
	Kern or track less by 1% em	Ctrl+Alt+Left Arrow
	Kern or track less by 10% em	Ctrl+Alt+Shift+Left Arrow
	Kern or track more by 1% em	Ctrl+Alt+Right Arrow
	Kern or track more by 10% em	Ctrl+Alt+Shift+Right Arrow
Leading	Adjust leading for the entire container	Drag a top or bottom handle
	Decrease leading by 100% or 2 pt.	Ctrl+− (minus)
	Decrease leading by 50% or 1 pt.	Ctrl+Alt+− (minus)
	Increase leading by 100% or 2 pt.	Ctrl+ +(plus)
	Increase leading by 100% or 2 pt.	Ctrl+Alt+ +(plus)

TEXT (cont'd)

Category	Activity	Shortcut
Paths	Attach to path	Ctrl+Shift+Y
	Convert to paths	Ctrl+Shift+P
	Flow inside path	Ctrl+Shift+U
	Run around selection	Ctrl+Alt+W
Point size	Decrease point size of selected text or a text container by one point	Ctrl+Alt+Shift+Down Arrow
	Increase point size of selected text or a text container by one point	Ctrl+Alt+Shift+Up Arrow

macintosh shortcuts

FreeHand offers lots of shortcuts that, once you learn them, will make your work easier. Many are described in the lessons in this book. This appendix is a quick reference to the default shortcuts in FreeHand for Macintosh computers.

KEYBOARD SHORTCUTS

FreeHand supports menu command shortcuts throughout the user interface. This section lists the default keyboard shortcuts for issuing commands. FreeHand 9's shortcuts can be customized by choosing File > Customize > Shortcuts. You can then select one of the predefined shortcut sets included with FreeHand, so you can use keyboard shortcuts you may already be familiar with from applications such as Adobe Illustrator, PageMaker, CorelDRAW, or QuarkXPress. You can also assign new keyboard shortcuts to frequently used commands to suit your own individual needs. The Customize Shortcuts dialog box provides a Print button that enables you to print a complete set of the current keyboard shortcuts.

note *O is the alpha character. 0 (zero) is the number.*

File menu

Command	Shortcut
New	Command+N
Open	Command+O
Close	Command+W
Save	Command+S
Save As	Command+Shift+S
Import	Command+R
Export	Command+Shift+R
Print	Command+P
Preferences	Command+Shift+D
Quit	Command+Q

EDIT MENU

Command	Shortcut
Undo	Command+Z, F1
Redo	Command+Y
Cut	Command+X, F2
Copy	Command+C, F3
Paste	Command+V, F4
Cut Contents	Command+Shift+X
Paste Inside	Command+Shift+V
Copy Attributes	Command+Shift+Option+C
Paste Attributes	Command+Shift+Option+V
Duplicate	Command+D
Clone	Command+=
Select All	Command+A
Select All in Document	Command+Shift+A
Find and Replace Text	Command+Shift+F
Find and Replace Graphics	Command+Option+E

VIEW MENU

Command	Shortcut
Fit Selection	Command+0 (zero)
Fit to Page	Command+Shift+W
Fit All	Command+Option+0 (zero)
Magnification › 50%	Command+5
Magnification › 100%	Command+1
Magnification › 200%	Command+2
Magnification › 400%	Command+4
Magnification › 800%	Command+8
Previous Custom View	Command+Option+1
Preview or Keyline	Command+K
Fast Mode View	Command+Shift+K
Flash Anti-alias	Command+Option+Shift+G
Panels	F12 or Command+Shift+H
Toolbars	Command+Option+T
Page Rulers	Command+Option+M
Text Rulers	Command+/
Snap to Point	Command+'
Snap to Guides	Command+\
Snap to Grid	Command+;

MODIFY MENU

Command	Shortcut
Object	Command+I
Stroke	Command+Option+L
Fill	Command+Option+F
Text	Command+T
Document	Command+Option+D
Transform: Scale	Command+F10
Transform: Move	Command+M
Transform: Rotate	Command+F13
Transform: Reflect	Command+F9
Transform: Skew	Command+F11
Transform Again	Command+,
Bring to Front	Command+F
Move Forward	Command+[
Move Backward	Command+]
Send to Back	Command+B
Align	Command+Option+A
Align Again	Command+Shift+Option+A
Join	Command+J
Split	Command+Shift+J
Blend	Command+Shift+B
Join Blend to Path	Command+Shift+Option+B
Rasterize	Command+Option+Shift+Z
Lock	Command+L
Unlock	Command+Shift+L
Group	Command+G
Ungroup	Command+U

TEXT MENU

Command	Shortcut
Smaller Size	Command+Shift+‹
Larger Size	Command+Shift+›
Type Style › Plain	F5 or Command+Shift+Option+P
Type Style › Bold	F6 or Command+Option+B
Type Style › Italic	F7 or Command+Option+I
Type Style › Bold Italic	F8 or Command+Shift+Option+O
Effect › Highlight	Command+Shift+Option+H
Effect › Strikethrough	Command+Shift+Option+S
Effect › Underline	Command+Option+U
Align Left	Command+Shift+Option+L
Align Right	Command+Shift+Option+R
Align Center	Command+Shift+Option+M
Align Justified	Command+Shift+Option+J
Special Characters › Em Space	Command+Shift+M
Special Characters › En Space	Command+Shift+N
Special Characters › Thin Space	Command+Shift+T
Special Characters › Discretionary Hyphen	Command+−
Editor	Command+Shift+E
Spelling	Command+Shift+G
Run Around Selection	Command+Option+W
Flow Inside Path	Command+Shift+U
Attach to Path	Command+Shift+Y
Convert to Paths	Command+Shift+P
Xtras Repeat	Command+Shift++ (plus)

WINDOW MENU

Command	Shortcut
New Window	Command+Option+N
Toolbars › Main	Command+Option+T
Toolbars › Toolbox	Command+7
Object Inspector	Command+I
Stroke Inspector	Command+Option+L
Fill Inspector	Command+Option+F
Text Inspector	Command+T
Document Inspector	Command+Option+D
Layers Panel	Command+6
Styles Panel	Command+3
Color List Panel	Command+9
Color Mixer Panel	Command+Shift+C
Tints Panel	Command+Shift+Z
Halftones Panel	Command+H
Align Panel	Command+Option+A
Transform Panel	Command+M
Xtras › Operations	Command+Shift+I
Xtra › Xtra Tools	Command+Shift+X

DRAWING AND EDITING

Command	Shortcut
Clone	Command+=
Close a Cut Path	Control+Knife tool
Cut Contents	Command+Shift+X
Deselect All	Tab
Grabber Hand	Spacebar
Group	Command+G
Paste Inside	Command+Shift+V
Preview or Keyline	Command+K
Select All in Document	Command+Shift+A
Select All on Page	Command+A
Snap to Guides	Command+\
Snap to Point	Command+'
Thicker Stroke	Command+Option+›
Thinner Stroke	Command+Option+‹
Variable Stroke/ Calligraphic Pen Size Down	1 or Left Arrow
Variable Stroke/ Calligraphic Pen Size Up	2 or Right Arrow
Ungroup	Command+U

GENERAL

Command	Shortcut
Export	Command+Shift+R
Help Cursor	Help
Import	Command+R
Next Page	Command+ Page Down
New Window	Command+Option+N
Pause Screen Redraw	Command+.
Previous Page	Command+Page Up
Zoom In Magnification	Command+ Spacebar+click
Zoom Out Magnification	Command+Option+ Spacebar+click

PANELS AND TOOLS

To display this	Use
Align	Command+Option+A
Arrowhead Editor	Option+Select Arrowhead
Bezigon Tool	8 or Shift+F2
Blend	Command+Shift+B
Color List	Command+9
Color Mixer	Command+Shift+C
Columns Inspector	Command+Option+R
Copyfit Inspector	Command+Option+C
Dash Editor	Option+Select Dash pop-up
Document Inspector	Command+Option+D
Ellipse tool	3 or Shift+F3
Fill Inspector	Command+Option+F
Freehand tool	5 or Shift+F5
Grabber Hand tool	Spacebar
Halftones panel	Command+H
Hide/show all open panels	Command+Shift+H
Knife tool	7 or Shift+F7
Layers panel	Command+6

PANELS AND TOOLS (cont'd)

To display this	Use
Line tool	4 or Shift+F4
Object Inspector	Command+I
Paragraph Inspector	Command+Option+P
Pen tool	6 or Shift+F6
Pointer tool	0 (zero) or Shift+F10
Polygon tool	2 or Shift+F8
Rectangle tool	1 or Shift+F1
Page rulers	Command+Option+M
Spacing/Horizontal	Command+Option+K
Stroke Inspector	Command+Option+L
Styles panel	Command+3
Text tool	. (period) or A or Shift+F9
Text toolbar	Command+Option+T
Toolbox	Command+7
Transform	Command+M

CONSTRAINING TOOLS

Tool	Shortcut	Action
Pointer	Shift+Pointer tool	Constrain the movement of a selected object to 45-degree increments of the Constrain angle.
Lasso	Command+Lasso tool	Constrain the lasso path to a straight line.
Text	Shift+Text tool	Constrain the text container to a square.
	Shift+Option+Text tool	Constrain a text container to a square text block.
Rectangle	Shift+Rectangle tool	Constrain a rectangle to a square.
	Option+Rectangle tool	Draw a rectangle from its center.
	Shift+Option+Rectangle tool	Draw a square along the Constrain angle from its center.
Polygon	Shift+Polygon tool	Draw and constrain based on the Constrain angle.
Ellipse	Shift+Ellipse tool	Constrain an ellipse to a circle.
	Option+Ellipse tool	Draw an ellipse from its center.
	Shift+Option+Ellipse tool	Draw a circle along the Constrain angle from its center.
Line	Shift+Line tool	Draw a line along the Constrain angle.
	Option+Line tool	Draw a line from its center.
	Shift+Option+Line tool	Draw a line along the Constrain angle from its center.
Crop	Shift+Crop tool	Constrain the crop area to a square.
Text	Shift+Option+Text tool	Constrain the text block to a square text block.
Freehand	Option+Freehand tool	Draw a straight line.
	Shift+Option+Freehand tool	Draw a straight line along the Constrain angle.
	Command+Freehand tool	Erase a path while drawing.
Pen	Shift+Pen tool	Extract a point handle along the Constrain angle.
Knife	Option+Knife tool	Cut along the Constrain angle.
	Control+Knife tool	Close a cut path.
Trace	Shift+Trace tool	Constrain the trace selection to a square area.
	Shift+Option+Trace tool	Constrain the trace selection to a square text block.
Page	Shift+Page tool	Constrain the page to horizontal or vertical movement.
	Shift+Page tool	Drag a corner of the page, resizing it proportionally.
	Shift+Option+Page tool	Drag a corner of the page to resize the page to a smaller or larger predefined page size.
Arc	Shift+Arc tool	Constrain the angle of the arc along the Constrain angle.
Bezigon	Shift+Bezigon tool	Constrain point placement along the Constrain angle.
Rotate	Shift+Rotate tool	Rotate in 45-degree increments from 0 degrees.
	Control+Rotate tool	Rotate around the center of the object.
	Control+Shift+Rotate tool	Rotate in 45-degree increments from 0 degrees.
Reflect	Shift+Reflect tool	Reflect in 45-degree increments from 0 degrees.
	Control+Reflect tool	Use the center of the object as the reflect axis.
	Control+Shift+Reflect tool	Reflect in 45-degree increments from 0 degrees.

CONSTRAINING TOOLS (cont'd)

Tool	Shortcut	Action
Scale	Shift+Scale tool	Scale proportionally from center.
	Control+Scale tool	Scale from the center of the object.
	Control+Shift+Scale tool	Scale proportionally from the center of the object.
Skew	Shift+Skew tool	Skew along the Constrain angle.
	Control+Skew tool	Skew from the center of the object.
	Control+Shift+Skew tool	Constrain skewing from the center of the object.
Smudge	Option+Smudge tool	Smudge from the center of an object.

Note: The Constrain angle defaults to 0 degrees. Choose Modify › Constrain to set a different angle.

TEXT

Category	Activity	Shortcut
Auto-expansion	Switch on and off	Double-click a side or bottom handle
Baseline	Shift down by one point	Command+Option+Down Arrow
	Shift up by one point	Command+Option+Up Arrow
Containers	Adjust word spacing for the entire container	Option+drag a side handle
	Reduce the size to fit text	Double-click the link box
Cursor placement: Char	Previous character	Left Arrow
	Next character	Right Arrow
Cursor placement: Word	Previous word	Command+Left Arrow
	Next word	Command+Right Arrow
Cursor placement: Line	Previous line	Up Arrow
	Next line	Down Arrow
	Beginning of line	Home
	End of line	End
Cursor placement: Sentence	Beginning of sentence	Command+7
	End of sentence	Command+1
Cursor placement: Paragraph	Beginning of previous paragraph	Command+Up Arrow
	Beginning of next paragraph	Command+Down Arrow
Cursor placement: Story	Beginning of story	Command+Home
	End of story	Command+End
Delete	Delete the previous word	Ctrl+Shift+Backspace
	Delete the next word	Ctrl+Shift+Forward space
Horizontal scale	Increase horizontal scale by 5%	Command+Keypad 6
	Decrease horizontal scale by 5%	Command+Keypad 3

435

TEXT (cont'd)

Category	Activity	Shortcut
Kerning	Adjust range kerning for the entire container	Drag a side handle
	Kern or track less by 1% em	Command+Option+Left Arrow
	Kern or track less by 10% em	Command+Shift+Option+Left Arrow
	Kern or track more by 1% em	Command+Option+Right Arrow
	Kern or track more by 10% em	Command+Shift+Option+Right Arrow
Leading	Adjust leading for the entire container	Drag a top or bottom handle
	Decrease leading by 100% or 2 pt.	Command+− (minus)
	Decrease leading by 50% or 1 pt.	Command+Option+− (minus)
	Increase leading by 100% or 2 pt.	Command++(plus)
	Increase leading by 100% or 2 pt.	Command+Option++(plus)
Paths	Attach to path	Command+Shift+Y
	Convert to paths	Command+Shift+P
	Flow inside path	Command+Shift+U
	Run around selection	Command+Option+W
Point size	Decrease point size of selected text or a text container by one point	Command+Shift+Option+Down Arrow
Showing or hiding UI	Spelling panel	Command+Shift+G
	Text Editor	Command+Shift+E or Option+Text tool
Text selection: Character	Extend left one character	Shift+Left Arrow
	Extend right one character	Shift+Right Arrow
Text selection: Word	Extend left one word	Command+Shift+Left Arrow
	Extend right one word	Command+Shift+Right Arrow
Text selection: Line	Extend up one line	Shift+Up Arrow
	Extend down one line	Shift+Down Arrow
Text selection: Sentence	Extend to beginning of sentence	Command+Keypad 8
	Extend to end of sentence	Command+2
Text selection: Paragraph	Extend to beginning of paragraph	Command+Shift+Up Arrow
	Extend to end of paragraph	Command+Shift+Down Arrow
Text selection: Story	Extend to beginning of story	Command+Shift+Home
	Extend to end of story	Command+Shift+End

FreeHand is designed to be easy to learn and use for people familiar with other graphic applications. This appendix is a quick reference to help you convert the terms and techniques found in other applications to the FreeHand equivalents.

BASIC TERMINOLOGY

Although the drawing and editing techniques you use in FreeHand are similar to those in other applications, there are differences in the terminology used to describe the tools and controls involved. This terminology is often the most confusing issue an Adobe Illustrator or CorelDRAW user will encounter when learning to use FreeHand. Here are some common terms that may help you understand FreeHand operations.

Feature	Terminology FreeHand	Adobe Illustrator	CorelDraw
Working with paths	Points	Points	Nodes
Adding color	Color Mixer, Tints Panel, Color List	Paint Styles palette Fill and Stroke	Colors
Clipping paths	Paste Inside	Mask	Power Clips
Effects and add-ins	Xtras	Filters	Effects
Path operations	Operations	Pathfinder Filters	Shaping
Gradients	Gradients	Gradients	Fountain Fills
View modes	Keyline, Preview	Artwork, Preview	Wireframe, Normal

KEYBOARD SHORTCUTS

Many of the keyboard shortcuts you are familiar with in other applications may have the same functions assigned in FreeHand by default (for example, Save, Print, and 100% View), and as you work with FreeHand, you can easily learn the other shortcuts for the features you use frequently.

Perhaps the quickest way to take full advantage of the efficiency and power keyboard shortcuts can offer is to use the shortcuts you already know from another application. Choose File > Customize > Shortcuts and select one of the predefined shortcut sets from the menu at the upper right.

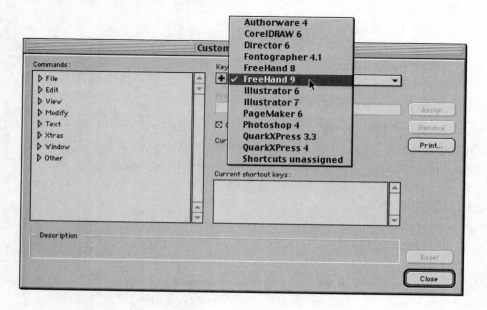

For example, if you are familiar with the keyboard shortcuts used in Macromedia Director, Authorware, Adobe Illustrator, Photoshop, PageMaker, CorelDraw, or QuarkXPress, select any of these from the Shortcuts Setting menu. Your familiar keyboard commands are now available, assigned to the equivalent functions and commands in FreeHand.

You can also assign your own keyboard shortcuts to frequently used commands to suit your individual needs. First, select a command from the list on the left. The current shortcut key or keys are displayed at the bottom right (if any are assigned). You can add your own shortcuts to this list or even delete any of the ones currently assigned and replace them with your own choice. By default, FreeHand will warn you if the shortcut you have entered is already being used by another command. (Make sure that the Go to conflict on assign button remains on so FreeHand can continue to provide these warnings.)

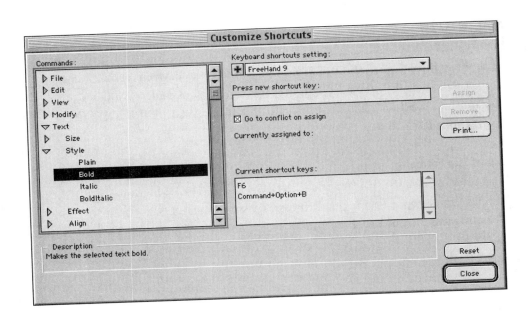

The Customize Shortcuts dialog box also provides a Print button that enables you to print a complete set of the current keyboard shortcuts.

FILE FORMATS FREEHAND SUPPORTS

You may have artwork created in other applications that you would like to convert to FreeHand. FreeHand provides extensive support for various graphic file formats on both Windows and Macintosh platforms. Here are the formats supported for each platform.

WINDOWS

Import File Formats:
EPS; Illustrator 1.1, 88, 3.0, 4.0, 5.5, 6, and 7 (Windows and Macintosh); CorelDRAW 7 and 8; Photoshop 2.5, 3.0, 4.0, and 5.0; Acrobat PDF 4; FreeHand 5, 5.5, 7, 8, and 9 (Windows and Macintosh); DCS 1 and 2; DXF; RTF; ASCII; TIFF; GIF; JPEG; PNG; Targa; BMP; WMF; EMF

Export File Formats:
Macromedia Flash; Generic EPS (RGB and CMYK); EPS for Photoshop; Photoshop 5 (PSD); EPS for QuarkXPress; Illustrator 1.1, 88, 3.0, 4.0, 5.5, 6, and 7 (Windows and Macintosh); FreeHand 5, 5.5, 7, and 8 (Windows and Macintosh); DCS 2; RTF; ASCII; TIFF; GIF; JPEG; PNG; Acrobat PDF; Targa; BMP; WMF; EMF

MACINTOSH

Import File Formats:

EPS; Illustrator 1.1, 88, 3.0, 4.0, 5.5, 6, and 7 (Windows and Macintosh); Photoshop 2.5, 3.0, 4.0, and 5.0; Acrobat PDF 4; FreeHand 5, 5.5, 7, 8, and 9 (Windows and Macintosh); DCS 1 and 2; DXF; PICT; PICT2; RTF; ASCII; TIFF; GIF; JPEG; PNG; Targa; BMP

Export File Formats:

Macromedia Flash (SWF); Generic EPS (RGB and CMYK); Photoshop 5 (PSD); EPS for Photoshop; EPS for QuarkXPress; Illustrator 1.1, 88, 3.0, 4.0, 5.5, 6, and 7 (Windows and Macintosh); FreeHand 5, 5.5, 7, 8, and 9 (Windows and Macintosh); DCS 2 EPS; PICT; PICT2; RTF; ASCII; TIFF; GIF; JPEG; PNG; Acrobat PDF; Targa; BMP

If you ever encounter a file format that FreeHand does not directly support, check to see if your other application can import or export an intermediate file format that FreeHand can import or export. If importing into FreeHand is the issue, a good place to start might be PDF; any application that supports printing can potentially create a PDF file, which FreeHand can then import.

FreeHand resources

There are a number of FreeHand resources, both on and off the Internet, that have proven valuable to countless users around the world. This appendix is a list of some popular FreeHand resources.

ADDITIONAL BOOKS

FreeHand Visual QuickStart Guide, by Sandee Cohen (Peachpit Press)
Real World FreeHand, by Olav Martin Kvern (Peachpit Press)
Digital Drawing, by David Bergsland (Del Mar Publishing)

WEB SITES

http://www.macromedia.com/software/freehand
This official FreeHand Web site contains news, product information, reviews, downloads, support information, a gallery of FreeHand artwork by high-profile companies, and much more.

http://www.macromedia.com/support/freehand
FreeHand Technotes are the most comprehensive source of technical information, answers to frequently asked questions and more. If you have questions or problems, this is a great place to start.

http://www.FreeHandSource.com
This site by Ian Kelleigh is the best resource for FreeHand outside of Macromedia. There are valuable tips, news, downloads, history, links and much more. The site design looks eerily like FreeHand itself.

OTHER RESOURCES

FreeHand Mailing List: to subscribe, email a message to *listserv@galileo.uafadm.alaska.edu*, and in the body of the email, enter SUBSCRIBE FREEHAND-L

FreeHand Newsgroup: *news://forums.macromedia.com/macromedia.freehand*

index

Macromedia tech support number: 415-252-9080

LICENSING AGREEMENT